DESIGN XXVII.

A Rural Church.

Fig. 137.

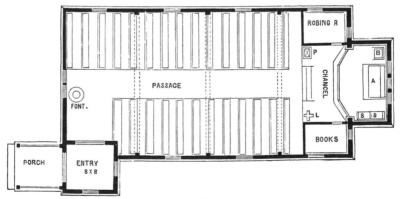

Fig. 138.

VICTORIAN COTTAGE RESIDENCES

by
Andrew Jackson Downing

With a New Preface by
Adolf K. Placzek

Dover Publications, Inc.
New York

𝔍𝔑𝔖ℭℜ𝔍𝔅𝔈𝔇,

WITH SINCERE REGARD,

TO

ROBERT DONALDSON, ESQ.,

OF BLITHEWOOD, ON THE HUDSON.

Arbiter Elegantiarum.

DOVER ARCHITECTURAL SERIES
Adolf K. Placzek
General Editor

Copyright © 1981 by Dover Publications, Inc.
All rights reserved under Pan American and International Copyright Conventions.

Published in Canada by General Publishing Company, Ltd., 30 Lesmill Road, Don Mills, Toronto, Ontario.
Published in the United Kingdom by Constable and Company, Ltd., 10 Orange Street, London WC2H 7EG.

This Dover edition, first published in 1981, is an unabridged republication of *Cottage Residences; / or, / A Series of Designs / for / Rural Cottages and Cottage Villas, / and their / Gardens and Grounds. / Adapted to / North America* in the 1873 edition, with additional material by Henry Winthrop Sargent and Charles Downing, edited by George E. Harney, as published by John Wiley and Son, New York.

International Standard Book Number: 0-486-24078-9
Library of Congress Catalog Card Number: 80-68351

Manufactured in the United States of America
Dover Publications, Inc.
180 Varick Street
New York, N.Y. 10014

PREFACE

TO THE DOVER EDITION

Andrew Jackson Downing (1815–52), America's first great landscape gardener, turned the taste of his generation toward the informal or "natural" garden and landscape. He was also the propagator and pioneer designer of the small inexpensive detached house—the cottage—in a nonurban setting. This type of dwelling in all its variations—Gothic, bracketed, Italianate, "rustic"—created the American suburb and, as has been said, made over the face of the land. This he did not through an active architectural practice, but through his enormously successful books: *A Treatise on the Theory and Practice of Landscape Gardening Adapted to North America* (1841), *The Architecture of Country Houses* (1850, Dover 22003-6) and, above all, *Cottage Residences*. One of the most widely used books in American architectural literature, it was first published in 1842. Many editions followed (1844, 1847, 1852) during Downing's lifetime. His premature death in 1852—he drowned in the Hudson River while trying to save fellow passengers after a shipwreck—did not slow the success of his book (editions of 1853, 1856, 1860, 1863 and on). The edition chosen for reprint here is that of 1873, which contains, for the first time, the historically interesting and useful additions by Henry Winthrop Sargent and Charles Downing.

Adolf K. Placzek

New York City, June, 1980

PREFACE

In revising this work of Mr. Downing's, and preparing it for its Fifth edition, it has been found necessary to make some changes both in the Architectural and Horticultural departments in order to bring the work forward to the requirements of the present day.

In the Architectural department these changes have been chiefly with regard to the estimates of the cost of the several designs—the prices of labor and materials being now double, and in some cases more than double, what they were twenty years ago, making it necessary to give new estimates based upon the prices of to-day—and these alterations have been made by means of notes placed in brackets where they were found necessary, so that Mr. Downing's original matter has been preserved just as he wrote it.

It will be interesting to compare the new estimates with the old, and note the difference between what it costs to build a house now and what it cost then; though it is but fair to say that the greater proportion of the increase has come about since the war, and in consequence of it. Whether, after our country shall have fully recovered from the evils thereby occasioned, we shall again return to anything like the former prices, is a question very difficult to determine; the probabilities are, however, that building will never be a great deal cheaper than now,—at least never again so cheap as it was before the year 1861.

With regard to the Horticultural department of the book, the necessary changes in the lists of flowers, and fruits, and shrubs, and trees were so great that it was found impossible to follow the plan of adding notes, because so many of the varieties recommended in the former editions have become obsolete, or rather have been superseded by the great variety of newer ones which have come

up and taken their place in the popular favor;—accordingly, in
most instances it has been necessary to completely rewrite those
lists. They were furnished for this edition, very carefully classi-
fied, by Mr. H. W. Sargent and Mr. Charles Downing.

Mr. Sargent has added some very interesting suggestions concerning Terrace Gardens, which follow Mr. Downing's chapter
on gardens at page 243, and are illustrated by pictures of his
own beautiful one at Wodenethe, in Fishkill Landing, and by a
plan of the new and very promising one of Judge Monell, in the
same neighborhood.

Mr. Hatfield has contributed a pretty design for a river cottage
(see page 213). Messrs. Vaux and Withers were the designers of
Judge Monell's cottage, illustrated on page 206, and Mr. Arthur
Gilman has given us the plans and views of his own house recently
erected on Staten Island.

The rest of the designs were all made by the editor; and all
will, he thinks, give a fair idea of the styles and plans for cottages
that are acceptable at the present day.

It is hoped that the design for a small Rural Church may not be
thought out of place even in a book purporting to be devoted to
cottages.

G. E. H.

Newburgh, January, 1873.

PREFACE.

A HEARTY desire to contribute something to the improvement of the domestic architecture and the rural taste of our country, has been the motive which has influenced me in preparing this little volume. With us, almost every man either builds, or looks forward to building, a home for himself, at some period of his life; it may be only a log-hut, or a most rustic cottage, but perhaps also a villa, or a mansion. As yet, however, our houses are mostly either of the plainest and most meagre description, or, if of a more ambitious, they are frequently of a more objectionable character— shingle palaces, of very questionable convenience, and not in the least adapted by their domestic and rural beauty to harmonize with our lovely natural landscapes.

Now I am desirous that every one who lives in the country, and in a country-house, should be in some degree conversant with domestic architecture, not only because it will be likely to improve the comfort of his own house, and hence all the houses in the country, but that it will enlarge his mind, and give him new sources of enjoyment.

It is not my especial object at this moment to dwell upon the superior convenience which may be realized in our houses, by a more familiar acquaintance with architecture. The advantages of an ingeniously arranged and nicely adapted plan, over one carelessly and ill-contrived, are so obvious to every one, that they are self-evident. This is the ground-work of domestic architecture, the great importance of which is recognized by all mankind, and some ingenuity and familiarity with practical details are only necessary to give us compact, convenient, and comfortable houses, with the same means and in the same space as the most awkward and unpleasing forms.

But I am still more anxious to inspire in the minds of my readers and countrymen livelier perceptions of the BEAUTIFUL, in everything that relates to our houses and grounds. I wish to awaken a quicker sense of the grace, the elegance, or the picturesqueness of fine forms that are capable of being produced in these by Rural Architecture and Landscape Gardening—a sense which will not only refine and elevate the mind, but open to it new and infinite resources of delight. There are perhaps a few upon whose souls nearly all emanations of beauty fall impressionless; but there are also many who see the Beautiful, in nature and art, only feebly and dimly, either from the want of proper media through which to view her, or a little direction as to where she is to be found. How many, too, are there, who even discover the Beautiful in a picture or a statue, who yet fail to admire her, rounding with lines of grace, and touching with shades of harmony all common nature, and pervading silently all material forms! "Men," says Goethe, "are so inclined to content themselves with what is commonest, so easily do the spirit and the sense grow dead to the impression of the Beautiful and the Perfect, that every person should strive to nourish in his mind the faculty of feeling these things, by everything in his power, for no man can bear to be wholly deprived of such enjoyment; it is only because they are not used to taste of what is excellent, that the generality of people take delight in silly and insipid things, provided they be new. For this reason, every day one ought to see a fine picture, read a good poem, hear a little song, and, if it were possible, to speak a few reasonable words."

It is in this regard that I wish to inspire all persons with a love of beautiful forms, and a desire to assemble them around their daily walks of life. I wish them to appreciate how superior is the charm of that home where we discover the tasteful cottage or villa, and the well designed and neatly kept garden or grounds, full of beauty and harmony,—not the less beautiful and harmonious, because simple and limited; and to become aware that these superior forms, and the higher and more refined enjoyment derived from them, may be had at the same cost and with the same labor as a clumsy dwelling, and its uncouth and ill-designed accessories.

More than all, I desire to see these sentiments cherished for their pure moral tendency. " All BEAUTY is an outward expression of inward good," and so closely are the Beautiful and the True allied, that we shall find, if we become sincere lovers of the grace, the harmony, and the loveliness with which rural homes and rural life are capable of being invested, that we are silently opening our hearts to an influence which is higher and deeper than the mere *symbol;* and that if we thus worship in the true spirit, we shall attain a nearer view of the Great Master, whose words, in all his material universe, are written in lines of Beauty.

And how much happiness, how much pure pleasure, that strengthens and invigorates our best and holiest affections, is there not experienced in bestowing upon our homes something of grace and loveliness—in making the place dearest to our hearts a sunny spot, where the social sympathies take shelter securely under the shadowy eaves, or grow and entwine trustfully with the tall trees or wreathed vines that cluster around, as if striving to shut out whatever of bitterness or strife may be found in the open highways of the world. What an unfailing barrier against vice, immorality, and bad habits, are those tastes which lead us to embellish a home, to which at all times and in all places we turn with delight, as being the object and the scene of our fondest cares, labors, and enjoyments; whose humble roof, whose shady porch, whose verdant lawn and smiling flowers, all breathe forth to us, in true, earnest tones, a domestic feeling that at once purifies the heart, and binds us more closely to our fellow-beings!

In this volume, the first yet published in this country devoted to Rural Architecture, I am conscious of offering but a slight and imperfect contribution to this important subject, which I trust will be the precursor of more varied and complete works from others, adapted to our peculiar wants and climate. The very great interest now beginning to manifest itself in rural improvements of every kind, leads us to believe and to hope, that at no distant day our country residences may rival the " cottage homes of England," so universally and so justly admired.

The relation between a country house and its " surroundings " has led me to consider, under the term residences, both the architectural and the gardening designs. To constitute an agreeable whole, these should indeed have a harmonious correspondence, one with the other; and although most of the following designs have not actually been carried into execution, yet it is believed that they will, either entirely or in part, be found adapted to many cases of every-day occurrence, or at least furnish hints for variations suitable for peculiar circumstances and situations.

A. J. D.

Newburgh, N. Y., June, 1842.

CONTENTS.

DESIGN III.

A COTTAGE IN THE POINTED, OR TUDOR STYLE.

DESIGN IV.

AN ORNAMENTAL FARM-HOUSE.

DESIGN V.

A COTTAGE VILLA IN THE BRACKETED MODE.

DESIGN VI.

AN IRREGULAR VILLA IN THE ITALIAN STYLE, BRACKETED.

DESIGN VII.

AN IRREGULAR COTTAGE IN THE OLD ENGLISH STYLE.

DESIGN VIII.

A VILLA IN THE ITALIAN STYLE.

DESIGN IX.

COTTAGE IN THE ITALIAN, OR TUSCAN STYLE.

NEW DESIGNS FOR COTTAGES, ETC.,
BY THE EDITOR AND OTHERS.

FURTHER HINTS ON THE GARDENS AND GROUNDS OF COTTAGE RESIDENCES.

ADDENDA.

COTTAGE RESIDENCES.

ARCHITECTURAL SUGGESTIONS.

"True Taste is an excellent economist. She confines her choice to few objects, and delights to produce great effects by small means; while False Taste is forever sighing after the new and rare; and reminds us, in her works, of the scholar of Apelles who, not being able to paint his Helen beautiful, determined to make her fine."

THERE are certain leading principles connected with architecture which earnestly demand our attention on the very threshold of the subject. In an indefinite manner they are, perhaps, acknowledged by all intelligent minds, but they are only distinctly and clearly understood by those who, having analyzed the expressions or characters inherent in various forms and modes of building, have traced the impressions derived, whether of utility or beauty, to their proper origin. When the mind has arrived at this point, the satisfaction it enjoys in an admirable work is proportionably greater; in the same manner (though in less degree) as the "devout astronomer" enjoys, with a far more intelligent and fervent rapture, his starry gaze, than the ignorant eye that sees only a myriad of lights hung above to dispel the gloom of midnight.

As the first object of a dwelling is to afford a shelter to man, the first principle belonging to architecture grows out of this primary necessity, and it is called the principle of FITNESS or *usefulness*. After this, man naturally desires to give some distinctive character to his own habitation, to mark its superiority to those devoted to animals. This gives rise to the principle of *Expression of* PURPOSE. Finally, the love of the beautiful, inherent in all finer natures, and its exhibition in certain acknowledged forms, has created the principle of the *Expression of Style*. In other words, all these principles may be regarded as sources of beauty in domestic architecture; Fitness being the *beauty of utility;* Expression of Purpose, the *beauty of propriety;* and Expression of Style, the *beauty of form and sentiment*, which is the highest in the scale. We shall say a few words in illustration of our ideas on each particular division.

Fitness, or use, is the first principle to be considered in all buildings. Those, indeed, who care very little for any other character in a dwelling, generally pride themselves upon the amount of convenience they have been able to realize in it; and nothing could be in worse taste than to embellish or decorate a dwelling-house which is wanting in comfort, since the beautiful is never satisfactory when not allied to the true.

In a dwelling-house, our every-day comfort is so entirely dependent on a convenient arrangement of the rooms, or plan of the interior, that this is universally acknowledged to be the most important consideration. To have the principal rooms or apartments situated on the most favorable side of the house with regard to aspect, in order that they may be light, warm, or airy, and, in respect to view, that they may command the finest prospects, are desiderata in every kind of dwelling. In all climates the stormy quarters are the worst aspects, and the fair weather quarters the best ones. Thus, in the Middle States, a south-west aspect (all other things being equal) is the best for the finer rooms, and a north-east the most disagreeable. In hot climates, a north exposure may be agreeable on account of its coolness, but in all temperate latitudes, a southern one is more desirable for the entire year.

In arranging the different apartments of a cottage or villa, great variations will naturally arise out of the peculiar circumstances, mode of living, or individual wants of the family by whom it is to be inhabited. Thus, a small family living a secluded life, or one composed of infirm persons, would prefer to have their sleeping apartments, their kitchen, and other conveniences, on the same floor with the parlor or living-room, even at the expense of one or two handsome rooms, for the sake of the greater convenience in conducting domestic affairs, and the greater ease and comfort thereby realized. On the other hand, a family fond of social intercourse, and accustomed to entertain, would greatly prefer, in a cottage or villa of moderate size, to have several handsome apartments, as a drawing-room, library, dining-room, etc., occupying almost exclusively the principal floor, placing the kitchen and its offices in the basement, and the bed-rooms in the second story. This arrangement would perhaps be less convenient in a few respects for the family, but it would be more elegant and more satisfactory for the kind of residence intended—each department of the house being complete in itself, and intruding itself but little on the attention of the family or guests when not required to be visible, which is the *ideal* of domestic accommodation. A kitchen on the first floor has the advantage of being more accessible, and more completely under the *surveillance* of the mistress of the house, but, on the other hand, it is open to the objection of being occasionally offensive in the matter of sound, sight, and smells; unless, in the case of large houses, where these may be excluded by long passages and double doors. Some families have a literary taste, and to them a library would be an indispensable apartment, while others, caring less for books, would in the same space prefer a bed-room. We mention these circumstances to show in what a relative sense the term fitness, as regards accommodation, must be used, and how many peculiar circumstances must be considered before we can pronounce decidedly upon the merits or demerits of a plan. What may be entirely fit and convenient for one, would be considered quite unsuitable for another. Hence the great difficulty of arranging plans exactly to suit all wants. And hence the importance to all persons, and especially ladies, who understand best the principle of convenience, of acquiring some architectural knowledge. There are doubtless many desiring to build a cottage, who will find no one of the plans hereafter submitted precisely what they want, and this will be found to arise mainly from their having certain peculiar wants growing out of their habits or position, for which no artist, not familiar with these, could possibly provide.

There are some rules of fitness of nearly universal application. Thus a dining-room should obviously have connected with it, either a pantry or a large closet, or both; and it should be so placed as to afford easy ingress and egress to and from the kitchen. The drawing-room, parlor, or finest apartment, should look out on the most beautiful view, either over a distant prospect, if there be such, or, if not, upon the fine home landscape of trees, lawn, or flower-garden. A library may occupy a more secluded position, and requires less attention to outward circumstances, as the *matériel* from whence it dispenses enjoyment is within itself. Again, there are other minor points more generally understood, which may be considered under this principle, and to which we need scarcely allude. Among these are the construction of proper drains to the kitchen and basement, the introduction of water-pipes, cisterns, etc. A bathing-room requires little space, and may be easily constructed in any cottage, and its great importance to health renders it a most desirable feature in all our houses. No dwelling can be considered complete which has not a water-closet under its roof, though the expense may yet for some time prevent their general introduction into small cottages.

In a country like ours, where the population is comparatively sparse, civil rights equal, and wages high, good servants or domestics are comparatively rare, and not likely to retain their places a long time. The maximum of comfort, therefore, is found to consist in employing the smallest number of servants actually necessary. This may be greatly facilitated by having all the apartments conveniently arranged with reference to their various uses, and still further by introducing certain kinds of domestic labor-saving apparatus to lessen the amount of service required, or to render its performance easy. Among those which we would, from experience, especially recommend for cottages, are the rising cupboard or dumb waiter, the speaking-tube, and the rotary pump.

The rising cupboard is only required in the case of a basement kitchen, and in this instance it will be found to render the labor of carrying the dinner to and from the kitchen much easier than that experienced in bringing it from a kitchen on the same floor, with less risk of broken china or dishes. The unsightly appearance of a cupboard rising through the floor in a corner of the dining-room is obviated by having it enclosed by a fixed case, like a small sideboard, and its construction we shall show hereafter.

Speaking-tubes are merely common tin tubes, one and a half inch in diameter, terminated by mouth-pieces, one of which is in the kitchen, the other in the desired apartment. They will usually only be required in two rooms, viz., the dining-room and the family bed-room, and in constructing the house they may be introduced and led through the partitions at a very trifling cost. They save much time and labor, as by their aid we may be able to communicate our wants in a whisper from the chamber floor to the kitchen, and have them answered with less loss of time than would be required by the ordinary use of the bell only, to bring the servant to our room to learn our wishes.

The rotary pump may be considered as supplying the place in a cottage of the extensive arrangement of water-pipes introduced in the best mansions for supplying the upper or chamber story with water. A rotary pump, placed in some convenient position in the hall of the chamber floor of a cottage, and communicating by a leaden pipe with a cistern outside, may be said to place an abundant supply of water within a few steps of every bed-room on that story. This, it is evident, will save much labor in carrying water daily, to say nothing of the comfort of having a fresh supply within reach at any moment. The introduction of a complete set of water-pipes in a house is expensive, and to keep them in repair is a considerable additional tax, but the comparative cheapness and efficiency of the rotary pump (which is the neatest and most complete apparatus) render it, or something of this same description, an almost indispensable convenience in a cottage of more than one story.

The universally acknowledged utility of closets renders it unnecessary for us to say anything to direct attention to them under this head. In the principal story, a pantry or closets are a necessary accompaniment to the dining or living room, but are scarcely required in connection with any of the other apartments. Bed-rooms always require at least one closet to each, and more will be found convenient. One, or sometimes two, may always be provided, in a chamber having a fire-place, by enclosing the space on one side of the chimney-breast, and in all cottage villas, or villas of good size, one or two bed-rooms should be provided with dressing-rooms attached, which will be found to add greatly to the real comfort of the apartment. Some persons, however, have such a passion for closets, that they not unfrequently destroy all the merit of a plan, by cutting up the interior so as to afford them in abundance. A plan of very moderate size will perhaps only afford a few rooms of good size and proportion, which would be injured or destroyed by cutting off many closets. It is far better to substitute wardrobes, or movable closets, than thus to sacrifice *all* space and elegance of arrangement to convenience.

The mode of construction, and the materials employed, are also comprised under the head of fitness. In this country, from the great abundance and cheapness of wood, it has, until within a few years, been almost the only material employed in constructing country houses : but as timber has grown scarcer in the forest it has also become dearer, until, in many parts of the Atlantic States, stone or brick is equally economical. Wood is acknowledged by all architects to be the worst material for building, and should never be employed when it is in the power of the builder to use any other. Its want of durability, the expense of

painting it and keeping it in repair, and its-frailness and
liability to decay by the action of the weather, are all very
serious objections to it as a material for dwelling-houses.
A cottage of wood is, from the thinness of the exterior,
necessarily warmer in summer and colder in winter than
one built of more solid materials. Filling-in with brick
decreases this objection, but does not entirely remove it.
In point of taste, a house built of wood strikes us the least
agreeably, as our pleasure in beholding a beautiful form is
marred by the idea of the frailness of the material composing that form. We are aware that the almost universal
prevalence of wooden country houses in the United States
has weakened this impression, but the strength with which
it strikes an European, accustomed to solidity and permanence in a dwelling, is the best proof of the truth of our
remark. And even in this country, the change of feeling
which is daily taking place on this subject, shows very
plainly in how little estimation wood will be held as a
building material, compared with brick or stone, by the
next generation.

Brick is the next best material to wood, and is every day
coming into more general use. The walls formed of it, if
well constructed, have a solidity and permanence appropriate for a country house, and requiring little cost to
keep it in repair. The offensive hue of red brick walls in
the country is easily removed by coloring them any agreeable tint, which will also render them dryer and more permanent. Brick and stucco (that is, a wall built of rough
brick, and coated exteriorly with a cement) is, when well
executed, one of the best materials for cottages or villas.
It is much warmer and dryer than wood, or even stone, and
is equal to the latter in external effect, when marked off
and colored to resemble it. We have no doubt that in a

short time it will have a very general preference in most sections of the country.*

Stone is generally conceded to be superior, on the whole, to any other material for building. This is owing to its great durability and solidity, both in expression and in reality; and to its requiring no trouble to keep it in repair, as it suffers little or no injury from the action of the elements.

When houses are built of brick or stone, the interior plastering should never be put directly upon the inner face of the wall, as is sometimes done by careless or ignorant mechanics : but the lathing upon which it is formed should always be separated from the solid wall by what is technically called "furring off," which leaves a space of two or more inches between the solid wall and that of plaster. This vacuity is, of course, occupied by air, which is a better non-conductor than any wall, prevents effectually the penetration of all dampness, and renders the wall warmer than would three times the same thickness of solid material.

When we are necessarily restricted to the employment of a certain material, both fitness and good taste require that there should be a correspondence between the material used and the style adopted for the building. Heavy and massive architecture—a temple, a castle, or a mansion— should be built of stone only, or some solid enduring substance, but cottages in some light and fanciful styles may with more propriety be erected in wood, that material

---

* The common hydraulic cements of New York are unfit for plastering the exterior of houses, and many persons who have only seen these employed (mixed perhaps with dirty, instead of sharp, clean sand), suppose that all cements are equally liable to crumble by exposure to damp and frost. The cement (or hydraulic limes) of Connecticut and Pennsylvania are greatly superior for stucco or external plaster, becoming, when well applied, nearly as firm and durable as stone. [The brick and stucco mode of building walls has not come into very general use in this country. ED.]

being in harmony with the expression of the form and out-lines. There cannot well be a greater violation of correct taste than to build a Gothic castellated villa with thin wooden boards. It is a species of counterfeit coin which will never pass current with cultivated minds. De Tocque-ville, in his remarks on the spirit in which the Americans cultivate the arts, says, " When I arrived for the first time at New York, by that part of the Atlantic Ocean which is called the Narrows, I was surprised to perceive along the shore, at some distance from the city, a considerable num-ber of palaces of white marble, several of which were built after the models of ancient architecture." His surprise was still greater, however, when he went the next day to inspect the temple that had particularly attracted his notice, to find that its imposing portico was supported by huge *columns of painted wood.*

Something might be said on the subject of fitness, with regard to the furniture and interior decoration of our dwelling-houses. This is a great charm about a country house, fitted up or furnished simply, appropriately, and comfortably. A profusion of mirrors, of gilding, or of chairs and sofas, too magnificent except for show, strikes us disagreeably amid the freshness, the silence, and sim-plicity of that nature which quietly looks us in the face at every window of a house in the country.

The *expression of purpose* in architecture is conveyed by features in a building, or by its whole appearance, suggest-ing the end in view, or the purpose for which it is intended. A church, for example, is easily known by its spire, or a barn by its plain large doors, and the absence of chimneys, and the reason acknowledges a satisfaction in finding them to be what they appear, or, in other words, with the *truth-fulness* of their expression. Whatever, therefore, tends to heighten expression of purpose, must grow out of some quality which connects itself in the mind with the use for which it is designed, and a genuine mode of increasing our admiration of any building is to render it expressive of the purpose for which it is built.

Although, at first thought, it would appear that persons would be little likely to fall into error in violating the truthfulness of a building, yet examples do not unfrequently occur. Some of our dwelling-houses are so meagre and comfortless in their exteriors, that one might be fairly pardoned for supposing them barns, and, on the other hand, we have seen stables so decorated with green shutters and pilasters that they have actually been mistaken for dwelling-houses. A blind passion for a particular style of building may also tend to destroy expression of purpose. It would certainly be difficult for a stranger in some of our towns, where the taste for Grecian temples prevails, to distinguish with accuracy between a church, a bank, and a hall of justice.

Not only should the whole house have a general character denoting the end in view, but every portion of it should be made, as far as possible, to convey the same impression. The various useful features entering into its composition should all be expressive of the end for which they are intended, and should appear to answer their purpose. Thus large windows indicate spacious and well-ventilated apartments, and although propriety requires the windows of the principal rooms to be made larger than those of the chamber story, yet the latter should not be shorn of their due proportions so as to be expressive of imperfect accommodation. One of the most common errors which of late has crept into our suburban builders' heads, is the introduction of short attic windows into the second or third story of their houses. However satisfactory such dwellings may otherwise be, the expression of low and confined chambers, conveyed by these cramped windows, destroys all pleasure in contemplating their exteriors.

The prominent features conveying expression of purpose in dwelling-houses, are the chimneys, the windows, and the porch, veranda, or piazza; and for this reason, whenever it is desired to raise the character of a cottage or villa above mediocrity, attention should first be bestowed on those portions of the building.

The chimney-tops, in all countries where fires are used, are decidedly expressive of purpose, as they are associated with all our ideas of warmth, the cheerful fireside, and the social winter circle. The learned Bishop Hall says,

> "Look to the towered chimnies, which should be
> The wind-pipes of good hospitalitie."

"In every human habitation," says Loudon, "these chimney-tops ought to be conspicuous objects, because they are its essential characteristics. They distinguish apartments destined for human beings from those designed for lodging cattle. They also distinguish a dwelling-house from a manufactory or workshop, by their size, number, form, or disposition." As chimney-tops are thus so essential a part of dwelling-houses, we should endeavor to render them pleasing objects, and increase their importance by making them ornamental. The clumsy mass of bricks should be enlivened and rendered elegant by varying its form, ornamenting its sides and summit, or separating the whole into distinct flues, forming a cluster, in modes of which there are a multitude of suitable examples in the various styles of architecture. The chimney-tops generally occupy the highest portions of the roof, breaking against the sky boldly, and, if enriched, will not only increase the expression of purpose, but add also to the picturesque beauty of the composition.

The porch, the veranda, or the piazza, are highly characteristic features, and no dwelling-house can be considered complete without one or more of them. The entrance door, even in the humblest cottage, should always be a conspicuous feature in its front, and it may be rendered so by a porch or veranda of some kind, which will serve to keep the entrance dry and warm in inclement weather. In all countries like ours, where there are hot summers, a veranda, piazza, or colonnade is a necessary and delightful appendage to a dwelling-house, and in fact during a considerable part of the year frequently becomes the lounging apartment of the family. Hence a broad shady veranda suggests ideas of comfort, and is highly expressive of purpose. For the same reason, bay or oriel windows, balconies, and terraces, added to villas, increase their interest, not only by their beauty of form, but by their denoting more forcibly those elegant enjoyments which belong to the habitation of man in a cultivated and refined state of society.

The *color* of buildings may very properly be made to increase their expression of truthfulness. Thus a barn or stable, being regarded entirely in a useful point of view, may have a quiet, unobtrusive tone of color, while a cottage or villa should be of a cheerful, mellow hue harmonizing with the verdure of the country. A mansion may very properly have a graver color than a cottage, to be in unison with its greater dignity and extent. There is one color, however, frequently employed by house-painters, which we feel bound to protest against most heartily, as entirely unsuitable and in bad taste. This is *white*, which

is so universally applied to our wooden houses of every size
and description. The glaring nature of this color, when seen
in contrast with the soft green of foliage, renders it
extremely unpleasant to an eye attuned to harmony of
coloring, and nothing but its very great prevalence in the
United States could render even men of some taste so
heedless of its bad effect. No painter of landscapes that
has possessed a name was ever guilty of displaying in his
pictures a glaring white house, but, on the contrary, the
buildings introduced by the great masters have uniformly
a mellow softened shade of color, in exquisite keeping with
the surrounding objects.*

We shall quote on this subject some remarks in point by
Uvedale Price, whose name is of high authority.† "One
of the most charming effects of sunshine is its giving to
objects not merely light, but that mellow golden hue so
beautiful in itself, and which, when diffused as in a fine
evening over the whole landscape, creates that rich union
and harmony so enchanting in nature and Claude. In any
scene, whether real or painted, when such harmony prevails,
the least discordancy in color would disturb the eye: but
if we suppose a single object of a glaring white to be introduced, the whole attention, in spite of all our efforts to the
contrary, will be drawn to that one point; if many such
objects be scattered about, the eye will be distracted among
them. Again (to consider it in another view), when the
sun breaks out in gleams, there is something that delights
and surprises in seeing an object, before only visible, lighted
up in splendor, and then gradually sinking into shade; but

---

* To render the effect still worse, our modern builders paint their Venetian
window-shutters a bright green! A cool dark green would be in better taste, and
more agreeable to the eye, both from the exterior and interior.

† "Essays on the Picturesque."

a whitened object is already lighted up; it remains so when everything else has retired into obscurity; it still forces itself into notice, still impudently stares you in the face. An object of a sober tint, unexpectedly gilded by the sun, is like a serious countenance suddenly lighted up by a smile; a whitened object like the eternal grin of a fool." There may be a little sarcasm in the tone of these remarks, but that they are strictly true every fine colorist will admit.

As it is difficult to convey in words a proper idea of delicate shades of color, and as we think the subject one of very great importance in domestic architecture, we have given specimens on the opposite page of six shades of color highly suitable for the exterior of cottages and villas.* A, B, and C, are shades of gray, and D, E, F, of drab or fawn color, which will be found pleasing and harmonious in any situation in the country. Stuccoed or cemented buildings should be marked off in courses, and tinted to resemble some mellow stone; Bath, Portland stone, or any other of the light free-stone shades, are generally most agreeable.

A person of correct architectural taste will carry his feeling of artistical propriety into the interior of his house, and confer on each apartment, by expression of purpose, a kind of individuality. Thus, in a complete cottage-villa, the hall will be graye and simple in character, a few plain seats its principal furniture; the library sober and dignified, or bookish and learned in its air; the dining-room cheerful, with a hospitable sideboard and table; the drawing-room lively or brilliant, adorned with pictures or other objects of art, and evincing more elegance and gayety of tone in its colors and furniture. The bed-rooms would be simple, or only pretty, with abundant ventilation, and ceilings of full height, and not low or contracted.

---

*Because the colors in the plate do not correspond to the colors mentioned in the text, the plate has been omitted from this reprint edition.

We have thus sketched the ground-work upon which architecture rests, fitness and expression of purpose, but architecture which goes no further is only a useful, not a *fine art.* It is only *building.* The true artist breathes a life and soul, *which is beauty*, into the dead utilitarian materials, stone and wood, and they speak a language that is understood as readily as that of animate nature. The mechanic blocks out the stone from the quarry, he even gives to it the semblance of the human form, but only the sculptor moulds the cold marble into a passion or a sentiment that endures for ages, and strikes men of speech dumb with its voiceless eloquence. A Greek temple or an old cathedral speaks to the soul of all men as audibly as could a Demosthenes. Even a Swiss chalet, with its drooping, shadowy eaves, or an old English cottage, with its quaint peaked gables, each embodies a sentiment in its peculiar form which takes hold of the mind, and convinces us that, in some way or other, it has a living power. To reproduce the beautiful in this manner, and to infuse a spirit and a grace in forms otherwise only admirable for their usefulness, is the *ideal* of architecture as an art of taste, and its inspiration may be seen here and there in some humble nook-hidden cottage, as well as in the dome of St. Peter's.

As all the satisfaction which the reason experiences in building as a useful art arises from fitness and expression of purpose, so all the delight which the imagination receives from architecture as an art of taste is derived from *beauty of form*, and from the *sentiment* associated with certain modes of building long prevalent in any age or country.

Aside from certain styles of architecture which have received the approbation of all men for their acknowledged beauty, and which are generally followed by architects, there are also some leading rules which should govern us in the composition of buildings in any style, however simple, because they are inherent sources of beauty, common to all styles.

The first of these is the principle of Unity, a principle of the highest importance in all works of art. There should be a unity of design in all portions of the same building, showing, by a correspondence of its various parts, that they all originated in the same mind; a unity of style, avoiding the introduction, in an established mode, of any portions or members not in keeping with that mode; and a unity of decoration, evinced in the appropriate application of enrichment to the whole, rather than to a single part of an edifice. These rules of Unity are not unfrequently violated by architects, but always at the expense of the beauty and perfection of their works, as no artist is superior to principles.* The production of a *whole* follows as the result of attention to the principles of Unity, and our pleasure in every work of art is enduring precisely in proportion as it forms a perfect whole. Unity is the principle of *Oneness*, and its violation always shocks a tasteful and consistent mind. As an example of the violation of unity of style, we might refer to a number of country chapels or churches within our knowledge, where a Grecian portico and Gothic or pointed windows occur in the same composition! Or, to illustrate the like in unity of decoration or of design, how many country dwellings have we all seen, with a highly elegant colonnade in front, accompanying bare sides, without the least corresponding enrichment in the windows!

The next principles of composition are those of *Uniform-*

---

* "Every opportunity should be taken to discountenance that false and vulgar opinion, that rules are the fetters of genius; they are fetters only to men of no genius."—SIR JOSHUA REYNOLDS.

ity and of *Symmetry;* two words which frequently pass as synonymous in common language.

Uniformity in building is the repetition of the same forms in the different portions or sides of a building. " A hut may be recognized as a work of art, however rude or anomalous its form; because, according to human experience, its sides, its roof, and its door could never have been arranged so as to form a hut by chance. Such a hut is satisfactory as a work of art, but nothing more; but a hut in a square form gives additional satisfaction by the regularity of its figure, which gives an idea not only of art, but of cultivated or improved art. There can be no doubt, therefore, that the love of regularity is strongly implanted in the human mind; since regularity is the first principle which displays itself in the works of man, composed with a view to beauty." * Hence, those persons who have the least taste or imagination will be found to prefer a plain square or cube, above all others, for a house, as being the first principle of beauty which they are able to discover in architecture.†

As Uniformity is the balance of two regular parts, so the principle of Symmetry may be defined the balance of two irregular parts; in other words, Uniformity in works of art is *artistical regularity;* Symmetry, *artistical irregularity.* There are irregular buildings without symmetry, but in all irregular compositions entirely satisfactory, it will generally be found that there is a kind of hidden proportion which one-half of the whole bears to

---

* *Architectural Magazine,* i. 221.

† As, besides this, a square or parallelogram is the most economical form in which a house can be built, and as a small house does not easily permit irregularity, we have adopted it in designing the greater number of cottages which follow, but we have endeavored to raise them above mere uniformity, by adding such characteristic ornaments as to give also some *variety* to the compositions.

the other, and it is this balance which constitutes symmetry.

A building may be highly irregular, it may abound in variety and picturesqueness, and yet be perfectly symmetrical. In the annexed rough sketch (Fig. 1), the pile of

FIG. 1.

building represented, which is full of irregularity, is also symmetrical, for if we divide it by the imaginary line a, the portion on the right balances that on the left; that is, though not in shape, yet in bulk and in the mass of composition; while in Fig. 2, which is a uniform or regular building, the portion to the right balances that on the left

FIG. 2.

both in form and bulk. Now almost all persons who have not cultivated a taste for architecture, or whose organizations are deficient in this faculty, would prefer a regular house to a symmetrically irregular one, because with them the reason only demands to be satisfied; but with more cultivated minds the taste and imagination are active, and call for a more lively and varied kind of beauty, and the irregular building would be chosen, as affording more intense and enduring pleasure.

As the principles of *Harmony*, *Variety*, etc., are intimately connected with, and may be said to grow out of, Unity, Uniformity, and Symmetry, we shall not in our present limits offer any remarks upon them.

The different styles in architecture are certain modes of building which have had their origin in different countries, and may be considered as standard forms of architectural beauty. They have, almost without exception, had their origin in some lofty enthusiasm of the age, which was embodied by the master artists of the time, generally in the enthusiasm of religion. To the pagan gods were reared the beautiful temples of the Greeks, and under the more spiritual influence of Christianity arose those Gothic cathedrals in which the ponderous stone was wrought in the most exquisite modifications of intricacy and beauty— those cathedrals which, says an eloquent writer, are "a blossoming in stone, subdued by the insatiable demand of harmony in man." In like manner the Oriental style, distinguished by its mosques and minarets, and the Egyptian, by its pyramids and cavernous temples, have all had their origin in the same lofty aspirations of the artist.

All domestic architecture, in a given style, should be a subdued expression or manifestation of that style adjusted to the humbler requirements of the building and the more quiet purposes of domestic life. Hence it would evidently be absurd to copy a cathedral in building a dwelling in the Gothic style, or a temple in a cottage after the Grecian mode.

Nearly all the modes of building in modern use may be referred to two original styles, of which they are only modifications or varieties, viz.: to the Grecian, in which horizontal lines prevail, and to the Gothic, in which vertical lines prevail; and there have not been wanting artists who have caught something of the spirit and beauty of the original masterpieces of art, and transfused them into the more domestic styles which have grown out of these to suit the wants of civilized life. Thus, although the pure Grecian style (the temple) was not intended, and is not suitable for domestic purposes, the Roman and the Italian styles, which are modified forms of it, are elegant adaptations of its characteristic forms to this purpose. The Italian style, by its verandas and balconies, its projecting roofs, and the capacity and variety of its form, is especially suited to a warm climate.

In the same manner the Swiss, the Flemish, and other continental modes of building, with exterior galleries, and wide horizontal cornices, are all variations of this mode, only differing in some peculiar adaptation to the climate of the country, or the customs of the people.

Neither has the Gothic been confined to the cathedral, where, as the noblest form, it exists in its grandeur and purity, but its beauty and picturesqueness have reappeared in the old English styles of domestic architecture. The most perfect examples are those of the castles and mansions of England of the time of the Tudors, but the whole of the cottage architecture of England is imbued with its spirit, and the manifestations are everywhere visible, in quaintly carved gables or verge boards, wreathed and clustered chimneys, beautiful windows ornamented with

tracery, and numberless other details, highly expressive
and characteristic.

In adopting any style for imitation, our preference
should be guided not only by the intrinsic beauty which
we see in a particular style, but by its appropriateness to
our uses. This will generally be indicated by the climate,
the site or situation, and the wants of the family who are
to inhabit it. In a high northern latitude, where it is evident colonnades and verandas would be unsuitable for most
of the year, the Italian or Grecian styles should not be
chosen; and in a tropical one, the warm, solid, comfortable
features of the old English architecture would not be necessary or appropriate. In a country like the middle portions of the United States, where the summers are hot and
the winters cold, there is sufficient latitude for the adop-
tion of various styles of building, and therefore more judgment or taste is requisite in the selection.

The different styles of architecture have been very aptly
compared to different languages, employed by various
architects to express their ideas, and which, when perfect,
always remain nearly fixed, and best express the wants
of a particular age or country. We may safely carry out
this illustration, and say that the temples and cathedrals
are the orations and epic poems, the dwelling-houses the
familiar epistles or conversations of the particular styles.

In expressing our architectural ideas by the medium of
a certain style or language, we shall succeed best, and our
efforts will afford most delight, the more nearly we approach to the nature of the circumstances under which the
style or language originated. Thus, if we talk pure Greek,
and build a Grecian temple for a dwelling, we shall be little
understood, or perhaps only laughed at by our neighbors.
It is not much better in the present day to recite an epic

poem by building a cathedral, or a heroic one by constructing a castle for our habitation. Let us rather be more sen-
sible, though not less graceful in our architectural utter-
ance, and express a pleasant, every-day language in an old
English mansion, a Rural Gothic cottage, or an Italian
villa.

For domestic architecture, we would strongly recommend those simple modifications of architectural styles,
where the beauty grows out of the enrichment of some
useful or elegant features of the house, as the windows or
verandas, rather than those where some strongly marked
features, of little domestic beauty, overpower the rest of
the building. The Rural Gothic style, characterized mainly
by pointed gables, and the Italian, by projecting roofs,
balconies, and terraces, are much the most beautiful modes
for our country residences. Their outlines are highly picturesque and harmonious with nature. Their forms are
convenient, their accessories elegant, and they are highly
expressive of the refined and unostentatious enjoyments of
the country. We have pointed out in another work the
objections that may fairly be urged against the false taste
lately so prevalent among us, in building our country
houses in the form of Greek temples, sacrificing thereby
the beauty of variety, much convenience, and all the comfort of low and shady verandas, to the ambitious display
of a portico of stately columns; and we are happy to see
that the fashion is on the decline. Let us hope speedily to
see in its place a correct taste springing up in every part of
the country, which shall render our cottage homes beautiful,
not by borrowing the features or enrichments of a temple
or palace, but by seeking beautiful and appropriate forms,
characteristic of domestic life, and indicative of home comforts.

Not a little of the delight of beautiful buildings to a cultivated mind grows out of the *sentiment* of architecture, or the associations connected with certain styles. Thus the sight of an old English villa will call up in the mind of one familiar with the history of architecture, the times of the Tudors, or of "Merry England," in the days of Elizabeth. The mingled quaintness, beauty, and picturesqueness of the exterior, no less than the oaken wainscot, curiously carved furniture, and fixtures of the interior of such a dwelling, when harmoniously complete, seem to transport one back to a past age, the domestic habits, the hearty hospitality, the joyous old sports, and the romance and chivalry of which, invest it, in the dim retrospect, with a kind of golden glow, in which the shadowy lines of poetry and reality seem strangely interwoven and blended.

So, too, an Italian villa may recall, to one familiar with Italy and art, by its bold roof lines, its campanile and its shady balconies, the classic beauty of that fair and smiling land, where pictures, sculptured figures, vases, and urns, in all exquisite forms, make part of the decorations and "surroundings" of domestic and public edifices. A residence in the Roman style (more suitable than the Grecian) may, by its dignified elegance of arrangement and decoration, recall to the classic mind the famed Tusculum retreat of Pliny. And one fond of the wild and picturesque, whose home chances to be in some one of our rich mountain valleys, may give it a peculiar interest by imitating the Swiss cottage, or at least its expressive and striking features. A great deal of the charm of architectural style, in all cases, will arise from the happy union between the locality or site, and the style chosen, and from the entireness with which the architect or amateur enters into the spirit and character of the style, and carries it through his whole work. This may be done in a small cottage, and at little cost, as well as in a mansion, at great expense; but it requires more taste and skill to achieve the former admirably, although the latter may involve ten times the magnitude.

DESIGN I.

A Suburban Cottage for a small Family.

WE have supposed this cottage to be situated in the suburbs of a town or village, and, for the sake of illustrating the treatment of a small portion of ground, we shall also imagine it to be placed on a lot of ground 75 feet front by 150 deep, which, at the time of commencing the building, has upon it no trees or improvements of any description.

By referring to the plan of the first floor of this cottage, Fig. 4, the reader will perceive on the left of the hall, the parlor, or living-room, 16 feet by 21 feet, having in communication with it, a pantry and a closet for books—each 4 feet by 8 feet. On the opposite side of the hall are, the kitchen, 14 feet by 16, and a bed-room 12 feet by 16 feet.

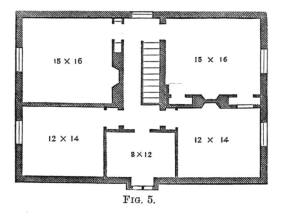

FIG. 5.

In the plan of the chamber floor, Fig. 5, there are four bed-rooms of good size, and one of small dimensions. Sufficient cellar room will be obtained under the living-room, closets,

DESIGN I.

A Suburban Cottage.

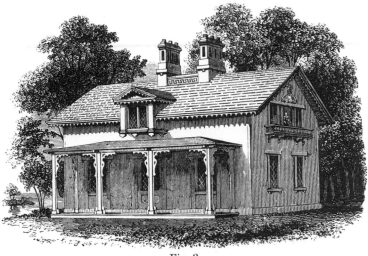

Fig. 3.

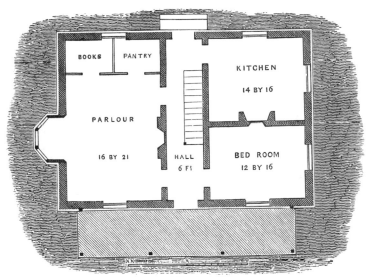

Fig. 4.

and hall, and it will not therefore be necessary to excavate for this purpose under the kitchen and first floor bed-room; a circumstance which will lessen the expense in building the foundation walls.

This simple cottage will be a suitable one for a small family, when the mistress wishes to have the management of the domestic affairs directly under her own personal care and supervision. In such a case it is indispensable to have the kitchen on the same floor with the living-room, though, if possible, not opening directly into it; as in the latter arrangement, the smell arising from the cooking would be in unpleasant proximity to the living-room. We have therefore placed it on the opposite side of the hall, though but a few steps from the living-room. In a cottage of this description, the master and mistress will generally prefer to have their own bed-room on the first floor, and we have accordingly placed it opposite the living-room.

Although this cottage is of very moderate size, yet, to a family of small means, leading a comparatively retired life, it will afford a great deal of comfort, and even a considerable degree of taste or neatness. The parlor or living-room is comparatively large; its outline is agreeably varied by the bay window opposite the fire-place—and the closet of books connected with it, indicating a certain degree of mental cultivation, may very fairly stand in the place of the library, which forms one of the suite of apartments in a larger cottage or villa. On the other hand, the pantry opening into the same apartment renders it equally eligible and convenient as a dining-room. However large our dwelling-houses may be, including every grade, from a cottage to a palace, if they are occupied by a family of moderate size, it will be found that more than one room is seldom used at a time, and that all the actual comforts of domestic life may be realized in a cottage of this class, containing only a single parlor or living-room, as well as in a mansion of a dozen apartments. "I must confess," says Cowley, "I love littleness almost in all things. A little cheerful house, a little company, and a very little feast." Whatever is necessary beyond this, arises either from a desire to enjoy a more luxurious style of living, or from the wish to entertain a larger circle of friends. Now as none of these are supposed to come within the wishes or means of the inmates of a cottage like the present, its accommodation will be found ample. And supposing one or two of the attic chambers occupied by younger members of the family, and another by a domestic or domestics, there will still remain a "spare room," which we shall suppose always neat and clean, ready for the friend or stranger who may enjoy the cordial welcome of the cottage.

In building this cottage, the kitchen should be provided with a brick drain, leading from the sink to some large drain at a distance from the house, or, in case this is impracticable, to a reservoir dug at a distance of forty or fifty feet from the house in a gravelly stratum, where the drainage may lose itself in the soil. [Cement pipes, or glazed stoneware pipes, laid in cement, with stench-traps of the same material attached to them near the house, or directly under, just beyond the rise, are now used in preference to the brick drains, being cheaper, and better for the purpose.—ED.] This reservoir may be of the size of a cistern of ordinary capacity, the sides built up with a dry wall, the top covered by flag stones, and the whole finally covered by soil. In order to prevent smells arising to the kitchen from the drain, it must be provided with a *smell-trap*, which is easily constructed. If the water

from the well, or cistern, or both, is introduced by a leaden
pipe and small pump into a corner of the kitchen over
the sink, it will add still further to the convenience of
performing the culinary labor of the dwelling.

As regards external effect, we think this cottage will be
allowed to be very pleasing to the eye. Aside from any
other quality, its uniformity will be a source of satisfaction
to a larger class of persons who do not relish irregularity
in any building. There are also several features entering
into the composition of this cottage which give it at once
the air of something superior in design to ordinary buildings of the same class. The first of these is the veranda,
ornamented by brackets between the supports, which shel
ters the entrance-door, and affords an agreeable place both
for walking in damp or unpleasant weather, and to enjoy a
cool shaded seat in the hotter portion of the season. The
second feature is the projection of the eaves, with the ornamental eave-board, which serves to protect the exterior
more completely than any other form against the effects
of storms, and gives character by its boldness and the deep
shadows it casts upon the building. The chimney-tops are
rendered sufficiently ornamental to accord with the degree
of decoration displayed in the other portions of the cottage;
and something of the bracketed character is kept up in the
dressing of the windows and door-frames. The projecting
dormer-window adds beauty and gives importance to the
entrance front.

If we suppose this cottage, stripped of its projecting
eaves, its bracketed veranda, its dormer-window, and the
little decoration visible in the chimney-tops and other
details, we shall have a building in the form of a parallelogram of the very plainest description. Such a building
would be distinguishable from a barn or outhouse only by

the presence of chimneys and windows of larger size, and would convey to the mind no impression whatever of refinement in its occupants. By a trifling additional outlay at the time of building, amounting from seven to ten per cent. on the whole cost, such a plain dwelling may be made the ornamental cottage shown in Design I., which we think would strike every observer as being tasteful and agreeable to the eye.

Construction.—This cottage, being light and somewhat fanciful in its character, may be built of wood filled in with brick. The roof should project twenty inches or two feet, and the roof of the veranda in proportion. A portion of this veranda is shown in Fig. 6, and a section of the pillars or

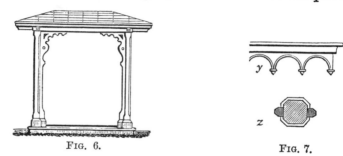

FIG. 6. FIG. 7.

supports in Fig. 7. z, The ornamental cornice which surrounds the building, is shown more in detail at y; the pendent portion being cut out of inch board, and the points terminated by acorns turned, and nailed on. The details y and z are to the scale of one-half of an inch to a foot.

Brick and cement would be a very suitable construction for this cottage, as the projecting roof would afford perfect security for the dryness and preservation of the walls. In this mode of building the roughest bricks may be used, and are really preferable, as affording a better surface for receiving and retaining the stucco than smooth ones. In many districts, where bricks are easily obtained, this kind of building will be found as cheap as wood.

It will be observed that in this design, and the seven others that follow, we have placed the chimneys in the interior, not in the exterior walls, a point of considerable importance, which is greatly overlooked by our builders. When a stack of chimneys is built in the outer walls, it seldom continues warm during the whole twenty-four hours, as it parts with its heat rapidly to the cold external air. Now as a good draught depends, in a great degree, on the warmth of the column of air, and this upon the heat of the chimney, it is evident that chimneys in the interior of a house must draw better than in the exterior walls. Besides this, a great deal of heat is retained in the body of the house by carrying the stacks of flues through it. And in point of external effect, it is much more pleasing to see the chimney-tops rising from the apex, or highest part of the roof, than from its lowest edge.

Estimate.—The estimated cost of this cottage, finished in a neat and suitable manner, is $1,800. This, as well as the estimates which follow, is intended to apply to the majority of situations in the Middle and Eastern States, where timber is comparatively scarce, and bricks of second quality, suitable for stuccoing upon, are worth about $4 per thousand. In districts where wood is much cheaper, the cost of erection would be much less if this material were wholly employed. [When the above estimate was made, labor and materials were about one-half the present prices. At the present writing, ordinary hard bricks are worth from $7.50 to $9 per thousand. Carpenters charge $2.50 to $3.50 per day, and masons from $3.50 to $4.50. This cottage in wood would cost about $3,600, and in brick, about $4,500.—ED.]

Laying out the ground.—As this cottage is decidedly ornamental in its character, it may fairly be presumed that it would be required that a considerable portion of the limited ground nearest the house should be rendered ornamental also. In the suburbs of a town or village, the more common kinds of vegetables may generally be purchased as cheaply as they can be raised by the inmates of such a cottage. The more delicate kinds of fruit, and a few of the earlier or finer kinds of vegetables may, however, be produced, of fine flavor, and with more satisfaction to the proprietor, on the spot. We have therefore devoted one-third of the area of the lot, Fig. 8, to the kitchen garden *a*, and the remaining two-thirds will remain to be occupied by the house, and for ornamental purposes. In order to separate these two portions, and to prevent the eye of a person looking from the house, or any of the walks across the little lawn *b*, from seeing the kitchen garden at the same time with the ornamental portion, we shall place an ornamental trellis across the lot at *c*, which may be covered by the following vines, remarkable for the beauty of their foliage and flowers, or for their fragrance, viz. :—

2 Chinese Twining Honeysuckles, blooming in June and October.		
2 Monthly Fragrant "	"	May to November.
1 Yellow Trumpet "	"	May to November.
1 Red " "	"	May to November.
1 Sweet-Scented Clematis,	"	August.
1 Virginian Silk, or Periploca,	"	July.
1 Chinese Wistaria,	"	May.
1 Climbing Boursalt Rose,	"	June.
2 Double Michigan Roses,	"	May to December.

These, after a couple of years' growth, will form a verdant barrier, which in no season, except winter, will be without flowers. Across the walks leading into the

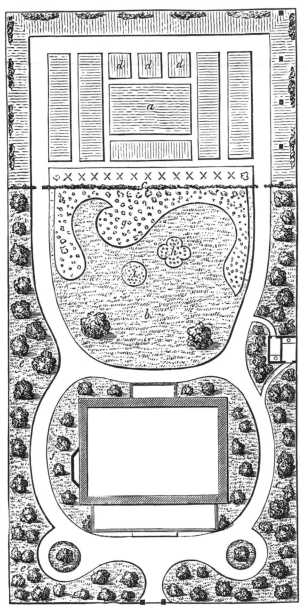

[Fig. 8.]

kitchen garden, the lattice fence may be continued in the form of light gates, and the vines may be trained so as to form archways overhead.

Around the exterior of the kitchen garden is a border 6 feet wide, which will be an excellent situation for a few choice fruit trees; because, if planted on this exterior border, they will not shade the beds devoted to vegetables, which, if planted in the middle of the compartment, they would soon do to such an extent as to render the situation unfit for raising a crop of any kind. On the right-hand border, which is the warmest aspect, we would advise the planting of some grape-vines, which may either be trained to the fence, or to a trellis placed four or five inches from the fence. These vines may consist of a Catawba, an Isabella, an Elsingburgh, and a Bland's Virginia, all hardy varieties, very productive, and requiring little care. [Instead of the Catawba, Isabella, and Bland's Virginia grapes, place Delaware, Israella, and Concord, which are more in favor now; and for the D'Aremberg Pear substitute the Beurre Bosc.—Ed.] On the other two outer borders there will be sufficient room for one tree of each of the following fruits, viz., a Bartlett, a Seckel, and a D'Aremberg Pear; a George the Fourth and a Snow Peach; an Imperial Gage and a Jefferson Plum; a Mayduke and a Downer's Late Red Cherry, and a Moorpark Apricot. In the same borders, and beneath these fruit trees, strawberries may be planted, making a bed about one hundred and twenty feet long, which, if kept in good condition, will be sufficient to supply a small family with this delicious fruit. The border to the right, containing the grape-vines, we shall suppose (except immediately around the vine) to be kept in grass, in which neat posts are set at the distance of twelve feet apart, for the purpose of stretching a line for drying clothes upon. These posts being half way between the frame or trellis, upon which the grapes are trained, and the walk, the line would be easily commanded by a person standing upon the walk. The space devoted to culinary vegetables we have merely indicated by beds four feet wide on the plan, leaving the occupant to apportion the same to their various uses, premising that the large bed in the centre, at *a*, is intended for asparagus; the three smaller ones, *d*, for sweet herbs; and the long bed, ×, behind the trellis, covered by ornamental vines, for the esculent rhubarb, which is so valuable an article for tarts or pies, that no cottage garden, however small, should be without it.

Such a thing as a *wall* for fruit trees, in a cottage garden, is nearly unknown in the United States, and therefore we need say nothing respecting training them to a wall. But a cottage garden is usually surrounded by a neat board fence or paling, painted some drab or inconspicuous color; and as the number of fruit trees that could be judiciously planted here is small, we would strongly advise the owner of this garden to train the branches to this fence, or to a trellis formed by nailing narrow strips of board, trellis-like, at a distance of four or five inches from the fence. The luxuriance and fruitfulness of trees planted as ordinary standards, in most parts of the country, is the very obvious reason why, except in gardens of the first class, a trained tree is so rarely seen; but, on the other hand, the superior size and beauty of the fruit raised in this way make it an object of considerable importance, when the number of trees is small. Besides this, the trees occupy so much less space, interfere so little with the growth of anything else that may be near or under them, and are so much more completely under the control of the gardener, that we are certain they would, if trained, afford ten times the satisfaction at all times beyond that derived from standard trees, cultivated, or rather left to grow, in the usual manner.

Proceeding now to the ornamental portion of the ground, we shall suppose the outer border, *e*, to be planted with a small mixed collection of handsome trees and shrubs, of such varieties as may be easily and cheaply procured. The trees may be planted at considerable distances, as a very few, when they have attained some size, will be sufficient for this limited surface. In the intermediate spaces, room will be found for quite a variety of shrubs, interspersed with several sorts of hardy roses. In the centre of each of the two small circles fronting the house, we will place a Norway spruce, one of the finest evergreens in this climate, as it preserves its rich green verdure unimpaired throughout the coldest winter. These firs, with two or three additional evergreens in the swell of the front border, will give a cheerful aspect to the entrance front of the cottage during the winter months.

The border marked *f*, in the plan, that directly surrounds the building, should be laid down in turf, which, if kept short, will be much more pleasing and satisfactory than if kept in a raw state by cultivation—partly from the greater appearance of permanence in a turf border, and partly from its greater neatness at all seasons. In this turf border may be planted a few choice shrubs, or roses, selecting such as are remarkable for beauty of leaf and flower, or for their fragrance; as from their nearness to the windows the latter may be enjoyed in the summer, while the windows are open through the whole house. There are about a dozen of these shrubs indicated on the plan, which we shall suppose to be the following:—

Blooms in

2 Pink Mezereon (*Daphne Mezereum*)..................March.
2 Sweet-Scented Shrub (*Calycanthus florida*)..........June.
2 Baron Prevost Rose (*Rosa Champneyana*).............June to Nov.
2 Fragrant Clethra (*Clethra alnifolia*)................August.
2 Purple Magnolia (*Magnolia obovata*)................April.
2 Missouri Currant (*Ribes aureum*)...................April.

These are all deliciously fragrant when in flower, and some of the number will be in bloom during the whole growing season.

Quite an area, *b*, in the rear of the house, is devoted to a lawn, which must be kept close and green by frequent mowings, so that it will be as soft to the tread as a carpet, and that its deep verdure will set off the gay colors of the flowering plants in the surrounding beds and parterre. This little lawn is terminated by an irregular or *arabesque* border, *g*, varying in width from four to fourteen feet. The irregular form of this border is preferable to a regular one on account of its more agreeable outline, and more especially for the reason that, to a person looking across the lawn from any part of the walk near the house, this variety of form in the boundary increases the apparent size of the area of turf which it encloses. To give still further variety and effect, we have introduced also the two small beds, *h* and *i*, cut in the turf, the former of which may be planted with monthly roses of any free-blooming sorts, and the latter may be filled with mignonette by sowing the seeds annually in April. The monthly roses will be covered with bloom all the season, and will stand the winter perfectly well in the open air anywhere south of Albany, with the trifling care of throwing a little straw or litter over them at the approach of winter, to protect them against the change of temperature.

It will be remembered that the kitchen garden is kept

out of view to a person standing at b, by the trellised screen c, covered with a luxuriant wreath of honeysuckles and other climbing plants, six or eight feet in height. We shall next suppose the arabesque border, g, devoted to a miscellaneous collection of perennial flowering plants, or herbaceous plants, as they are generally termed, arranging them so that those of a few inches in height shall be near the front margin of the border, those of a larger size the next, and so gradually increasing in size until the largest growing ones, perhaps three feet in height, shall be at the back of the border and farthest from the eye. It is not necessary to have costly varieties of plants, or a large collection, to render this border a handsome object to look upon, but, on the contrary, a few well-selected species, which may be procured for a trifling sum from a nursery, or the greater part of which may be had from the garden of some neighboring amateur, will serve to render this border rich and beautiful, in leaf and blossom, all the season. In the description of Design V., we shall give a list of the most ornamental varieties of border perennials, from which the reader may choose for this or any other garden. If, however, the occupant of this cottage should desire to be at little or no cost for border flowers, and still should wish to produce a considerable effect, it may be done by planting the bed with masses of the following showy perennials :—

Double red Ragged Robin.... (*Lynchis flos-cuculi.*)
Orange Chelone............. (*Chelone barbata.*)
Chinese Pinks............... (*Dianthus sinensis.*)
Bee Larkspur............... (*Delphinium elatum.*)
White Lily................. (*Lilium candidum.*)
Japan White Lily...... .... (*Hemeroallis japonica.*)
Early White Phlox........... (*Phlox suaveolens.*)
Late Purple Phlox.......... (*Phlox autumnalis.*)

Fragrant Blue Violet.........(*Viola odorata.*)
Blue Omphalodes...........(*Omphalodes verna.*)
Chinese White and Rose
    Pœonias.................(*Pœonia whitlejii and fragrans.*)
Hearts-ease or Pansy.........(*Viola tricolor.*)

Or, as a few seeds of ornamental annuals are easily and cheaply procured at the seed-shops, the variety may be increased by sowing the seeds of twenty or thirty species of the latter in the spaces that would be left between the masses of herbaceous plants, taking care to arrange them, with regard to height, in the same manner as the perennials, as otherwise the taller plants near the eye would hide the smaller and more delicate ones at the back of the border.

We trust the reader who has followed us in our description will acknowledge that this cottage, with its moderate accommodations and small lot of ground, may be made productive of a considerable degree of interest and beauty, as well as comfort and enjoyment. There is nothing in the plan of the house or garden that may not be realized by a family living upon a very small income, provided the members of the family are persons of some taste and refinement, who appreciate the value and pleasure of such a residence sufficiently to take a strong personal interest in it. The master of the premises we shall suppose capable of managing the kitchen garden, the fruit trees, the grass, and the whole of the walks, himself, with perhaps the assistance of a common gardener or laboring man for a day or two, at certain seasons of the year. The mistress and her daughter, or daughters, we shall suppose to have sufficient fondness for flowers to be willing and glad to spend, three times a week, an hour or two in the cool mornings and evenings of summer in the pleasing task of planting, tying to neat stakes, picking off decayed flowers, and removing weeds from the borders, and all other operations that so limited a garden may require.

A love for these floral occupations, so simple and so natural, that in all times and countries they have been the delight of the highest as well as the lowest, insensibly gains upon us as we become interested in the growth of plants and the development of the varied forms of beauty and grace with which every leaf, tendril, and blossom is replete; and the exercise involved in the pursuit thus soon becomes, also, a source of pleasure and mental satisfaction, and is not, as in many other cases, an irksome duty performed for the preservation of bodily health.

DESIGN II.

A Cottage in the English or Rural Gothic Style.

THE object in view in designing this cottage is internal convenience. There are many families mainly composed of invalids, or persons advanced in years, who have a strong preference for a plan giving the kitchen, and at least one bed-room, upon the same floor with the living rooms, and in which there is little or no necessity for ascending or descending stairs; an exercise which, though of little consequence to the young and robust, is of all others the most fatiguing to the infirm, or those in delicate health.

A glance at the plan of the first floor, opposite, Fig. 10, will show how we propose to realize this kind of accommodation in this dwelling. The kitchen is a wing, added in the rear, of one story in height. The situation on which this dwelling is placed has a prospect in one direction only, and the front, shown in the elevation, commands this view, the rear being nearly hidden by trees. On this front are situated two pleasant apartments, each 17 by 20 feet, opening from the vestibule or entrance hall by large double doors, which, when fully opened, will throw these two rooms and the vestibule into one large apartment. Some elegance is conferred on the parlor by the bay window, after the old English mode, projecting on the right side, which is balanced by a double window opposite in the dining-room. We would recommend the employment of a few large windows in the principal apartments, as there is

DESIGN II.

A COTTAGE IN THE ENGLISH OR RURAL GOTHIC STYLE.

Fig. 9.

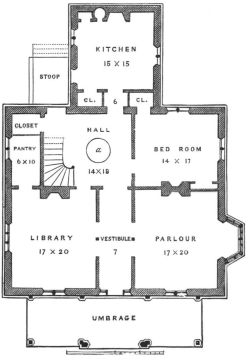

Fig. 10.

an appearance of pettiness, and a want of breadth, in rooms full of little windows, which is so common a feature in our country houses. It is always preferable, also, to light a room from two sides only, rather than three, as nothing is more unfavorable to the effect of interiors than cross lights proceeding from every direction.

The living-room, or library, commands a pantry of convenient size, in the rear of which is a closet opening into the hall. This hall is of ample size to serve as a dining-room, and this disposition would doubtless be preferred during at least part of the year, as it would allow the apartment on the left to be devoted entirely to a library. To make an *entrance* hall a dining apartment, is a very objectionable, though not unusual mode, as visitors, chancing to call at the dinner hour, cannot be shown into the parlor without passing the table, and perhaps discomposing the whole family. But in the present case, the door being closed between the entrance or vestibule and the dining hall, the table, *a*, and persons seated about it, would be completely private. There is a glazed back door opening to the rear of the house, near the left angle of this hall, and a door opening into the kitchen passage, *b*, on the right, and the hall also receives light from the window over this door, in the second story. This passage is formed by running a solid partition across the kitchen building, so as to admit of two doors, in order to prevent smells; one, an ordinary door opening into the hall, and the other a fly or spring door opening into the kitchen. This partition also gives room for the introduction of two convenient closets, one for the kitchen, and another for the bedroom.

In the plan of the second floor, Fig. 11, we have two large and two small bed-rooms. There is a dressing-room and closet communicating with the small bed-room on the left, and a closet for linen opening into the hall. The cellar plan is not given, as this would be very simple, and would probably not be required larger than the main building. Access would be had to it by steps going down

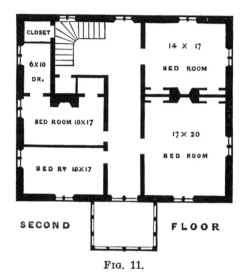

FIG. 11.

under the stone platform of the stoop on which the hall, back door, and the kitchen door open; and by stairs descending under the ascending staircase in the hall.

The elevation of this cottage is in the English cottage style, so generally admired for the picturesqueness evinced in its tall gables ornamented by handsome verge-boards and finials, its neat or fanciful chimney-tops, its latticed windows, and other striking features, showing how the genius of pointed or Gothic architecture may be chastened or moulded into forms for domestic habitations. The steep roofs are highly suitable for a cold country liable to heavy snows. A very pleasing mode of covering roofs of this kind is shown in the elevation, and the effect is produced by procuring the shingles of equal size, and cutting the lower ends before laying them on, in a semi-hexagon or semi-octagon shape, so that when laid upon the roof these figures will be regularly produced.

The English cottage style will admit of great irregularity and picturesqueness of outline, and is productive of beautiful effects when the composition forms a large group of building. In the present example we have only been able to show one of the simplest of its forms, which, however, is not destitute of expression of style. In the English examples a veranda is rarely seen, as the dampness of their climate renders such an appendage scarcely necessary. But its great utility in our hot summers makes it indispensable to every house, and we have introduced it on the entrance front, as affording in this position shelter, prospect, and an agreeable promenade. Over the porch is a pleasant balcony for the pointed window in the gable. As the spirit of Gothic architecture lies in vertical lines, a long unbroken horizontal line of veranda would destroy or mar the architectural character of the cottage.

We have, therefore, made the veranda two or three feet shorter at each end than the front, and have further broken the horizontal line, by the porch balcony, to the window in the front gable.

One of the most characteristic and beautiful features in rural Gothic architecture is the ornamental chimney shaft, sometimes rising singly, sometimes in clusters from the roof; often plain and square, or octagonal, but frequently wreathed and moulded in the most picturesque manner. The finest specimens of the old English chimneys are built of bricks, cast in moulds for the purpose, or stamped with ornaments. These bricks were until lately so highly taxed in England as to render them as expensive as cut stone, but they may be made very cheaply here.* We have built neat chimney shafts in an octagonal form of common bricks, by cutting them with a trowel in the desired form, and rubbing the faces smooth on a hard sand-stone before laying them; but this is more expensive than to employ bricks ready moulded for the purpose. Chimney-tops of artificial stone in handsome forms may also be had of various manufacturers in our principal cities, but they will seldom stand our trying climate at the north.

Construction.—This cottage should be built of brick and cement, colored in imitation of Bath or Portland stone; or of smooth brick, colored after some of the soft neutral tints described in a former page; or of quarried stone. The window-frames, the porch, and veranda, and the verge board, may be made of good seasoned wood, painted the same color as the walls, and sanded; or they may be grained in imitation of oak. Real oak would be preferable where economy is not an object. The label or drip-stones to the window may be made of moulded brick, or cut free-stone, after Fig. 25, of the next design. These windows are latticed casement windows, the plan and section of which are shown in Fig. 12.

In the gable, Fig. 13, the roof or cornice of which should project at least twenty inches over the wall, is shown a specimen of feathered tracery from one of the best examples, with its pinnacle and pendant. This may be cut out of thick plank,† and if thought too elaborate, may be simplified by omitting the minor details. If well executed it will have a rich effect.

---

* We trust that by the time this volume is out of press, some of our brickmakers will be able to offer moulded bricks of a variety of patterns, as the demand for such is every day increasing.

† Never (as is sometimes done by ignorant carpenters) out of inch boards.

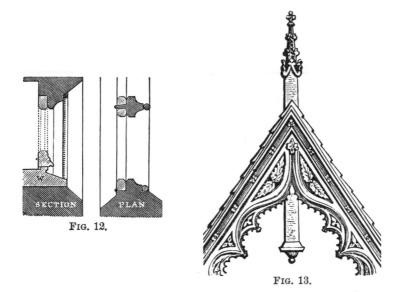

FIG. 12.

FIG. 13.

The porch and veranda are shown in detail in Fig. 14;
the detached portion on the right showing a part of the

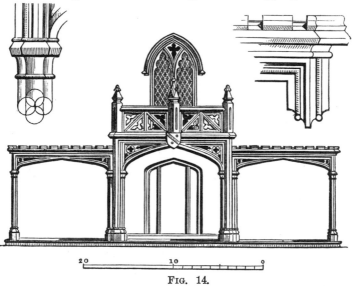

20   10   0

FIG. 14.

veranda cornice, and that on the left a portion of the
clustered column. (The sections of which are seen at the
lower ends of the drawing.)

Fig. 15 shows a pair of chimney shafts in the old
English style, which may be had in artificial stone, or cast iron.   A great variety
of forms are frequently collected together
in the same stack.

FIG. 15.

The shutters should be inside box shutters,
or shutter-blinds, painted and grained in
imitation of oak.

Estimate.—The cost of this cottage in
brick and stucco (bricks at $4) would be
$4,500.

[This design has been executed in various
parts of the country—sometimes for a trifle
more, but in several instances for less than this estimate.
It has lately been very carefully carried out in a residence
on Staten Island, N. Y., with elaborate details, for
$4,800.—*4th Edition.*] [At the present time the cost
of this cottage would be about $9,000.—ED.]

LAYING OUT THE GARDEN OF DESIGN II.

The situation where it is proposed to build this cottage
is about a mile from a country town, and the area of surface for the whole purpose is about an acre and a fourth.
This lot of ground is bounded by a street both in the front
and rear.   The entrance is at *a ;* the dwelling at *b ;* the
stable at *c.*   One-half of the whole surface, viz., that portion represented by right-lined plots in the rear of the
house, is devoted to a garden for fruits and vegetables, and
the whole remaining portion, comprising the space in front
and at the sides of the house, is laid out as a lawn, shrubbery, and flower-garden, in the picturesque manner.   The
carriage road, leading to the front door and to the stable, is

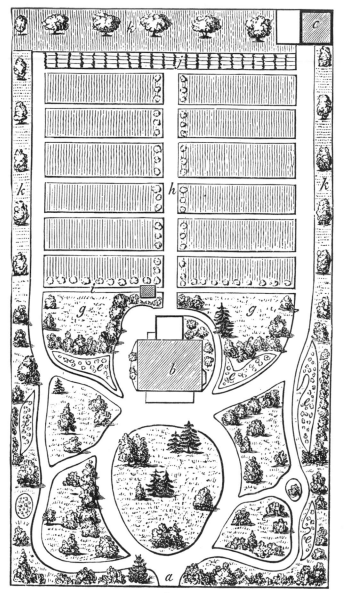

[Fig. 16.]

shown at *d ; e* designates irregular beds cut in the turf, and stocked with annuals and perennial flowers; *f*, a thick shrubbery belt, composed of syringos, mountain ashes, and lilacs, interspersed with the balsam fir and arbor vitæ, to give a cheerful appearance in winter. In the rear of the kitchen are planted two or three hemlocks and larches. Two plots of grass for bleaching and drying clothes are shown at *g*.

In the ornamental garden before the house, the whole surface, excepting the walks, and the flower-beds, *e*, is to be laid down in turf and kept neatly mown. This turf will give an appearance of much greater extent to the area than it could possibly have by any other arrangement, while it will be more agreeable to the eye through the whole year than any extensive disposition of parterre, or flower-beds, directly under the eye. A fresh verdant lawn, varied only by walks and green trees, is a delightful object at all seasons, and more especially in the middle of summer; while at the latter period flower-beds have frequently a dry and parched appearance, but poorly compensated for by the brilliancy of a few plants in bloom, which scarcely hide the surface.

The spiry-topped trees shown in these plots are chiefly the European Larch and the Balsam Fir, with one or two White Pines, all of which harmonize well with the architecture of the cottage. Among the round-headed trees we will only particularize the Osage Orange (*Maclura aurantiaca*), the Umbrella Magnolia (*M. tripetala*), the Weeping Ash (*Fraxinus excelsior pendula*), and the Silver Maple (*Acer dasycarpum*). Among the shrubs forming little thickets along the walks, we would introduce the Mezereon and the Cornelian Cherry, the pink and yellow flowers of which appear in March; the scarlet and blush Japan

Quince (*Cydonia Japonica*), the pink and double white Hawthorns, and the purple and white fruited Strawberry Tree (*Euonymus europeus*).

The walks should all be well gravelled; the carriage road being first excavated twelve inches deep, and one-half the depth on the bottom filled with small stones, in order to have it dry and firm at all seasons.

In the kitchen garden, the borders on the sides of the central walk, *h*, are occupied by two rows of currants and gooseberries. The currants are the Large White and Red Dutch, and the Naples or Black English. [Add the Cherry, White Grape, Victoria, and Versaillaise.—C. D.] The gooseberries are half a dozen of the best English sorts. Both currants and gooseberries must be kept well trimmed and thinned, to admit the air freely to every part of the plant, and the borders should be annually manured, as they require a rich soil to produce large fruit. On one side of the cross-walk, *i*, is a border devoted to raspberries, and planted with the large Red Antwerp and the White Antwerp, in equal quantities. [Omit the White Antwerp, and add Orange and Franconia.—C. D.]

Within the boundary fence of that half of the area comprising the kitchen garden, is a border fourteen feet wide on the sides, and twice that width on the rear, devoted to a small number of choice fruits. The walk, *j*, is covered by an arbor for grapes, and may contain, besides the native sorts, Catawba, Isabella, etc., a few vines of the Royal Muscadine, Sweet Water, and Black July, which are among the hardiest and most productive of the foreign varieties. [Substitute for the grapes mentioned above, the Delaware, Israella, Allen's Hybrid, Iona, and the Mottled. —C. D.] Nearly all the foreign grapes require much care to be raised in the open air. For a year or two after they come into bearing, the crops, it is generally remarked, are good, and the fruit fair; but in a few seasons more the mildew attacks the fruit, and frequently destroys every bunch, or renders it worthless.   The most successful practice for out-of-door culture appears to consist in laying down some of the long thrifty shoots each season, so as to have every year, or every other year, a succession of new roots—destroying those that have borne two good crops, and allowing the young rooted plants to take their place. Lime and marl are excellent manures for the grape.

DESIGN III.

A Cottage in the Pointed, or Tudor Style.

THIS edifice is designed for a situation on the bank of one of our boldest rivers. From its site the eye wanders over a richly cultivated country, dotted and sprinkled with luxuriant groups of wood; the wide, lake-like expanse of water, the sails floating lazily on its bosom, the tufted fringes of trees and shrubs in the foreground, and the distant hazy summits of blue in the horizon, are all fascinating elements of the beautiful, which make up the view from the point of its location. As in many of our finest natural situations for residences, nature has done so much here to render the scene lovely, that it would appear that man had only to borrow a few hints from the genius of the place, and the home features would all be rendered equally delightful. But how frequently do we see those who seem incapable of reading the wide and ever eloquent book of natural beauty, deforming its fair pages, written in lines of grace and softness, by rigid lines and hard mathematical angles, only too plainly indicative of the most primitive and uncultivated perceptions. Let us hope, by studying the character of the whole scene, to succeed better in improving a very small portion of it.

The arrangement of the cottage we propose for this place, differs from the previous ones in having the principal floor devoted almost entirely to pleasant apartments; the kitchen being below, and the bed-rooms above stairs. This renders the whole air of the house somewhat elegant.

DESIGN III.

A Cottage in the Pointed or Tudor Style.

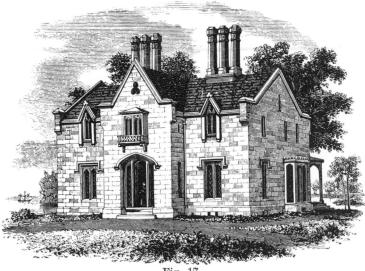

Fig. 17.

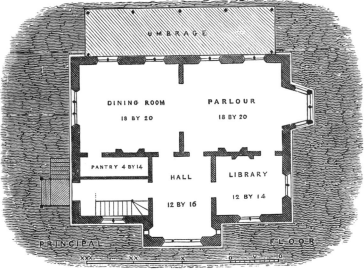

Fig. 18.

A cottage like this, although of moderate size, in the hands of a family of taste, may be made to produce a beautiful effect. While it is true, that

"Here no state chambers in long line unfold,
  Bright with broad mirrors, rough with fretted gold,
  Yet modest ornament with use combined,
  Attracts the eye to exercise the mind."

And while there are no superfluous and luxurious apartments, nor anything requiring the attendance of a retinue of servants, there is much here, compactly arranged, to render a home pleasant and attractive. The neat and spacious parlor, eighteen by twenty feet (see Fig. 18), is varied in its outline by an old English bay-window, one of those pleasant nooks, which, says Lord Bacon, "be pretty retiring places for conference," and has also windows opening quite to the floor of the veranda, and letting in a full expanse of the bright green lawn, and tufts of rich foliage that border it. This room would afford some scope for the "faire ladye" to exercise her taste in a simple, elegant, and harmonious style of fitting and furnishing; not by bringing from the shops the latest and most fashionable patterns of city chairs and tables, carpets and sofas,—which, we are sorry to say, are in most cases destitute of all appropriateness, and, in many, of all intrinsic taste and beauty,—but by selecting articles recommended by fitness in design, in order that they may be in harmony with the character of the house, and by a tasteful and comfortable character, that they may suit the more simple and unostentatious habits of country life.

The dining-room is of equal size with the drawing-room, and as the family who are to occupy this cottage villa live in a pleasant and social neighborhood, and are in the habit, occasionally, of entertaining a little party of their friends, they thought it desirable to make these rooms communicate by sliding doors, in order that they may, on such occasions be thrown into one. The rooms will then have a handsome effect, as the bay-window at the end of the parlor is balanced by a wide mullioned window at the end of the dining-room opposite, and the whole space between them is forty feet. For the convenience of the *ménage*, we have located a neat pantry directly in contact with the dining-room, and opening out of it, so that the china and plate, or the little delicacies of the larder, may be under the eye, or, what is better, under the lock and key of the mistress. As the kitchen is below stairs, in the ordinary mode the dishes will require to be brought up the stairs and across the staircase entry to reach the table. This is somewhat objectionable, inasmuch as a hot dinner is likely to become cooled in this long state of transition, the china is liable to become broken by an occasional misstep, and the privacy of the hall is unnecessarily intruded upon by the repeated coming and going of the domestics arranging the dinner. We shall endeavor to remedy these difficulties, by placing in the little space on the right hand of the door opening from the dining-room to the pantry, what is called a *rising cupboard* or *dumb waiter*, which will be found a more careful, more obedient and more unobtrusive " help " than any other in the house. The actual size of this cupboard need not be more than twenty inches by three and a half or four feet, which will just occupy the space in the pantry that is of little value for any other purpose. Or if it should be thought desirable to have it a little wider, the width may be increased by making a small recess in the wall of the house. Fig. 19 shows the manner in which the

pantry may be finished; the pantry being on the right
side, and the dumb waiter
(D W) on the left; the cupboard rising in the pantry to
the height of three feet, and
descending through the floor

FIG. 19.

to the closet in the kitchen. The mode of constructing
this is shown in the details of this design, Fig. 28.

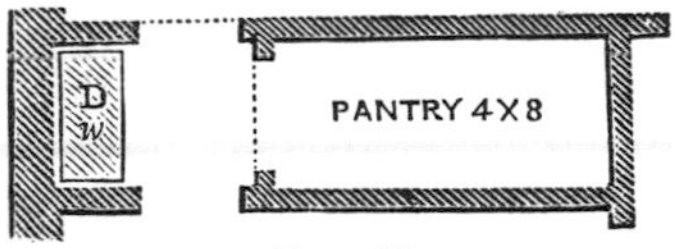

It will be seen on examining the plan of the principal
floor, that by placing the stairs in a separate passage communicating with the principal hall, this hall is left free
and unencumbered, and is in fact a pretty little ante-room,
twelve by sixteen feet. This is doubly advantageous, as
the servants are enabled to go from the basement to the
chamber story without passing through the principal hall;
thus making this single staircase to serve the purposes, in
a great measure, of the two frequently seen in the villas,
viz., the stairs in the hall used by the family, and the
private stairs chiefly used by the domestics. From this
passage also there is a private, or side entrance to the
house, by an outer door. The *hall* is lighted by two small
windows in the sides and by the semi-glazed door, as shown
in the perspective elevation.

We have as yet said nothing of the neat little library
on the right of the hall, twelve by fourteen feet in its
dimensions, where

"Selected shelves shall claim our studious hours."

But there is no portion of the house which, to a man fond
of those most cheerful and never tiresome companions,
good books, is more peculiarly the *sanctum* or "own room"
than the library, whether it be small or large. This,
though small, is sufficiently ample to contain all the *best*

books ever written; large enough for a comfortable ruddy fire in a damp or cold wintry day, and for an ample library round-table furnished with the necessary materials for writing and correspondence of all kinds. The gentleman who is to occupy this cottage has, besides the few acres on which this residence is erected, a farm where he practises agriculture in an amateur manner, and on his library shelves may therefore be found a few choice works on rural economy, such as "Loudon's Encyclopædias," "Low's Practical Agriculture," "Allen's American Farm-Book," and a number of others of similar character, and on the table lie the last numbers of our most valuable and interesting agricultural periodicals. The library, being fitted up in a plain and simple manner, answers admirably also as an office, into which persons who call to see the master of the house on business are readily shown from the hall without disturbing the family, who are occupying the dining-room or parlor.

The veranda, or umbrage, which is entered by windows opening to the floor of the two principal apartments, is a cool and shady place for a promenade, and, we need hardly repeat, commands the most delightful views, as this is the river front of the house.

In the plan of the second floor, which is before us, are accommodations for the family and their guests, Fig. 20, consisting of four excellent sleeping apartments, each with a small closet attached. Two of these are of ample size; and as it might be desirable to many to have in them a greater amount of closet room, it may be easily obtained by making a double partition between these apartments, which would allow of two large closets in the space thus formed. The bed-room, twelve by twelve feet, over the hall, is a pretty lodging apartment, opening through a picturesque old English oriel window on a balcony. The staircase shown in this plan gives access to the attic, where two servants' bed-rooms are located.

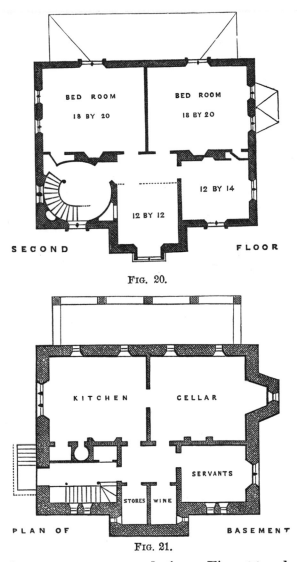

FIG. 20.

FIG. 21.

The basement accommodation, Fig. 21, shows an entrance into the staircase passage by a descent of steps; a kitchen, and cellar of good dimensions, a servants' sleeping room (which may be made a laundry if preferred), and a small store-room and wine-cellar conveniently located.

The exterior of this dwelling is designed after the old English architecture of the Tudor era, a style replete with interesting associations, as it is the genuine and most characteristic mode of building long ago prevalent in the finest country-houses of England, associated by "lay and legend ten times told" with all that is brightest and noblest in the history of our mother country. It is highly picturesque, abounding in the finest specimens with a rich variety of gables, turrets, buttresses, towers, and ornamental chimney-shafts, which form striking and spirited objects in domestic architecture, and harmonize agreeably with the hills and tree-tops, and all the intricacy of outline in natural objects. And finally the irregularity of its outlines, admitting future additions with facility, the substantial and permanent expression of its exterior, and the beauty and comfort indicated in the richness, variety, and size of its windows, all point out the old English style, in its various modifications, as admirably adapted by beauty and fitness for domestic purposes in a cold climate.

This cottage being of very moderate size, neither demands, nor would with propriety admit, a profusion of ornament, and we have, indeed, for the sake of economy, made it assume a character and a degree of decoration comparatively simple, still, however, preserving a very marked and distinct expression of the style. If we analyze its leading features, we shall find that character is conferred chiefly by the windows and the chimney-tops, the two most essential and characteristic features of dwelling-houses, as contrasted with buildings for any other purposes; and to which, as such, decoration should always be first applied rather than to any less essential or superadded features; for example, to columns or a colonnade. Chimney tops, since we cannot dispense with them, should always be rendered ornamental, both because strongly expressive of comfort, no house being tolerable in a cold climate without fires, and on account of their occupying the highest part of the building, and therefore being most likely to strike the eye agreeably, if appropriate, or offend it if ugly and unshapely in form. We have shown in this design one of the simplest forms of old English chimneys, many of which are extremely beautiful.*

An edifice in this style should be built of none but the most solid materials. Stone would be the most appropriate, as it has a substantial and durable character in keeping with the style, and next to this brick, or brick covered with the best cement, would be most suitable. To erect a dwelling in this style of so light and frail a material as wood, under any circumstances, would be a complete violation of good taste, as there would be an entire discordance or incongruity between the style adopted and the material employed. Where wood is the only material within our reach, some lighter and more suitable style should be adopted, and the result will then undoubtedly be more satisfactory.

A solecism in taste which we have several times witnessed with pain in this country, and which we will therefore caution our readers and the occupant of this cottage against, is the introduction of *green blinds*, or Venetian shutters, upon a building in the pointed, or the English cottage style. This kind of shutter, applied to the out-

---

* By an error in the engraving, the *base* of each stack of chimneys in the elevation of this design is made to appear too low ; a more correct proportion is shown in the details, Fig. 15.

side of buildings, belongs properly to the Venetian, Tuscan,
or Italian villas, where the architecture is lighter and more
fanciful, and the windows are frequently mere openings
for the circulation of air; but to cover a handsome or
quaint old English window, enriched by decorative mullions and window-heads, with an outside shutter belonging
to a totally different style of building, and painted a
bright green, is as revolting to a mind imbued with correct
principles of taste, as to cover the venerable head of a
staid gentleman of the old school with the flaunting head-
dress of an Italian peasant girl.   Outside shutters of any
description are barely admissible in this style of architecture, as they conceal one of the chief sources of interest in
the exterior.   But as the walls are thick, inside shutters,
or even inside blinds, are easily introduced.   The latter
may be made to fold into window casings like ordinary
box shutters, where they will serve the purposes of both
shutters and blinds, and will be found more convenient
and more appropriate than outside blinds, without violating correct principles of art.

The interior of this cottage may be finished in a very
simple manner.   But the effect will be far more consistent
and satisfactory if some attention is paid to keeping up
the pointed, or old English character, in the finish of at
least the principal apartments.   This may be done without
incurring any extra expense, merely by employing Gothic
or pointed mouldings and details in the trimmings of the
doors and windows, the forms of the cornices and chimney
pieces.   As there are now numerous examples of this style
of dwelling in the Middle States, there will be little or no
difficulty in procuring the necessary forms of designs,
moulds, and planes for a cottage of this kind.   A person
whose taste is sufficiently cultivated to induce him to desire

such a dwelling as this, will naturally inform himself of the actual effect, both as regards the interior and exterior finish, by inspection of the best example of the style within his reach; or, for a small sum, he may obtain from an architect the working drawings necessary for the complete execution of the whole, by the builders employed, in the most correct manner.

A harmonious and pleasing effect is produced in houses in the old English style, by painting and graining the wood-work in imitation of oak or black walnut. This is partly owing, no doubt, to the allusion thus awakened in the mind to the "old oaken wainscots," always so characteristic a feature in the antique houses in this style, but partly, also, to the mellow and furnished look which the warm and dark tone of the wood gives to the apartments. In an economical point of view, it has also the great recommendation of being kept clean and bright with one-twentieth part of the labor expended in maintaining wood-work, painted white, in its original purity.

Details.—In the construction of a cottage in the pointed style, attention should be paid to a unity of design in all parts of the building. One of the most essential principles in this style is the recognition of the arch, in some manner, in all the principal openings. In public buildings, all windows and doors terminate upward in the pointed arch; in domestic architecture this would often be inconvenient, as in the case of windows in apartments on the first floor, where inside shutters are required. The windows are generally therefore square-headed, but the principle of the arch appears in the moulded window tracery.

In Fig. 22 is shown a small portion of the veranda on the river front, with its appropriate columns, and the archway between.

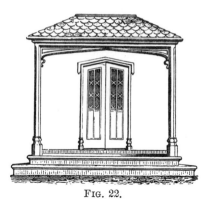

FIG. 22.

A portion of the balcony to the oriel window is shown in Fig. 23. In Fig. 24, is shown one of the dormer

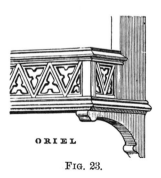

ORIEL

FIG. 23.

FIG. 24.

windows of the front elevation. For the section and plan of the lower windows, see Fig. 12, of Design I.

FIG. 25.

The section or profile of the land, or lintel of the window, is shown in Fig. 25; and that of the wall-coping, in Fig. 26; both to the scale of half an inch to a foot.

A stack of chimneys suitable for this cottage is shown in Fig. 27, which may be built of brick; the chimney tops being eight feet high above the base or square platform. The flues may be square or semicircular within (the latter is preferable), and ten or twelve inches in diameter. Circular flues are easily formed by building round a cylinder of tin, which is worked upwards by turning it with the hand as the chimney is carried up. The interior of the flue next the cylinder is covered with mortar in building, and the gradual withdrawal of the cylinder upwards leaves a smooth plastered surface.

FIG. 26.

FIG. 27.

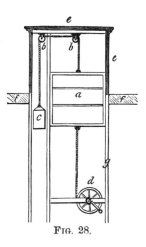

FIG. 28.

A section showing the construction of the rising cupboard, or dumb waiter, is shown in Fig. 28. In this section the floor of the pantry is indicated at f, the portion above being enclosed in a sort of sideboard or closet in the pantry, and the part below in a similar closet in the basement. At a, is the cupboard with three shelves. This cupboard, with the dishes it will contain, is balanced by the weight, *c*, at the end of a rope, passing over the pulleys, *b*, which are attached to the top of the cupboard. This, with a slight impetus, sends the loaded cupboard up to the top; it is drawn down by a small wheel and crank, *d*, with a similar cord or leathern strap attached to the bottom of the cupboard. This wheel and crank are fixed firmly at the bottom of the trunk in which the cupboard moves, and about a foot and a half above the floor of the kitchen. The top of the trunk, or that part above the floor, *f*, is disguised and rendered ornamental by the neat sideboard or closet covering it, which opens in front to allow the dishes to be taken out.

Estimate.—If this cottage is built of brick and stucco, with cut stone labels to the windows, and finished in a consistent and appropriate, though simple manner in the interior, it will cost about $3,500. Built of quarried stone, where the latter is not abundant, it would probably cost $4,800. [This cottage would cost $7,000 in brick, and if built of stone would cost $8,500 to $9,000.—ED.]

THE GROUNDS OF DESIGN III.

The situation of the ground, four acres in extent, upon which this dwelling is to be erected, we have already partly described. It is nearly a parallelogram, one end of which borders the public road and the other is bounded by the river. In its original state, before operations were commenced, the place appeared only a simple meadow, the land of fair quality, and the surface level, or nearly so, between the road and the site of the house, but sloping off to the river, in some parts gently, and in others more abruptly, about one hundred feet beyond the veranda on the river side of the house, at *h*, Fig. 29. The best soil for a garden appeared to be on the left of the property, and we accordingly located the kitchen garden, *f*, and the orchard of choice fruits, *g*, in this quarter.

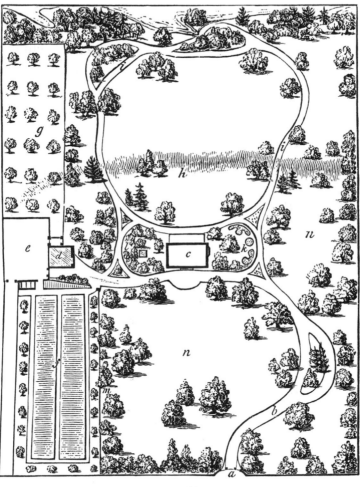

FIG. 29.

As it was not thought desirable by the owner of this place to expend much in keeping the place in order, be-yond what labor might be required in the kitchen garden,

few walks are introduced, except such as are actually
necessary or convenient. Of these the most essential in
every place is the entrance road, or Approach, *b*, which
leaves the public road, in this example, at *a*, that point
being indicated as most suitable by the situation of the
ground, and by the shelter and effect which will be given
to the entrance gate by two or three large trees found
growing there. There is a gravelled area in front of the
house, upon which carriages may turn, and at the extremity
of this road are the stable, *d*, and stable yard, *e*. Next to
the Approach, the most desirable walk is one for exercise,
leading over more secluded parts of the place, or to spots
enjoying beautiful or extensive prospects. In a place of
small extent, it is desirable to have this walk as long as
possible, which is generally effected by making the circuit
of the space offered, keeping at such a distance from
boundary fences that they may not be obtrusive. Such a
walk is shown at *i*, which, leaving the veranda on the
river front of the house, proceeds in easy curves, shaded
by occasional groups of trees, over the whole area between
the house and the river.

On the right of the house, looked out upon from the
bay-window of the parlor, is a small area of smooth turf,
surrounded by the walk, *k*, and containing some irregular
beds and circles, cut in the turf, devoted to choice flowers.
At *l*, on the left, is a corresponding walk, serving the
purpose of connecting the two principal walks, which is
thickly bordered with ornamental shrubbery. With the
exception of a few vines on the veranda, and shrubs near
the house, these two small walks, with their accompani-
ments of flowers and shrubs, comprise all the ornamental
details of the place requiring much care. All that portion of the grounds between the public road and the line

h, is in lawn or grass, and is kept short by repeated mowings during summer. At h is a slight paling fence,
rendered inconspicuous by painting it dark green. This
fence follows the lower line of the ridge, and from the
house is not visible, on account of the slope of the ground
just above that line; the fence being six or eight feet
below the level of the platform on which the house stands.
The area embraced between this fence and the river is also
in grass, but which here, however, is kept short by the
pasturage of a cow, or a few sheep.

Instead of this fence of pales a *sunk fence* or *ha-ha*
might be preferred, and where stone is abundant it would
not be more expensive. The construction of such a fence
will be easily understood by referring to the accompanying
section, Fig. 30, in which a is the level of the ground,

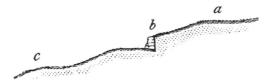

FIG. 30.

falling off gradually at b, where a wall three feet and a
half deep, open on the side facing the declining surface,
would form an effectual protection against cattle on the
lower side. It is evident from the section shown here, that,
to a person standing at a, the fence and depressed surface at
its bottom not being seen, there would be no apparent barrier or interruption to the view across the whole space to
the river. Such a fence, it should be remarked, must, as in
the present case, run *across* the surface to be looked over,
and not in any direction parallel to the line of vision. In

commencing the description of this place, it was remarked that the few fine trees already growing on it gave it a considerable degree of character. The majority of these were oaks and chestnuts of good size, and as the expression of dignity and picturesqueness inherent in these trees is in excellent keeping with the style of this dwelling, it will be advisable to maintain the character by planting chiefly round-headed trees, rather than drooping trees like the elm, which are mainly expressive of gracefulness. Near the house, a few Larches and Hemlocks are also introduced, as the spirited forms of these trees, contrasted with the round-headed ones, will add to the picturesque character of the architecture.

At the end of this section we shall give a list of the finest ornamental trees, classed according to height and other qualities, and another of shrubs, from which selections may be made for planting this and other designs. We shall, in relation to these, only remark at present that, in order to insure a rapid and vigorous growth to these trees, the holes, previously to planting them, should be thoroughly prepared by throwing out the soil two feet in depth, and from three to six feet in diameter, and mixing it intimately with a plentiful supply of compost or well-rotted manure, before returning it to the holes in planting. When a tree is planted in the ordinary manner without preparation, from the poverty of the soil, and the closeness of those portions of it adjacent to the roots of the newly moved tree, it requires a year or two to recover from the removal, and advances afterwards in its growth only in a feeble and tardy manner. On the other hand, where the holes are carefully prepared, the soil furnished with a plentiful supply of nutriment, and rendered loose and easily permeable by the light and air, as well as by the roots, the newly transplanted tree soon establishes itself, and makes rapid and luxuriant shoots. In many soils it will be found that this previous preparation will insure a growth more than four times as vigorous as that resulting from the usual hasty and careless mode of planting without preparation; and it is therefore better policy, where effect is speedily desired, to plant a few trees in the best manner, than a great number in the ordinary careless mode.

Another very erroneous practice, of frequent occurrence with planters of little experience in the United States, consists in planting the tree *too deep*. This is not only to the eye contrary to nature, and in violation therefore of correct taste, but it is destructive to the health of the tree, by placing the mass of young roots below the genial influence of the atmosphere. Treated in this manner, trees will frequently struggle against the adverse situation for years, without ever attaining any considerable degree of luxuriance.

If we observe a tree growing in a natural state after it has attained some size, we must at once remark that the base of the trunk, or that part nearest the ground, is much larger than the same trunk a few inches above; and that, in consequence of the development of roots just below this point, the tree *appears to stand on a base* a little elevated above the level of the ground above it. This gives it an appearance of strength and dignity, and connects it, by a natural transition, with the surface around it. Now a tree, however large, which has been planted too deep, presents no appearance of this kind, but rises out of the level ground without any base, in a manner precisely similar to a post. In order to prevent this appearance, it is advisable, in planting, to set out the trees on a hillock, a few inches raised above the surface, in order that they may, when the ground settles about them, have a natural appearance to the eye, and that the roots may also be placed in the most favorable condition.

We have arranged the trees to be planted on the lawn, in this design, as in most of the others, in the natural style of landscape gardening—that is, with a view to the production of natural beauty. This is effected by planting the trees in irregular groups, or singly, in a manner somewhat similar to that in which they occur in nature, avoiding straight lines and parallel rows, because such lines indicate a formal art, never found in natural landscape. At the same time, the effect will be not the less indicative of elegant art, which will be evinced—1st, In the employment of many exotic trees, or those obviously not natives of this part of the country, as the Horse Chestnut, or the European Linden; 2d, In the space allowed for the trees to develop themselves fully in the lawn from *h* to *a*, and in the more park-like forms which they will therefore assume in time; and 3d, In the manner in which these trees are arranged.* The latter consists in concealing all objects which would not add to the beauty of the scene by an irregular plantation, as, for example, the fence of the kitchen garden at *m*, or the outbuildings at *d;* in planting the borders of the Approach, and of all walks, so as to give an obvious reason (when none other exists) for the curves of such walks, as well as to shade or shelter them; and in contrasting these plantations by broad open glades of turf, *n*. On the river side of the

---

* Landscape gardening, as an art, does not consist, as many seem to suppose, in producing a counterfeit of nature, but in *idealizing* natural beauty in a lawn, park, or garden.

house, the trees should be so arranged as not to shut out any important portion of the prospect.

It is preferred in this design not to have any spot especially devoted to a flower-garden, but in its place to assemble a showy and select collection of flowers, in beds dug in the turf, bordering the walk *k*, near the house.   In this way the flowers are brought near the house, and their beauty enjoyed, without destroying the simplicity and general effect of the place by cutting off a separate place for a flower-garden.

In laying out the kitchen garden, *f*, the border within the boundary is devoted to fruit trees, as designated on the plan, with the exception of a small space in the corner adjoining the stable yard, *e*, for hot-beds.   There is a separate entrance for a cart or wagon to this yard, or to the kitchen garden, by a road on the left of the kitchen garden.   The interior of the latter is left free for growing vegetables ; and a select collection of fruit is planted in the small orchard, *g*.   This little orchard, together with the border set apart in the kitchen garden, if planted with the selection of fruit trees, seventy-four in number, given for this purpose in a succeeding page, will furnish a moderate supply to the family, through the greater part of the year. They are to be cultivated as standards, unless the proprietor prefers training them in the kitchen garden as espaliers, and the ground in the orchard, *g*, is to be devoted to potatoes, beets, turnips, or other roots, both for the purpose of turning the ground to account, and of promoting the growth of the trees.

List of the finest hardy Ornamental Trees of foreign and native growth, for planting in groups and masses.

CLASS I.

Deciduous Trees of the largest size, and of very rapid growth.

Cut-leaved Alder....................*Alnus laciniata.*
Norway Maple......................*Acer platanoides.*
Sugar   do. ....*do. saccharinum.*
Silver   do. ....*do. dasycarpum.*
Country   do. ....*do. campestre.*
Purple   do. ....*do. japonicum, atro-purpureum.*
Large Leaf Maple ....*do. macrophyllum.*
Hawk's Foot do. ....*do. laciniatum.*
Variegated Leaf Maple ....*do. foliis variegatis.*
Variegated Ash Leaf Maple..........*do. negundo variegata.*
Catalpa ....*Catalpa syringæfolia.*
Spanish Chestnut...................*Castanea vesca.*
European Ash ....*Fraxinus excelsior.*
Aucuba Leaf Ash ....*do. aucuba folia.*
Silver Leaf   do. ....*do. argentea.*
Pendulous   do. ....*do. pendula.*
American White Ash ....*do. americana.*
Three-Thorned Acacia ....*Gleditschia triacanthos.*
Tulip Tree ....*Liriodendron tulipifera.*
European Larch....................*Larix europœa.*
American do. ....*do. microcarpa.*
Griffith's   do. ....*do. Griffithii.*
False   do. ....*Pseudo larix kempferi.*
Oriental Plane, or Sycamore..........*Platanus orientalis.*
Lombardy Poplar ....*Populus dilitata.*
Silver Leaf Aspen or Abele ....*do. alba.*
Cotton Wood   do. ....*do. angulata.*
Yellow Locust.....................*Robinia pseud-acacia.*
Weeping Willow...................*Salix babylonica.*
Huntington do. ....*do. alba.*
American Linden ....*Tilia glabra.*
European   do. ....*do. europœa.*

Red-twigged Linden................ *Tilia rubra.*
American White or Drooping Elm.... *Ulmus americana.*
Scampston   do.   .... *do. scampstonii.*
Camperdown   do.   .... *do. camperdowniensis.*
Variegated   do.   .... *do. foliis variegatis.*
Purple   do.   .... *do. purpurea.*
English   do.   .... *do. campestris.*
Dutch or Cork-barked Elm........... *do. suberosa.*
Scotch or Wych Elm................ *do. montana.*

CLASS II.

Deciduous Trees of largest size, and of moderate growth.

White Horse Chestnut................ *Æsculus hippocastanum.*
Scarlet Maple....................... *Acer rubrum.*
Sycamore Maple .... *do. pseudo-platanus.*
Scotch Weeping Birch .... *Betula alba pendula.*
Cutleaf   do.   .... *do. laciniata.*
American Beech..................... *Fagus americana.*
Purple Leaf Beech.................. *do. purpurea.*
Copper Leaf   do. .... *do. ferrugiana.*
Crested Leaf do. .... *do. cristala.*
Weeping   do. .... *do. pendula.*
Torn Leaf   do. .... *do. asplenifolia.*
Kentucky Coffee-Tree............... *Gymnocladus canadensis.*
Sassafras .... *Laurus sassafras.*
Liquid Amber or Sweet Gum .... *Liquid amber styraciflua.*
Cucumber Magnolia .... *Magnolia acuminata.*
American White Oak .... *Quercus alba.*
American Scarlet do. .... *do. coccinea.*
Overcup Oak .... *do. macrocarpa.*
English do. .... *do. robur.*
Lucombe's Seedling Oak............ *do. ——lucombeana.*
Willow-leaved do. .... *do. phellox.*
American Cypress .... *Taxodium disticham.*
Weeping   do. .... *do. pendulum.*

CLASS III.

Deciduous Trees of medium size and rapid growth.

Buckeye or Western Horse Chestnut... *Pavia rubra.*
Pale Yellow Horse Chestnut .... *do. flavia.*

Weeping Ash....................... *Fraxinus excelsior pendula.*
Umbrella Magnolia................. *Magnolia tripetala.*
Large-leaved Magnolia..............   *do.   macrophylla.*
Osage Orange...................... *Maclura aurantiaca.*
Double-Flowering Cherry............ *Cerasus flore pleno.*
Ringlet Willow ....*Salix annularis.*
American Weeping Willow...........   *do. americana pendula.*
Kilmarnock   do.   ....   *do. kilmarnock.*
Rosemary   do.   ....   *do. rosemarifolia.*
Wahoo Elm .... *Ulmus alata.*

CLASS IV.

Deciduous Trees of medium size, moderate growth.

Papaw or Western Custard Apple .....*Anona triloba.*
Red Bird or Judas Tree............. *Cercis canadensis.*
White Flowering Dogwood........... *Cornus florida.*
Variegated   do.   .. ..   *do.   variegata.*
Blood Red   do.   ....   *do.   sanguinea.*
Scotch Laburnum .... *Cytissis alpinus.*
Persimmon or American Medlar....... *Dyospirus virginiana.*
Yellow Magnolia................... *Magnolia cordata.*
Chandelier Magnolia................   *do.   conspicua.*
Soulange's Purple Magnolia..........   *do.   soulangeana.*
Norberti's   do.   ....   *do.   norbertiana.*
Broad-leaved Euonymous............ *Euonymous latifolia.*
Sour Gum......................... *Nyssa villosa.*
Paper Birch....................... *Betula papyracea.*
Japan Ginko Tree.................. *Salsiburia adiantifolia.*
European Mountain Ash .... *Sorbus aucuparia.*
American   do.   ....   *do.   americana.*

Hardy Evergreen Trees.

SPRUCE FIRS.

Norway Spruce Fir................. *Abies picea.*
Double Black Spruce Fir............   *do.   nigra.*
Hemlock Fir ....   *do.   canadiensis.*
Douglas Fir.......................   *do.   Douglasii.*
Clambrasils Fir....................   *do.   clambrasiliana.*
Compact   do......................   *do.   compacta.*

Eleganta Fir	*Abies elegans.*
Finedons do.	do. *finedoniensis.*
Weeping do.	do. *inverta.*
Monstrous do.	do. *monstrosa.*
Dwarf do.	do. *pumila.*
Pigmy do.	do. *pygmæa.*
Hooker's do.	do. *hokeriana.*
Oriental do.	do. *orientalis.*
Vigorous do.	do. *firma.*

SILVER FIRS.

Lovely Silver Fir	*Picea amabilis.*
American do.	do. *balsamea.*
Cephalonican, or Mount Enos Fir	do. *cephalonica.*
Frazier's Silver Fir	do. *frazeri.*
Majestic do.	do. *grandis.*
California do.	do. *lasciocarpa.*
Noble do.	do. *nobilis.*
Nordman's do.	do. *nordmaniana.*
Common English Silver Fir	do. *pectinata.*
Siberian do.	do. *pichta.*
Spanish do.	do. *pinsapo.*
Balsam or Balm of Gilead Fir	do. *balsamea.*
White or Weymouth Pine	*Pinus strobus.*
Yellow do.	do. *variabilis.*
Austrian do.	do. *austriaca.*
Bentham's do.	do. *benthamiana.*
Lofty do.	do. *excelsa.*
California do.	do. *fremontiana.*
Lambert's do.	do. *lambertiana.*
Corsican do.	do. *laricio.*
Ponderous do.	do. *ponderosa.*
Spanish do.	do. *pyrenaica.*
Snow do.	do. *nivea.*
Sabine's do.	do. *sabiniana.*
Umbrella do.	*sciadopitys verticillata.*
English Yew	*Taxus baccata.*
Irish do	do. *hibernica.*
Short-leaf do.	do. *adpressa.*
Golden do	do. *aurea.*
Silver do	do. *argentea.*
Erect do.	do. *erecta.*

Fortune's Yew...................... *Cephalotoxus fortunii.*
The Yew-leaf Torryea................ *Torryea taxifolia.*
Californian do. .... *do. myristica.*
Chinese do. .... *do. grandis.*
American Arbor Vitæ................ *Thuya occidentalis.*
Crested do. .... *do. crestata.*
Gigantic do. .... *do. gigantea.*
Weeping do. .... *do filiformis.*
Golden do. .... *do. aurea.*
Siberian do. .... *do. plicata.*
Warren's do. .... *do. warreana.*
Japan do. .... *do. japonica.*
 do. do. .... *do. macrocarpa.*
Wootka Sound Thuiopsis .... *Thuiopsis borealis.*
Japan do. .... *do. dolabrata.*
Standish's do. .... *do. standishii.*
Charming do. .... *do. virens.*
Lawson's Cypress .... *Cupressus lawsonii.*
 do. Erect Cypress............... *do. do. erecta.*
 do. Graceful Cypress............ *do. do. gracilis.*
Chinese Juniper..................... *Juniperus chinensis.*
Weeping do. .... *do. oblonga pendula.*
Nepaul do. .... *do. squamata.*
Silver do. .... *do. glauca.*
Carpet do. .... *do. prostrata.*
Retinospora .... *Ericoides.*
 do. .... *Filifera.*
 do. .... *Leptoclada.*
 do. .... *Obtusa.*
 do. .... *Pisefera.*
 do. .... *Aurea.*
 do. .... *Plumosa.*

CLASS V.

Hardy Shrubs growing from 6 to 20 feet high.

Hercules Club.... .... *Aralia spinosa.*
Snow-Drop, or White Fringe Tree...... *Chionanthus virginica.*
Narrow leaved do. ...... *do. maritima.*
Laburnum, or Golden Chain.......... *Cytissus laburnum.*
Weeping do. .... *do. do. pendula.*

Yellow Bladder Senna.............. *Colutea arborescens.*
Pink Flowering Hawthorn........... *Crategus oxycantha, var.*
New Scarlet   do.   ....   *do.   do.   var.*
Double White   do.   ....   *do.   do.   floro pleno*
Cornelian Cherry.................... *Cornus mascula.*
European Strawberry Tree, or Burn-
        ing Bush...................... *Euonymus europæus.*
White Fruited   do.   ....   *do.   do.   fructu alba.*
Purple Flowering   do.   ....   *do.   atropurpureus.*
American   do.   ....   *do.   americanus.*
Silver Bell Tree.................... *Halesia tetraptera.*
Althea Frutex, or Rose of Sharon,
        many sorts and colors.......... *Hibiscus syriacus.*
Silvery Buckthorn.................. *Hippophæ rhamnoides.*
Chinese Kolreuteria................. *Kolreuteria paniculata.*
Snowy Flowered Mespilus............ *Mespilus botryapium.*
Glaucous, or Swamp Magnolia........ *Magnolia glauca.*
Carolina large flowering Syringo...... *Philadelphus grandiflorus.*
Common Fragrant   do.   ......   *do.   coronarius.*
Semi-double   do.   ......   *do.   semi-pleno.*
Hop Tree,.................... `.......... *Ptelea trifoliata.*
Venetian Sumac, or Purple Fringe
        Tree........................ *Rhus cotinus.*
Shrubby Yellow Robinia............. *Robinia frutescens.*
Silvery-leaved Shepherdia, or Buffalo
        Berry........................ *Shepherdia argentea.*
Three-leaved Bladder Nut............ *Staphylea trifoliata.*
White and Purple Lilacs............. *Syringa vulgaris.*
White and Purple Persian Lilacs...... *do. persica.*
Cut-leaved   do........   *do. laciniata.*
French Tamarisk.................... *Tamarix gallica.*
Snow-ball, or Guelder Rose..... .... *Viburnum opulus.*
Wayfaring Tree.................... *do.   lantana.*

CLASS VI.

Hardy Shrubs growing from 1 *to* 6 *or* 8 *feet high.*

Indigo Shrub...................... *Amorpha fruticosa.*
Dwarf White Horse Chestnut......... *Æsculus macrostachya.*
Groundsel Tree.................... *Baccharis halimifolia.*
Sweet-Scented Shrub................ *Calycanthus floridus.*

Fragrant Clethra	*Clethra alnifolia.*
Panicled Flowered Clethra	*do. paniculata.*
Red Flowering Bladder Senna	*Colutea arborescens.*
Scorpion Senna	*Coronilla emerus.*
Bloody-twigged Dogwood	*Cornus sanguinea.*
Cluster-flowered Cytissus	*Cytissus capitatus.*
Scarlet Japan Quince	*Cydonia japonica.*
Blush, or White do.	*do. alba.*
Pink Mezereon	*Daphne mezereum.*
White Mezereon	*Daphne m. album.*
Oak-leaved Hydrangea	*Hydrangea quercifolia.*
Heart-leaved Hydrangea	*Hydrangea cordata.*
Italian Yellow Jasmine	*Jasminum humile.*
Japan Yellow Globe Flower	*Kerria japonica.*
Common Privet, or Prim	*Ligustrum vulgare.*
Tartarian or Tree Honeysuckle	*Lonicera tartarica.*
White flowering do.	*do. alba.*
Black-berried do.	*do. nigrum.*
English fly do.	*do. xylosteum.*
Pink flowering Honeysuckle	*do. pulverulenta.*
Standish's do.	*do. Standishii.*
Dwarf Syringo	*Philadelphus nanus.*
Shrubby Cinquefoil	*Potentilla fruncosa.*
Double Purple Tree Pœony	*Pœonia moutan Banksia.*
Single Pink and Purple do.	*do. papaveracea.*
Double Rose-colored do.	*do. rosea.*
Rose Acacia	*Robina hispida.*
Shrubby Caragana	*do. caragana.*
Corymbose Spirea	*Spirea corymbosa.*
Sorb-leaved do.	*do. sorbifolia.*
Red flowering do.	*do. tomentosa.*
Panicled do.	*do. paniculata.*
Pretty flowering do	*do. bella.*
Fortune's do.	*do. callosa.*
do. white do.	*do. alba.*
Lance-leaved or Reevsi do	*do. lanceolata.*
do. do. or double do. do.	*do. do. fl. pl.*
Double flowering plum-leaved do.	*do. prunifolia.*
Nicondert Spirea	*do. niconderti.*
Germander-leaved Spirea	*do. chamædrifolia.*
Hawthorn-leaved do.	*do. crenata.*
Chinese do. do.	*do. sinensis.*
Elm do. do.	*do. ulmifolia.*

Billard's Rose Spirea................*Spirea Billardii.*
St. Peter's Wreath................... do. *hypericifolia.*
Plaited Viburnum...................*Viburnum plicata.*
Snowberry (white fruit)..............*Symphoria racemosa.*
Indian Currant (red do.).............. do. *glomerata.*
Rose weigela.......................*Weigela rosea.*
Splendid do .... do. *amabalis.*
Desbois's do....................... do. *Desboisii.*
Variegated leaved do............... do. *fol. variegata.*
White do. .... do. *alba.*
Isoline do. .... do. *Isolinii.*
Van Houte's do. .... do. *Van Houtii.*
Profuse flowering do................ do. *floribunda.*
Parsley-leaved yellow root............*Zanthoriza apiifolia.*
Dwarf double-flowering Almond......*Amygdalis pumila.*
   do. white do do ...... do. do. *alba.*
Purple-leaved Berberry..............*Berberris purpurea.*
Variegated-leaved Cornus............*Cornus variegata.*
Golden Bell Forsythia................*Forsythia verdissima.*
Rough-leaved Deutzia...............*Deutzia scabra.*
Slender-branched do. .... do. *gracilis.*
Double crenate-leaved do............. do. *crenata flore pleno.*

Evergreen Shrubs.

Tree Box....................... ...*Buxus arborescens.*
American Holly.... ....*Ilex opaca.*
European do., *rather tender at the north.* do. *aquifolium.*
Swedish Juniper....................*Juniperus suecia.*
Common Laurel, or Kalmia...........*Kalmia latifolia.*
American Rhododendron.............*Rododendron maximum.*

The following Rhododendrons, seedlings of Catawbiensis, are hardy:—

Album elegans.	Fastuosum flore pleno.
Atropurpureum.	Purpureum elegans.
Azureum.	Roseum elegans.
Bicolor.	Pictum.
Delicatissimum.	Standishii.

And the following newer Shrubs are desirable acquisitions to our gardens:—

Andromeda floribunda.	Mahonia Bealii.
Mahonia japonica.	do. intermedia.
Berberis Mahonia.	

Selection of very choice Fruits for the small Orchard of 74 trees.

CHERRIES.

1 Knight's Early Black.
1 Mayduke.
1 Tartarian.
1 Downer's Late.
1 Coe's Transparent.
1 Belle d'Orleans.
1 Rockport.
1 Bigarreau of Mezel.
1 Kentish.
1 Reine Hortense.

PEARS.

2 Bartletts.
2 Seckel.
2 Beurré Bosc.
1 Dearborn's Seedling.
1 Winter Nelis.
1 Bloodgood's Early.
1 Beurré d Anjou.
1 Lawrence.
1 Rostezier.
1 Tyson.
1 Sheldon.
1 Dana's Hovey.
1 Doyenne d'Eté.
1 Beurré Giffart.
1 Manning's Elizabeth.
1 Doctor Reeder.

PLUMS.

1 Coe's Golden Drop.
1 Washington.
1 Green Gage.
1 Imperial Ottoman.
1 Jefferson.
1 Reine Claude de Bavay.
1 McLaughlin.
1 Prince's Yellow Gage.
1 Transparent Gage.

1 Dennison's Superb.
1 Purple Favorite.

PEACHES.

2 George the Fourth.
2 Early Newington.
2 La Grange.
1 Early York.
1 Large White Cling.
1 Crawford's Late.
1 Old Mixon Freestone.
1 Troth's Early Red.
1 Large Early York.
1 Early Beatrice.

APPLES.

1 Newtown Pippin.
1 Yellow Harvest.
1 Fall Pippin.
2 Baldwin.
1 Rhode Island Greening.
1 Yellow Bell Flower.
1 Northern Spy.
1 Primate.
1 Mother.
1 Gravestein.
1 Porter.
1 Red Astrachan.
1 Melon.
1 Hubbardston Nonsuch.
1 Jonathan.
1 Wagener.

APRICOTS.

1 Moor Park.
1 Breda.

NECTARINES.

1 Early Violet.
1 Downton.

Total, 74

DESIGN IV.

An Ornamental Farm-House.

In designing this farm-house we have had two objects in view; first, to offer to the large class of intelligent farmers a plan of a house of moderate size, somewhat adapted in internal accommodation to their peculiar wants; and second, to give to the exterior, at little additional cost, some architectural beauty. The first object, it is evident, must ever be the principal one in a farmer's dwelling, and therefore everything should yield to such an interior arrangement as will give the greatest amount of comfort, and the maximum of convenience, in performing in-door labor. But beyond this, there is no reason why the dwelling-houses of our respectable farmers should not display some evidences of taste, as well as those of professional men, or persons in more affluent circumstances. The farmers are really the most independent men in our community, as their wealth is less liable to fluctuation than that of any other class; and if the amount they wish to expend upon a dwelling is less than that within the means of some others, they are generally able, on the other hand, by having abundance of stone or timber on their own premises, to build at a greatly reduced cost. By bestowing some degree of ornament on farm-houses, we shall hope to increase the interest and attachment which the farmer and his family have for their home, and thereby to improve his social and domestic state. A man who is content to live in a clumsy, badly contrived, and uncouth habitation, will generally be found to care little for his home, or to have in his heart but a scanty flow of genial domestic sympathies. This love of home, and with it all the tender affections bound up in that endearing word, will be sure to grow with every step we take to add to its comforts or increase its beauty, and if we feel a species of affection for the goodly trees we have planted, which, growing along with us, seem like old and familiar friends, we must acknowledge a still greater attachment to a dwelling that we have built, and which becomes our own home,—whether it be a cottage or a mansion,—if there is an air of taste lurking about it, and breathing out from vine-covered porch or open window casement.

We are especially anxious that the farmer should cultivate a taste for improving his home, including under this term his dwelling, and his garden or grounds, as we are confident that in so doing he will unconsciously open to himself and his family new sources of enjoyment, beyond such as are *directly* derived from their beauty and convenience. It is unquestionably true, that we learn to appreciate the beauty of nature in proportion as we become familiar with the beauty of art. Now, although we do not expect farmers to possess a gallery of pictures or statuary, yet they have a scarcely less instructive field open to them whilst tastefully disposing their gardens and grounds, in studying the various developments of beauty that occur and become familiar to the mind in these and all other employments, unfolding the order and harmony of a well-regulated rural home. And we will venture to assert that no person, however small his original knowledge, has followed these occupations thoughtfully for half a dozen years, without having his appreciation of the beauty of all nature, and especially the beauty of trees, forests, hills, and rivers, a thousand-fold increased.

DESIGN IV.
An Ornamental Farm House.

Fig. 31.

PRINCIPAL FLOOR

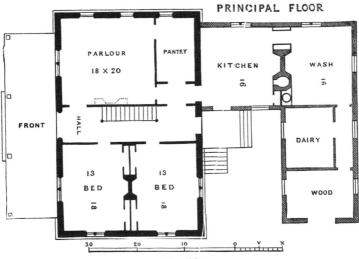

Fig. 32.

By referring to the plan of the principal floor, Fig. 32, it will be seen that the main building, thirty by forty-six feet, is two stories in height, and contains on this floor a hall, a parlor, two bed-rooms, and a large pantry. The parlor, or sitting-room, is an excellent apartment, suitable for any occasion, and the pantry being placed between it and the kitchen, either of these rooms may be used to dine in; while the passage, with two doors between the parlor and the kitchen, prevents the noise of the latter from being heard in the former.

The kitchen, wash-house, dairy, and wood-house, on the same level with the main building, are contained in an L-form addition in the rear, one story in height. The kitchen is sixteen feet square, and opens also by a back door, upon a broad stone platform, under which the steps next the main building descend to the cellar. The wash-room is sixteen feet square, and has by the side of the fire-place a circular copper boiler set, for boiling the clothes. There is a passage from the wash-room, communicating directly with the wood-house. The dairy may, if it is thought advisable, be sunk three feet below the level of the wash-house, and paved with flag-stones, in order to keep it cool; and there may be a raised shelf of stone all around it, on which to place pans of milk. In this case it would be entered by descending four or five steps. The wood-house has a large door, to facilitate unloading from the wood wagons.

The plan of the second story, Fig. 33, affords three good bed-rooms, closets, etc., and a small bed-room; and above this story is an ample garret for drying various seeds and vegetables.

The cellar is large, being of the same size as the main building, and on the side next the carriage-road should be placed a *slide*, wide enough to receive a cart-load of roots, which will save much labor and time usually occupied in carrying them in baskets.

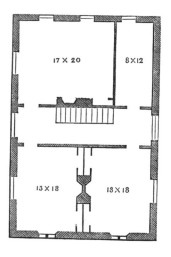

FIG. 33.

This dwelling is supposed to be constructed of rough stone, or stone partially smooth on the face, but not laid in regular courses. Such stone is abundant throughout a great portion of the United States, and makes excellent walls.

We have given the preference to the *Rural Pointed* style in composing the exterior of this dwelling, partly on account of the large lofts or garrets, so useful to the farmer, afforded by the steep gables and roofs, and partly on account of its intrinsic beauty and picturesque effect when built of stone even in this simple manner. We have introduced a *veranda* in the same style in front, because such a feature is as necessary to the comfort of a farm-house as a villa in this country.

Where all the out-buildings are to be erected at the same time with the dwelling-house, something of the same style should be evinced in the construction. It is not necessary, to attain this, that ornamental verge-boards or windows, or other minor details, should be introduced in barns or the like structures, but it will be sufficient if attention is paid to repeating the same general forms in the *outlines* of the buildings, and of these the form of the roof or gables is most essential.

In some districts, wood is the only material which comes

within reach of the farmer. When this is the case it would be better to adopt another style for the exterior, of a lighter character. We would recommend the simple projecting roof, and the general style of Design I., omitting some of the ornamental details. The arrangement of the rooms would require no material alteration, whatever style of architecture may be adopted for the interior ; and a farm-house built in the plainest manner, preserving the arrangement exactly, would still have all the merit of this part of the design, of whatever value it may be considered.

It is evident that to some families another parlor, or a common eating-room, but little superior to the kitchen, might be thought desirable. This would be easily obtained by converting the *rear bed-room* into a *dining-room*, and keeping the *parlor* (which is now intended to serve the purpose of dining-room also) as a show apartment, or *best room.* Such a plan might suit the fancy of those who take pleasure in keeping the best and most comfortable room in their house shut except when they see strangers, but we cannot recommend it as consonant with good taste, and that unaffected, genuine hospitality, which ought to characterize "plain country folks."

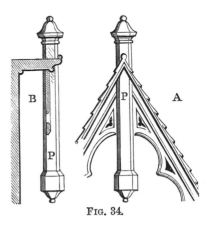

FIG. 34.

Details of construction.— The construction of this building will be easily understood by merely inspecting the elevation, as it is extremely simple. In Fig. 34, the verge-board and cornice are shown more in detail, to the scale of $\frac{1}{2}$ inch to a foot. In this, A is the front view of the top of gable, and B, the profile or section of the same. P is the pendant which perforates the ridge of the roof, and terminates the gable by what is termed a hip-knob, or finial. The roof, in this design, projects about a foot beyond the walls of the house. The veranda is supported by octagonal posts or pillars, the openings between which are ornamented at the top by single arches cut from 2-inch plank. All the exterior wood-work of this building (except sashes and doors) should be painted three coats of the same color as the stone, or a few shades lighter, and painted.

Estimate.—The cost of this building, supposing the stone to be found on the farm, and all the materials to be drawn by the farmer, will not exceed $1,700. [The cost now would be about $4,000.—ED.]

The Ornamental Portion of the Farm.

The *ferme ornée* is a term generally applied to a farm, the whole or the greater part of which is rendered in some degree ornamental by intersecting it with drives, and private lanes and walks, bordered by trees and shrubs, and by the neater arrangement and culture of the fields. But it may also be applied to a farm with a tasteful farm-house, and so much of the ground about it rendered ornamental as would naturally meet the eye of the stranger, in approaching it the first time.

It is evident that the farm proper, in the present case, may consist of 50 or 500 acres. We have only shown in the annexed engraving, Fig. 35, a plan of a few acres immediately surrounding the house, and consisting of the entrance lawn *a*, about one and a quarter acres bordering the entrance road or approach *b*, the orchard *c*, the

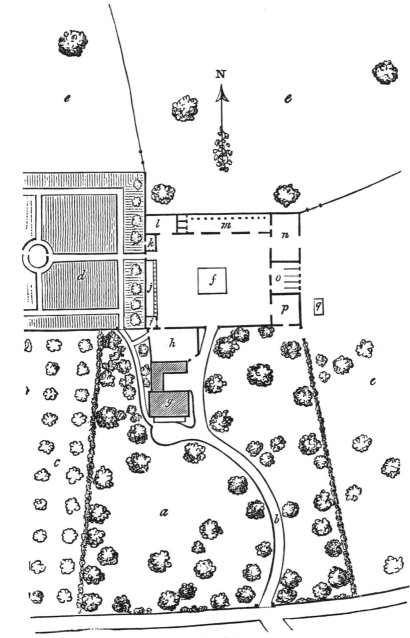

[Fig. 35.]

kitchen garden *d*, adjoining fields, in grass or under the plough *e*, and the yard for the out-buildings *f*.

At *g* is shown the house, and in the rear of the kitchen, wash-house, etc., is the kitchen yard *h*. The out-buildings, or farmery, are arranged around three sides of a square, open to the south, and consist of the piggery *j*, the tool-house communicating with the garden *k*, open shed for carts, ploughs, etc., *l*, cow-house with three calf-pens attached at the end *m*, barn *n*, stable for horses *o*, wagon-house *p*, and corn crib *q*. The surface of the yard descends slightly on all sides to the centre *f*, where the manure heap is kept. This collection of out-buildings is much more complete and extensive than will be found connected with most farms in this country, but we have given it with a view of exhibiting what ought to be aimed at as a desideratum in accommodation on every extensive farm; and it will be found easy to diminish the amount of buildings and sheds to as many as would occupy only one side of the yard, if the farm be small, or to such a number as can be afforded.

This plan will require but little description, as the ornamental grounds have no intricacy of detail. The effect of the view from the house across the entrance lawn *a*, would be pleasing, and its expression would be that of simply natural or pastoral beauty. The trees might be of the finest native species, selected from the woods on the farm, as nothing is more beautiful than our fine drooping Elms, Tulip-trees, Oaks, and Ashes. Or some additional interest may be given to the place by introducing a few Horse Chestnuts or European Lindens around the house and along the approach. The trees we would plant in natural groups, as indicated on the plan, as this would not only evince a more cultivated taste in a farmer than straight lines, but it would also add to the apparent extent of the whole area devoted to ornamental trees, by giving it an irregular and varied boundary of foliage.

This acre and a quarter devoted to ornament may also be rendered profitable: 1st, by mowing the grass over the whole surface : or secondly, by keeping it short, by pas-turing it with favorite animals. In the case of mowing, when no animals are admitted, a few flowering shrubs and plants may be cultivated directly around the house. But if it is preferred to pasture the area, it would be necessary to confine all small shrubs and plants to a certain portion of the kitchen garden devoted to this purpose.

There are some farmers who would be willing to devote an acre around their house to some kind of lawn, or purpose superior to a common field, who are yet not sufficiently alive to the beauty and dignity of fine forest trees to be willing to plant the latter. Such may substi-tute fruit for forest trees, and even arrange them in the same manner, planting those most symmetrical and pleasing in their forms, as the cherry and pear, near the house and the Approach ; and those which are unsightly in growth, nearest the boundary.

The beauty of a farm will be greatly enhanced by introducing verdant hedges in the place of stone or wooden fences, at least in all situations near the house. The best plant to be had in the nurseries for this purpose is the Buckthorn (*Rhamnus cathartica*), a native shrub, much hardier and better than the English hawthorn for our climate. Almost any of our native thorns in the woods make good hedges, and the farmer may gather the seeds and raise them himself. South of the latitude of New York city, the best hedge-plant is the Osage Orange (*Maclura aurantiaca*).

If the ground is previously well prepared by repeated ploughings and manuring, and proper care is taken to head back the young plants the first year or two, to make a thick bottom, and to trim them twice a year afterwards, an excellent hedge may be obtained in five years. No person, we hope, who has once seen a handsome deep green hedge, forming a dense close surface, enlivened with blossoms in the spring and berries in the autumn, will grudge the little annual care necessary to substitute this for at least a small part of his unsightly wall, or "post and rail."

Wooden and stone fences near the house may be rendered ornamental by planting the Virginia creeper (*Ampelopsis*), or five-leaved ivy, at short distances along the fence. This vine is common over a large portion of the Union, and will quickly form a beautiful mantle of verdure, concealing the wall in summer with its rich and luxuriant green, and in autumn with its bright scarlet foliage.

When the eye commands from the house a view beyond the ornamental lawn, the latter may be pleasingly connected by planting or preserving, here and there, in the adjoining fields, a few of the same forest trees that are growing on the lawn, thus avoiding too strongly marked a contrast between the latter area and the farm-lands, and showing something of a unity of design and purpose.

The orchard near the house is an apple orchard, and we give a selection of one hundred trees for the purpose of planting it with the most valuable sorts, including a number of sweet apples for feeding stock.

		Ripens in
2	Early Bough	August.
2	Yellow Harvest	July.
2	Esopus Spitzenberg	Nov. Feb.

Ripens in

4 Boston Russet.........................May.
6 Fall Pippin...........................Sept. Dec.
4 Jersey Sweet..........................Aug. Nov.
2 Jonathan.............................Dec. Feb.
6 Baldwin..............................Nov. May.
2 Lady Apple...........................Nov. March.
4 American.............................Dec. Feb.
6 Ladies' Sweeting......................Nov. March.
2 Newtown Pippin.......................Dec. May.
3 Golden Sweeting ....Sept. Oct.
8 Rhode Island Greening ....Nov. March.
2 Summer Paradise......................Aug. Sept.
4 Swaar...............................Dec. March.
4 Yellow Belle Fleur.....................Oct. Jan.
4 Winesop ....Nov. March.
4 Campfield............................Nov. March.
2 Dominie.............................Nov. March.
2 Hubardston Nonsuch....................Dec. March.
2 Gravestein...........................Sept. Oct.
4 Northern Spy.........................Feb. May.
4 Porter...............................Sept. Oct.
3 Melon...............................Oct. March.
3 Wagener............................Nov. Feb.
4 Peck's Pleasant.......................Nov. March.
4 Summer Pippin.......................Sept.

DESIGN V.

A Cottage Villa in the Bracketed Mode.

WE trust that the exterior of this villa will generally please, as, although it is simple in form, we have endeavored to add to its domestic, comfortable air a more forcible and elegant expression than rectangular buildings generally possess. The strongly-marked character which it has is derived mainly from the bold projection of the roof, supported by ornamental brackets, and from the employment of brackets for supports in various other parts of the building.

This bracketed mode of building, so simple in construction and so striking in effect, will be found highly suitable to North America, and especially to the Southern States. The coolness and dryness of the upper story, afforded by the almost veranda-like roof, will render this a delightful feature in all parts of our country where the summers are hot, and the sun very bright during the long days of that season. Indeed, we think a very ingenious architect might produce an *American cottage style* by carefully studying the capabilities of this mode, so abounding in picturesqueness and so easily executed.

In actual fitness for domestic purposes in this country, we think this bracketed mode has much to recommend it. It is admirably adapted to the two kinds of construction which must, for some time, be the most prevalent in the United States—wood, and brick covered by an external wash. Its comparative lightness of character renders it well suited for wood, and the protection afforded by the projection of the roof will give complete security and dry-ness to the walls, rendering good stucco or cement in such a situation as durable as stone. The facility of its construction is an additional circumstance in its favor, as the details are extremely simple—the ornamental brackets, which are the principal features of decoration, being cut out of pine or oak plank, two inches thick, and one or two patterns serving for the whole exterior.

Extending the roof in the manner shown in this design gives expression and character at once to the exterior, and the broad and deep shadows thrown by the projection are not only effective and pleasing to the artistic eye, but they increase the actual comfort of the chamber apartments; a projection of from thirty inches to three feet serving as a hood to shelter the windows from the summer sun during all the sultry portions of the day; while in winter, the sun being low in position, this effect will not be felt when it is not desirable.

On entering the hall (see plan of principal floor, Fig. 37), we find on the left an oval dining or living room, lighted by a large and handsome window on the side, and another in front; the latter finished with a window-seat. There are two pantries, or closets, in this room, in the spaces formed by the ovals in front, and the opposite end of the room may be finished with shallow closets for plate, glass, or valuable china. At the opposite end of this room is a door opening into the passage *b*, which communicates with the stairs to the kitchen (under the main stairs), and also with the open air, by the door on the veranda. At the left of this passage is the water-closet (W. C.).

DESIGN V.

A Cottage Villa in the Bracketed Mode.

Fig. 36

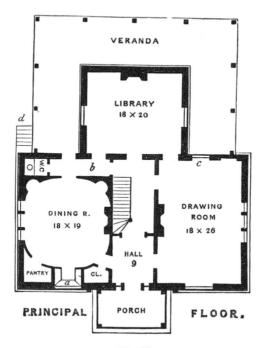

Fig. 37.

On the opposite side is the parlor or drawing-room, occupying the whole space, eighteen by twenty-six feet. This room is of very handsome size, and if well finished would make a splendid apartment. The ceiling should be thirteen or fourteen feet high, and might be supported by a bracketed cornice, tastefully executed in plaster, to harmonize with the character of the exterior. Our own taste would lead us to prefer greatly, in all cases, the simplicity and dignity of a single large apartment of this kind in the country, to two apartments connected by folding or sliding doors. In the latter the single room, considered by itself, is comparatively of no importance, because it is evidently only one-half of the architect's idea, and the *coup d'œil* of the whole is greatly injured by the partition still remaining after the doors are open. A large room like this drawing-room will, on the contrary, be a complete whole in itself, and regarding its effect, either with or without company, it will be found much more satisfactory than that of the two smaller ones connected. Access to the veranda from this room is afforded by the window at its further end, *c*, which is a casement window opening to the floor, and may therefore be used as a door.

At the end of the hall a door opens into the library, eighteen by twenty feet, which is a cool, airy apartment, shaded by the veranda that surrounds it on three sides. It communicates directly with the drawing-room by one door, and with the passage *b*, leading to the veranda, by another.

On the second floor are five bed-rooms, Fig. 38. The two bed-rooms on the right being connected by a door, one of them may be used as a nursery, and the other as a family bed-room. Three bed-rooms for servants may be finished in the attic story, which will be lighted by the

windows in the gable. There is a handsome balcony,
which is entered upon from the casement-window, at the
end of the hall in this story, shaded by the broad overhanging roof, and two other balconies which accompany,
in a similar manner, the large windows in the two principal bed-rooms on either side of this hall. These two large
windows are each composed of three compartments, and
the middle compartment of that on the right, against
which the partition of the nursery abuts, is made solid
on the inside, which still gives one window, or compartment of moderate size, for each room.

The basement accommodation, Fig. 39, consists of a

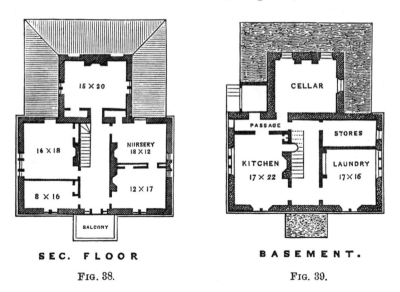

SEC. FLOOR

FIG. 38.

BASEMENT.

FIG. 39.

kitchen, laundry, store-room, and cellar. The basement
story is raised about three and a half feet above
ground, with areas built around the windows, to admit
an abundance of light. The outer entrance to this story
is by the steps descending under the veranda, indicated
on the left of this plan.

The chimneys in this elevation are bold and striking, and show what would be in good keeping with the style of the house. Their construction is simple. They are each covered on the top by two flat coping-stones, of bold projection, the smoke escaping on two sides (Fig. 42). Chimneys built in this manner are much more likely to draw well than those with an open top, in the common mode. This form, however, is not by any means essential, and square flues in a body, with a bold cornice supported on bricks projecting as brackets, or separate detached flues carried up in clusters, with heavy tops, would also be suitable for a building in this style.

Variation of this design as constructed in wood.—The foregoing engravings being in illustration of this design as built of solid materials, we introduce another elevation, Fig. 40, to show its appearance constructed of wood. The common mode of *siding* is sufficiently well understood by every one, but in this elevation a less general mode is shown, which consists in tongue and grooving the boards, nailing them vertically on the frame, and covering the joint by a strip one or two inches wide. We suggest this mode as a variation, as it makes a very warm and dry house, and the effect is good. Fig. 45 is a section to the scale of half an inch to a foot, showing this kind of siding.

There are, perhaps, some families who would much prefer a bed-room to the library, in our previous plan of the principal floor. We have therefore, in the annexed Fig. 41, shown how this wing, originally intended for a library, may, by a little variation in the plan, be made to afford a pleasant bed-room, with a closet adjoining, and a pretty little boudoir opening either into the bed-room or the drawing-room, as may be thought best. If this variation should be preferred to the original plan of this floor, it will only

be necessary to carry through the partitions introduced in
this wing, which will make a similar alteration in the plan
of the second and basement stories so easily understood,
that it will not require any further plans in illustration.

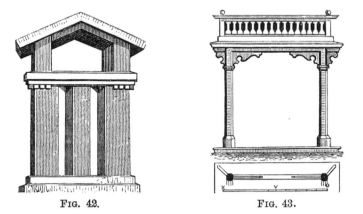

FIG. 42.   FIG. 43.

Details.—A portion of the porch in Fig. 43 shows the
manner of ornamenting this part of the building by
brackets.   Four varieties of brackets, suitable for the roof
supports of buildings in this style, are seen in the accompanying Fig. 44.   In this engraving, drawn to the scale of
half an inch to a foot, A represents the boldest form, suitable for the corners or angles of the building; B, one of
lesser size, proper for the projection of the gables; c is
another variation, employed in the bold projection of the
gable in front, over the porch, and D is a form employed
for eave brackets, when it is thought advisable to continue
them along the whole line of roof, as in the next design.
In the following engraving, *a* represents a moulding, and
b the roof and cornice above the bracket.   The most
complete mode would undoubtedly be to employ cut-
stone brackets in a building like this composed of stone or
solid materials; but if made of good sound wood, and

DESIGN V.*

As Constructed in Wood.

[Fig. 40.]

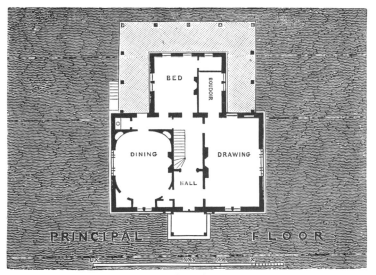

[Fig. 41.]

thoroughly painted and sanded to resemble the stone or stucco, it will answer as well.

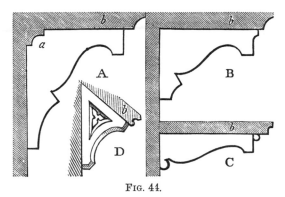

FIG. 44.

In Fig. 45 is seen a section of the mode of siding alluded to in our variation of this design *in wood*, which needs no further explanation.

FIG. 45.

It will be observed that the supports to the veranda in the rear of this dwelling are simple octagonal posts, ornamented with brackets at the top, and that the brackets being a characteristic feature in this style or mode, it is introduced wherever a support is really or apparently necessary, as in the case of the balconies to the windows, etc. And in a building in this mode, the unity of design should be further preserved by carrying out the boldness of character in all portions of the building, by projecting the roofs, verandas, porches, etc., in a proportionate degree, and by introducing few and bold mouldings and ornaments.

Some character is given to the roof in this design by employing shingles of a uniform size, and rounding the lower ends before laying them on the roof.*

---

* The principle of *expression of purpose* demands that the *roofs* of buildings should be shown, and rendered ornamental. In snowy countries especially, a

We have designated a *water-closet* in this design. A water-closet does not actually require a space larger than three by four or five feet, and it may therefore be introduced in the first or second story of almost every house, although we have only shown it in two or three of these designs. If properly constructed, and its accompanying cistern kept supplied with water, it will be found entirely free from odors of any kind, and therefore a very great desideratum in every house. The better way is to employ a first-rate plumber from the city to fit it up completely while the house is in progress. In order to explain the principle of its construction, we extract the following description of one of a simple and very efficient kind from the "Encyclopædia of Cottage, Farm, and Villa Architecture," p. 18.

"The water-closet may be variously arranged; but as one of the best and cheapest modes, and one the least likely to go out of order, we give the following: The cistern, Fig. 46, *a*, may be at any distance from the seat *b*, provided it be on a higher level by four or five feet. The basin, *c*, may be an inverted hollow cone, truncated, and joined to a piece of cylindrical tube, inserted in a closed leaden vessel, technically called a smell-trap, *d*. In the side of *c*, at *e*, is a hole or vertical opening passing obliquely through the sides of the basin, and communicating with the cistern *a* by the pipe *f*. The water in the cistern is prevented from running off through this

---

moderately steep roof is necessary to sustain the pressure, and shed the snow perfectly, and it should always, therefore, be boldly exposed, and rendered ornamental in domestic architecture. Some of our builders seem to have a farcical horror of a roof or a chimney-top (derived from the study of Greek temples!), and conceal both by costly and elaborate balustrades and parapets, in many cases at an expense sufficient, if judiciously applied, to have given a superior character to the whole building.

pipe by a nicely fitting valve at g.   When it is desired to
allow the water to rush down into
the basin, it is only necessary to pull
the string h; which, if the cistern
be at a distance, may pass over
several pulleys, according to the
number of angles in its course.   In
order to insure the descent of a
quantity of water to the basin every
time it has been used, a cord i, may
be joined to h, and passed over the
pulley at k, and the end of this cord
may be fixed to the upper part of
the door of the water-closet at such
a distance from the hinge, say a foot,

FIG. 46.

as will suffice to lift up the valve g; or the same purpose
might be effected by a lever which would be acted upon
every time the door was opened.   In every case where it
is intended that a common or lever valve should be
operated on by a door, the latter ought to have a spring-
bolt to shut it, lest at any time it should be left open by
neglect."   There are several late improvements in water-
closets now to be had of the best plumbers in New York.
The waste-pipe from the water-closet should leave the
house by a properly fitted under-ground drain, and should
either terminate in a covered drain or sewer, at a considerable distance, or in a well or cistern for liquid
manure, the contents of which may be turned to valuable
account.

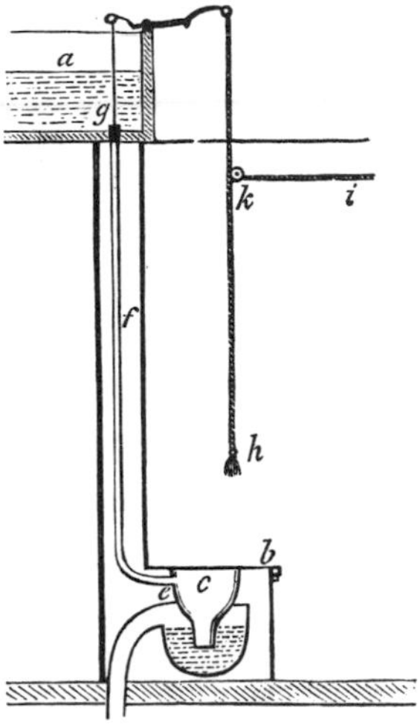

Estimate.—This cottage-villa may be built of brick and
stucco or of wood, in the best manner, at a cost of about
$5,500.   With cut freestone trimmings, it would cost
$6,000.   [At present the cost would be, in wood, about

$6,500, and in brick, with freestone trimmings, about
$8,500.—ED.]

Laying out the Ground.

The situation for which this cottage is designed borders
the public road, and contains about two acres, which are
nearly level. At the back of the garden, Fig. 47, is a steep
hill, *a*, the side covered with trees, which is ascended by a
walk, *b*, leading to a rustic summer-house on the top at *c*,
from whence a prospect of the surrounding country is
obtained.

The house is at *d*, and the objects in laying out the
ground were to create an airy, cheerful aspect around the
house, especially in front; to preserve a view of the steep
picturesque hill from the veranda in the rear, and with the
appearance of a good deal of ornamental effect to retain
about one acre, or nearly half the level ground, for a
kitchen garden, *e*, and a fruit garden, *f*.

In order to give an air of some extent and elegance
about the house, the whole surface in this neighborhood
not devoted to the kitchen and fruit gardens is laid
down in lawn, *g*, to be kept neatly mown, with the exception of the long borders, *h*, devoted to a miscellaneous
collection of flowers; the circular beds filled with verbenas, petunias, and monthly roses, three plants which will
bloom the whole summer, and have a brilliant effect from
the drawing-room windows; and the two beds, *j*, filled
with choice double dahlias. In the turf is planted a number of the finest species of ornamental trees and shrubs,
some being allowed to grow alone and assume all their
beauty of development, and others planted in groups, or
thickets, for effect or shelter. The novice will be assisted

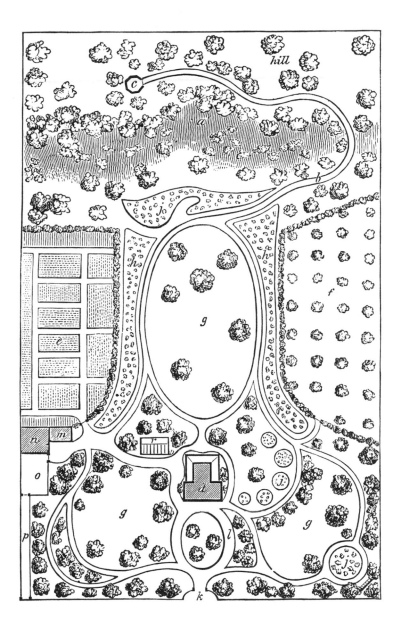

[Fig. 47.]

in making a selection of these trees and shrubs by referring to the list given at page 74. Some of the less hardy and robust of these trees and shrubs, being planted in groups in this way, will require that the surface around each tree for a small area of about two feet in diameter be kept loose by culture, to promote their growth, until they attain considerable size.

The entrance gate is shown at *k*, and there is a large oval of turf, around which to turn carriages, immediately before the door. The carriage road, *l*, after approaching the entrance to the kitchen, for the convenience of delivering heavy articles, leads to the carriage-house, *m*, adjoining which are the barn and stable, *n*, and the stable yard, *o*, the latter communicating directly with the public road by the lane, *p*.

The kitchen and fruit gardens are enclosed on three sides by hedges of the *privet* or *prim*, a rapid-growing plant which forms a thick hedge in three years, has neat foliage and flowers, and is easily cultivated from slips or cuttings planted in March or April. These verdant fences will scarcely appear barriers, and a spectator standing on the veranda in the rear of the house, and looking over the open oval lawn, *g*, bordered by the flower borders, and these backed by the deep green hedges, would scarcely be impressed with that idea of confinement which this moderate space would otherwise convey.

A detached green-house is shown at *r*, which, like the dwelling-house, fronts due south. This green-house is 14 feet wide by 40 feet long, and has a lean-to, or shed, at the rear, which affords a cover for the furnace, with a place for fuel, and a long narrow apartment for a gardener's seed-room, tool-room, or work-room, the latter being a place absolutely necessary in every residence of the size of half an acre, if appropriated to ornamental purposes. Not only the front, but also both the ends of this green-house should be glazed, as the sun will then, in the course of the day, shine on all sides.   In the Middle or Eastern States, where the winters are severe, it will be found a great economy of both fuel and labor to have light shut-ters made for all the sashes in a green-house detached like this one.   When the sun is shining, the shutters can be speedily removed, and in cold dull days and at night the glass may be kept covered, which will prevent the house from losing its heat rapidly.   No green-house in this country, where even the wintry sun is brilliant, will require a particle of fire while the sun shines, and by the aid of shutters we may preserve the warmth of the green-house, collected during the afternoon, through a considera-ble portion, and often the whole of the night.

The hill-side *a*, in its original state, was sprinkled over with trees, tufts of grass, ferns, etc., and was disfigured by the presence of a number of rough piles of rock.   In order to render them ornamental, a quantity of hardy climbers, as the Trumpet vine (*Bignonia*), the coral or trumpet Honeysuckles, the double-flowering Bramble, and the Virginia creeper, may be planted at the foot and among these rocks, and they will in two or three seasons render them highly picturesque by enwreathing them with beautiful garlands of foliage and flowers.

As the lawn will be a great source of beauty in all places of this kind, it is important that attention should be paid to this feature early in the preparation of the grounds.   No lawn will retain its freshness and verdure throughout our hot summers, unless particular attention is paid to two circumstances.   The first of these is the preparation of a *deep* soil before it is sown or laid down in grass; the second consists in frequent mowings. When there is a large surface to be kept in lawn, the soil may be rendered suitable by manuring and ploughing thoroughly beforehand with the sub-soil plough, or by going through the same furrow three times in ploughing the soil. When the area is small, it may be trenched with the spade. The roots of the grasses strike much deeper in a mellow prepared soil than persons are generally aware, and are thereby enabled to stand a severe drought, when, if sown in the ordinary mode, they would have dried up and the foliage become brown in a short time. A rich soil for a lawn is not desirable, but rather a deep one, capable of retaining moisture for a long time. Wood ashes will be found an excellent top-dressing for invigorating a worn-out lawn.

Frequent mowing is necessary to insure that velvet-like appearance so much admired in English lawns. To perform this operation neatly, the mower must be provided with a scythe, the blade of which is very broad, and hung nearly parallel to the surface of the lawn; and the mowing should always be performed, if possible, after a shower, or a heavy dew, while the grass is yet damp. The best mixture of grass-seeds in use among us, and to be had at our seed-shops, is the same as composes the natural growth of our commons, and the turf by the road-sides, viz., Red top and white Clover (*Agrostis vulgaris* and *Trifolium repens*). They should be sown thickly for a lawn, at the rate of three bushels of the former and six quarts of the latter to the acre.*

The five circular beds *i*, are supposed to be each ten or

* Mr. Loudon recommends the following mixture of grasses for a lawn, viz., *Agrostis vulgaris var. tenuifolia, Festuca duriuscula, F. ovina, Cynosurus cristatus, Poa pratensis, Avena flavescens*, and *Trifolium minus*.

fifteen feet in diameter, and cut in the turf. It is proposed to fill these with plants, each bed with the same genus, and cultivate them in such a manner that, when full grown, they shall cover the whole surface of the bed. They will then present a mass of rich leaves and blossoms, and the raw earth not being seen, these beds will connect themselves much more harmoniously with the surrounding turf or lawn, than if only partially covered with plants. Nothing is more unsightly than raw flower-beds near the windows of the house in midsummer, and we therefore greatly prefer the beauty of a few rich circles or groups like these, to the lean and parched appearance which long beds of miscellaneous flowers exhibit when placed in direct proximity to the dwelling.

The trailing *Verbenas* and *Petunias* are very showy plants, blooming perpetually during the whole season, and are therefore admirably adapted to this purpose. As they will not stand our winters, they must be treated as annuals; or preserved by taking small plants up in pots, in autumn, and keeping them in the green-house or a frame, planting them out again in April. The following varieties are recommended :—

VERBENAS.

Ada Snow (delicate blush).
Blue Bonnet (purplish blue).
Brightness (scarlet crimson).
Crimson King (brilliant crimson).
Capt. Tottinger (scarlet crimson.
Defiance (dazzling scarlet).
Mrs. Field (scarlet crimson).
White Beauty (pure white).
Scarlet Gem (brilliant scarlet).
Purple Standard (dark purple).
Richard Cobden (deep purple).
Purple Crown (rich purple).

Imperatrice Elizabeth (striped).
Reliance (bright ruby).
Ultramarine (deep blue).
Robinson's Defiance (scarlet).
St. Margaret (crimson).
Hermione (blue).
Beauty Supreme (pink).
Sir Seymour (white).

PETUNIAS.

Anita.
Adrienne.
Excellent.

Bayswater,   *Eclipse.*
The Bride.   *Rosy Morn.*
Striata Superba,   *King of Crimsons.*
Countess of Ellesmere.   *New White.*
Kermesina,   *Lady Alice Peel.*
Hebe.

A great number of beautiful monthly roses, including the Noisettes, the common China or Bengal, and the Tea and the Bourbon varieties, may be procured in the nurseries. These require a rich loamy soil, where they will bloom in great profusion all the summer, and until winter frosts overtake them. The Bourbon roses are especially remarkable for the size, the abundance, fragrance, and the beauty of their blossoms. The following selection includes some of the most desirable sorts, all everblooming or monthly.

HYBRID PERPETUAL ROSES.

Duke of Wellington, *dark crimson.*
Lord Clyde, *crimson shaded with purple.*
Alfred Colomb, *brilliant crimson.*
Charles Lefebvre, *brilliant red.*
General Jacqueminot, *brilliant crimson.*
General Washington, *brilliant rosy crimson.*
Madame Charles Wood, *briliant rosy red.*
Senateur Vaisse, *brilliant light crimson.*
John Hopper, *rosy crimson and rose.*
Jules Margottin, *vivid rosy carmine.*
Victor Verdier, *deep carmine.*
Charles Verdier, *rose bordered with white.*
Madame George Paul, *brilliant rose.*
Alba Mutabilis, *white tinged with rose.*
Louise Darzeus, *pure white.*

BOURBON ROSES.

Acidalie, *white, often tinged with rose.*
Baronne Genella, *lilac pink.*
Bouquet de Flore, *deep carmine.*
Catherine Guillot, *very bright rose.*
Dupetit Thonars, *dark crimson.*
Louise Odier, *bright rose.*
Marguerite Bonnet, *beautiful flesh white.*
Model de Perfection, *bright rose.*
Monsieur Jard, *crimson.*
Queen, *rosy fawn.*
Rev. H. Dombrain, *brilliant carmine.*
Souvenir de la Malmaison, *large pale flesh.*
Louis Chaix, *scarlet crimson.*
Hermosa, *rose-colored pink.*

BENGAL ROSES.

Mrs. Bosanquet, *pale flesh.*
Louis Philippe, *deep crimson.*
Agrippina, *bright crimson.*

Cramoise Superior, *bright crimson.*
Eugene Beauharnais, *dark amaranth.*
Clara Sylvan, *pure white.*
Madame Beron, *rosy crimson.*
Lady Warrender, *pure white.*
Archduke Charles, *rose changing to crimson.*
Double White Daily.

NOISETTE ROSES.

Aimée Vibert, *pure white.*
Augusta, *sulphur yellow.*
Lamarque, *pale yellow.*
Jaune (Desprez), *creamy blush.*
Jeanne d'Arc, *pure white.*
Baronne de Maynard, *pure white.*
Celine Forestier, *fine bright yellow.*
Fellemberg, *bright crimson.*
Solfaterre, *deep sulphur yellow.*
Triomphe de Rennes, *canary yellow, deep centre.*

TEA-SCENTED ROSES.

Devoniensis, *creamy white.*
Climbing Devoniensis, *creamy white.*
Adam, *rose.*
Alba rosea, *white shaded with rose.*

Comte de Paris, *flesh-colored rose.*
Comtesse Onvaroff, *rose tinted with pink.*
Duc de Magenta, *fine rosy salmon.*
Glorie de Dijon, *fawn, tinted with salmon and rose.*
Homer-rose, *centre salmon.*
Isabella Sprunt, *pure yellow.*
Jaune d'Or, *yellow.*
Louise de Savoie, *fine yellow.*
Madame Falcot, *nankeen, changing to yellow.*
Madame Charles, *bright yellow, centre salmon.*
Madame Willermoz, *white, salmon centre.*
Madame William, *rich yellow.*
Marshal Niel, *deep brilliant yellow.*
Moire, *flesh, and shaded with fawn.*
Rubens, *creamy white-flesh centre.*
Souvenir d'Eliza Varden, *creamy white tinted with rose.*
Souvenir d'Ami, *salmon, shaded with rose.*
Triomphe de Guillot, *white, shaded with rose and salmon.*
Vicomtesse Decazes, *yellow, centre shaded with copper.*

Nearly all the varieties of China Roses may be culti-vated in the open air, with a trifling covering of straw or litter, over the tops in winter, to prevent their being injured by sudden thawing after severe frosts.

The two flower borders, *h,* being each more than one hundred and fifty feet long, will contain a large collection of flowering plants, both annuals and perennials. The latter, being more permanent and more showy, are to be chiefly employed, but small spaces should be left at inter-vals along the borders to allow the sowing of annuals, as the latter bloom profusely during midsummer and autumn, when comparatively few perennials are in flower. We have already remarked that, in order to attain the most beautiful effect from such flower borders, two rules must be observed : the first is, to arrange the plants so that the taller and coarser growing shall be farthest from the front of the border, the smallest near the walk; and the second, that the collection should consist of a due proportion of plants blooming in the different months through the whole season.   As to perform this will perhaps require more knowledge of the habits of herbaceous plants than many of our readers possess, we give the following list for the purpose of assisting them in stocking beds of this description, so as to produce satisfactory results.

LIST OF PERENNIAL BORDER FLOWERS,

Arranged according to their period of blooming, with their height.

FLOWERING IN APRIL

CLASS I.

From 6 to 12 inches.

Anemone thalictroides, pl.   Double wood Anemone; white.
Adonis vernalis.   Spring flower Adonis; yellow.
Corydalis cucularia.   Breeches flower; white.
Anemone pulsatilla.   Pasque flower; blue.
Anemone hepatica, pl.   Double Hepaticas; blue.
Viola odorata, pl.   Double white and European Violets.
Omphalodes verna.   Blue Venus Navelwort.
Polemonium reptans.   Greek Valerian; blue.
Phlox stolonifera.   Creeping Phlox; red.
Primula veris.   The Cowslip; yellow and red.
Primula polyantha.   The Polyanthus; purple.
Primula auricula.   The Auricula; purple.
Viola tricolor.   Heart's Ease, or Pansy; many colors and sorts.
Viola grandiflora.   Purple Pansy.
Phlox subulata.   Moss Pink Phlox.
Phlox nivea.   White Moss Pink.
Gentiana acaulis.   Dwarf Gentian; purple.

CLASS II.

From 1 to 2 feet high.

Phlox divaricata.   Early purple Phlox.
Saxifraga crassifolia.   Thick-leaved Saxifrage; lilac.
Dodecatheon meadia.   American Cowslip; lilac.
Dodecatheon meadia alba.   American Cowslip; white.
Pulmonara virginica.   Virginian Lungwort; purple.
Alyssum saxatile.   Golden basket; yellow.
Trollius europeus.   European Globe flower; yellow.

MAY.

CLASS I.

From 6 to 12 inches high.

Alyssum saxatile compactum.   Golden Alyssum.
Veronica gentianoides.   Gentian-leaved Speedwell; blue.
Arabis alpina.   White Arabis.
Jeffersonia diphylla.   Two-leaved Jeffersonia; white.
Aubrietia delbroides.   Pale violet.
Lysamachia nummularia.   Trailing Loose-strife; yellow.
Myosotis palustris.   Forget-me-not; blue and yellow.
Myosotis palustris alba.   Forget-me-not; white.
Convallaria majalis.   Lily of the Valley; white.
Saponaria ocymoides.   Basil-like Soapwort; red.
Phlox pilosa.   Hairy Phlox; red.
Houstonia cærulea.   Blue Houstonia.

CLASS II.

From 1 to 2 feet high.

Coronilla varia.   Changeable Coronilla; pink.
Pæonia tenuifolia.   Fine-leaved Pæony; red.
Corydalis formosa.   Showy Corydalis; red.
Veronica spicata.   Blue-spiked Speedwell.
Pentstemon ovata.   Oval-leaved Pentstemon; blue.
Pentstemon atropurpureus.   Dark purple Pentstemon.
Orobus niger.   Dark purple Vetch.
Anchusa Italica.   Italian Bugloss; blue.
Ranunculus acris, pl.   Double Buttercups; yellow.
Tradescantia virginica.   Blue and white Spiderwort.
Lupinus polyphyllus.   Purple Lupin.
Iris siberica.   Siberian Iris; blue.
Lupinus Nootkaensis.   Nootka Sound Lupin; blue.
Hesperis matronalis, alba, pl.   The Double White Rocket.
Corydalis nobilis.   Yellow, with brown dots.
Phlox suaveolens.   The white Phlox, or Lychnidea.
Phlox maculata.   The purple-spotted Phlox.

Lupinus perennis et rivularis.   Perennial Lupins ; blue.
Lychnis flos cuculi, pl.   Double Ragged-Robin ; red.
Aquilegia canadensis.   Wild Columbine ; scarlet.
Pæonia tenuifolia, flore pleno.   Double-leaved fennel.

CLASS III.

2 *feet and higher.*

Papaver orientalis.   Oriental scarlet Poppy.
Iris florentina.   Florentine Iris ; white.
Pæonia albiflora.   Single white Pæony.
Hemerocallis flava.   The yellow Day-lily.

JUNE.

CLASS I.

From 6 to 12 inches high.

Asperula odorata.   White, fragrant.
Potentilla rosea.   The Rose-colored Potentilla.
Potentilla mayeana.   Mayes' Potentilla ; light rose.
Spirea filipendula, pl.   Double Pride of the Meadow ; white.
Cypripedium pubescens.   Yellow Indian Moccasin.
Viscaria vulgaris, pl.   White and Red Viscaria.
Eschscholtzia californica.   Golden Eschscholtzia ; yellow.
Lychins fulgens.   Fulgent Lychins ; red.
Dianthus chinensis.   Indian pinks ; variegated.
Verbena multifida.   Cut-leaved Verbena ; purple.
Verbena Lamberti.   Lambert's Verbena ; purple.
Iris Susiana.   Chalcedonian Iris ; mottled.
Iberis sempervirens.   White candytuft.
Papaver croceum.   Golden Poppy.
Lotus corniculatus.   Yellow and pink.
Aquilegia caryphilloides.   Columbine ; striped.
Aquilegia jucunda.   Columbine ; white and blue.
Aquilegia formosa tricolor.   Columbine ; striped, blue and white.
Aquilegia hybrida californica.   Columbine ; a reddish violet.

CLASS II.

From 1 *to* 2 *feet high.*

Spirea lobata. Siberian spirea; red.
Spirea ulmaria, pl. Double Meadow Sweet; white.
Spirea ulmaria variegata. Meadow Sweet; leaves variegated.
Spirea japonica. Japan Spirea; pure white.
Delphinium grandiflorum, pl. Double dark blue Larkspur.
Delphinium chinensis album. Chinese Larkspur; white.
Delphinium chinense, pl. Double Chinese Larkspur; blue.
Dianthus hortensis. Garden Pinks; many double sorts and colors.
Caltha pulustris, pl. Double Marsh Marigold; yellow.
Polemonium cœruleum and album. Common white and blue Greek Valerian.
Campanula persicifolia, pl. Double peach-leaved Campanula; white.
Campanula persicifolia cerulea, flore pleno. Double peached-leaved Campanula;
    blue.
Antirrhinum majus. Red and white Snap Dragons.
Geranium sanguineum. Bloody Geranium; red.
Geranium ibericum. Violet and purple.
Œnothera fruticosa. Shrubby Evening Primrose; yellow.
Dianthus caryophyllus. The Carnation, of many colors.
Campanula grandiflora. Large blue Bellflower.
Campanula grandiflora alba. Large white Bellflower.
Campanula coronata. Crowned campanula.
Clematis integrifolia. Austrian blue Clematis.
Asphodelus ramosus. Branching Asphodel; white.
Pentstemon speciosa. Showy Pentstemon; blue.
Lychnis viscaria roseo pleno. Silene; double pink.
Pyrethrum roseum, double and single. Feverfew; red and pink.
Salvia rubicunda. Sage; reddish violet.
Salvia bicolor. Sage; white and blue.

CLASS III.

2 feet and higher.

Aconitum napellus, variegata. Purple-and-white Monk's Hood.
Aconitum napellus. Monk's Hood; purple.
Aconitum tenuifolia. Cut-leaved aconitum; light blue.
Campanula ranunculoides. Nodding Bellflower? blue.
Verbascum phœniceum. Purple Mullein.
Clematis erecta. Upright Clematis; white.

Linum perenne. Perennial Flax ; blue.
Linum perenne album. Perennial Flax ; white.
Linum Lewisii variegata. Flax, Lewis' variegated.
Pœonia Humei. Double blush Pæony.
Pœonia fragrans. Double fragrant Pæony ; rose.
Pœonia Whitleji. Double white Pæony.
Gaillardia aristata. Bristly Gaillardia ; yellow.

JULY

CLASS I.

From 6 to 12 inches high.

Pentstemon Richardsonii. Richardson's Pentstemon ; purple.
Pentstemon pubescens. Downy Pentstemon ; lilac.
Campanula carpathica. Carpathian Bellflower ; blue.
Campanula carpathica alba. Carpathian Bellflower ; white.
Sedum populifolium. Poplar-leaved Sedum ; white.
Dianthus deltoides. Mountain Pink ; red.
Dianthus del toides alba. Mountain Pink ; white.
Veronica maritima. Maritime Speedwell ; blue.
Lychnis lapponica. Reddish Pink.

CLASS II.

From 1 to 2 feet high.

Pentstemon campanulatum. Bell-flowered Pentstemon ; lilac.
Pentstemon cobea. Large foxglove-like flowers ; whitish.
Pentstemon grandiflora. Large foxglove-like flowers ; lilac.
Pentstemon speciosa. Showy Pentstemon ; red.
Pentstemon roseum. Rose-colored Pentstemon.
Monarda didyma. Lemon-scented balm ; scarlet.
Potentilla atrosanguinea. Dark red Potentilla.
Potentilla Hoopwoodiana. Scarlet and white Potentilla.
Funkia Sieboldii. Lilac Funkia.
Coreopsis Atkinsonia. Atkinson's Coreopsis ; yellow.
Aquilegia glandulosa. Glandular Columbine ; striped.
Aquilegia cerulea. Beautiful light blue and white.
Phlox Brownii. Brown's Phlox ; red.
Dictamnus Fraxinella. Purple Fraxinella.
Dictamnus alba. White Fraxinella.
Anchusa officinalis. Common Bugloss ; blue.

Œnothera Fraseri.   Fraser's Evening Primrose ; yellow.
Œnothera macrocarpa.   Large-podded Evening Primrose ; yellow.
Campanula trachelium, pl.   Double white and blue Bell Flower.
Potentilla Russelliana.   Russell's Cinquefoil ; red.
Delphinium speciosum.   Showy Larkspur; blue.
Campanula macrantha.   Large blue Bell-flower.
Chelone Lyoni.   Purple Chelone.
Chelone barbata.   Bearded Chelone ; orange.
Dracocephalum grandiflorum.   Dragon's head ; purple.
Oroleus lathyrorides.   Violet blue.
Achillea millifolia rubra.   Double milfoil ; red.

CLASS III.

2 *feet and higher.*

Delphinium elatum.   Bee Larkspur; blue.
Delphinium formosum.   Large dark-blue, white eye.
Delphinium Hendersonii.   Large deep-blue, white eye.
Delphinium hyacinthaflora.   Semi-double; light blue and white.
Delphinium Madame Gerard Leigh.   Semi-double; light blue, white eye.
Pentstemon digitalis.   Missouri Pentstemon ; white.
Hibiscus palustris.   Single Hibiscus; red.
Lychnis Chalcedonica.   Single and double scarlet Lychnis.
Lythrum latifolium.   Perennial Pea ; purple.

AUGUST.

CLASS I.

From 6 *to* 12 *inches high.*

Corydalis formosa.   Red Fumitory.
Phlox carnea.   Flesh-colored Phlox.
Lychnis coronata.   Chinese orange Lychnis.
Lychnis haageana.   Bright scarlet Lychnis.

CLASS II.

From 1 *to* 2 *feet high.*

Geum Quellyon.   Scarlet Geum.
Gaillardia aristata.   Bearded Gaillardia; yellow.

Phlox Alcordi.   Alcord's Phlox ; purple.
Catananche cærulea.   Blue Catananche.
Catananche bicolor.   White and blue Catananche.
Asclepias tuberosa.   Orange Swallowwort.
Veronica carnea.   Flesh-colored Speedwell.
Veronica alba.   White Veronica.
Gaillardia bicolor.   Orange Gaillardia.
Hemerocallis japonica.   Japan day-lily ; white.
Funkia marginata.   Beautiful striped foliage.
Dianthus superbus.   Superb fringed Pink ; white.
Lobelia cardinalis.   Cardinal flower; red.
Lythrum Salicaria.   Willow Herb ; purple.
Liatris squarrosa.   Blazing Star ; blue.
Liatris scariosa.   Spikes of reddish purple globe flowers.
Coreopsis tenuifolia.   Five-leaved Coreopsis ; yellow.
Phlox Van Houttei.   Van Houtte's Phlox ; purple and white, striped.
Phlox gràcalis.   Blush and rose, crimson eye.
Phlox Madam Nerard.   Blush and white, crimson eye.
Phlox Roi de rose.   Rosy purple, crimson eye.
Phlox Surprise.   White pencilled, with rosy lilac and crimson eye.
Phlox Venus.   White, shaded with rose.
Phlox Gem.   Deep blush, dark eye.
Phlox John Baillie.   Dark rosy purple.
Phlox Mrs. Hare.   Pure white, violet crimson eye.
Phlox Lady Elizabeth Home.   French white, vermilion eye.
Phlox Juliette Russell.   White, crimson eye.
Phlox Triomphe de Twickle.   Crimson and white, striped.
Phlox Alphonse Karr.   Deep crimson.
Phlox Professor Kock.   Light vermilion, dark eye.
Phlox Madame Lacerf.   Clear paper white.
Phlox Madame Andry.   White, crimson eye.
Phlox Madame Autin.   Deep vermilion.
Phlox Mr. Thibeaut.   Rosy crimson, dark eye.
Phlox Minerva.   Rosy lilac, crimson centre.
Phlox Spectabalis.   Lilac, veined with purple.
Phlox la Comte.   Shaded rose, white centre.

CLASS III.

2 feet and higher.

Campanula pyramidalis.   The pyramidal Bell-flower; blue and white.
Yucca filamentosa.   Adam's Thread ; white.

Yucca flaccida. Flaccid Yucca; white.
Phlox paniculata. Panicled Phlox; purple and white.
Epilobium spicatum. Purple-spiked Epilobium.
Anemone japonica. Japan anemone; rose color.
Cassia Marylandica. Maryland Cassia; yellow.

SEPTEMBER AND OCTOBER.

CLASS I.

From 6 to 12 inches high.

Achillea ptarmica, pl. Double Milfoil; white.
Aster linifolius. Fine-leaved Aster; white.
Gentiana Saponaria. Soapwort Gentian; blue.
Sedum Sieboldtii. Japan Sedum; pink.

CLASS II.

From 1 to 2 feet high.

Coreopsis grandiflora. Large yellow Coreopsis.
Eupatorium celestinum. Azure blue Eupatorium.
Phlox Wheeleriana. Wheeler's Phlox; red.

CLASS III.

2 feet and higher.

Aster macrophyllus. Broad-leaved Aster; white.
Eupatorium aromaticum. Fragrant Eupatorium; white.
Liatris elegans. Elegant Blazing Star; purple.
Liatris spicata and scarrosa. Blue Blazing Stars.
Aster novæ-angliæ. New-England Aster; purple.
Echinops ritro. Globe thistle; blue.
Chrysanthemum indicum. Artemisias, many sorts and colors.

DESIGN VI.

An Irregular Villa in the Italian style, bracketed.

THIS design shows a villa in the Italian style, of moderate size. It is highly irregular, and while it will, on
account of the great picturesqueness and variety growing
out of this circumstance, be much more pleasing to a portion of our readers, a great number of persons, who only
judge of a dwelling-house by a common-sense standard,
will probably prefer a more regular and uniform building,
like one of the previous designs. The latter class will
find no good reason for any extra cost incurred in creating
an irregular villa like this, as a more regular one would
afford the same comfort and convenience; but persons who
have cultivated an architectural taste, and who relish the
higher beauties of the art growing out of variety, will give
a great preference to a design capable of awakening more
strongly emotions of the beautiful or picturesque, as well
as the useful or convenient. We might illustrate the natural progress in taste in the fine arts which all persons
make, and their relative capacity of enjoying different
degrees of art, by a familiar example drawn from music.
Most persons, having an ear for music, but who have never
cultivated a taste for it, will be found greatly to prefer
simple airs, because the simple rhythm of *melody* is distinct, and easily understood; the more intricate beauties of
harmony abounding in fine musical compositions, are only
intensely felt and enjoyed when our perceptions are en-
larged and heightened by education.

DESIGN VI.

A VILLA IN THE ITALIAN STYLE, BRACKETED.

Fig. 48.

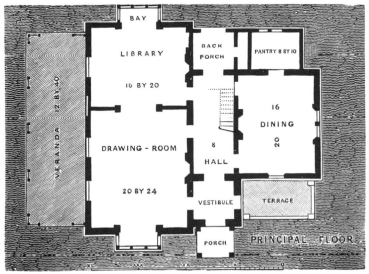

Fig. 49.

The Italian mode is capable of displaying a rich domestic character in its balconies, verandas, ornamental porches,
terraces, etc.   The square tower, or *campanile*, is a prominent feature in villas in this style, and frequently confers
on the Italian compositions a character of great boldness
and dignity.   The projecting roof and the round-arched
window are also characteristic features.

The present design is intended for a situation where it
is desired to preserve the whole of the fine view from the
windows of the drawing-room unobstructed, and the entrance front is accordingly made on the adjoining side.
After reaching the porch, see Fig. 49, we enter the vestibule which occupies the lower floor of the tower, and from
thence the hall, leading through the building, and terminating in a back porch of one story in height.   Adjoining
the latter is a closet for stores.

On the left of this hall is an elegant drawing-room 20 by
24 feet, connected with a library 20 by 16 feet.   At either
extremity of these rooms is a handsome projecting window
in the Italian mode, giving an air of dignity to the apartments, and in front are three casement windows opening to the floor of the veranda, both for the purpose of
allowing an uninterrupted view, and affording easy communication.

On the right of the hall is the dining-room, 20 by 16
feet.   A pantry or store-room, 8 by 10 feet, opens into this
room.   In front is a pretty little terrace, ornamented with
a few vases of terra cotta, or artificial stone.

The chamber floor of this design shows three bed-rooms,
20 by 16 feet, each with a pleasant balcony at one of its
windows, and two smaller bed-rooms.   In the attic story
are three bed-rooms for servants, lighted by the windows
shown in the gables.   From the attic a small staircase

leads through the half-story (with square windows) to the upper story of the campanile or tower, whence an extensive prospect of the country for many miles round is enjoyed.

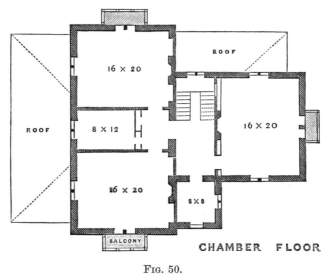

FIG. 50.

The kitchen of this villa is placed beneath the dining-room; and ample cellarage, wine and store rooms, are obtained under the main body of the house, at the other side of the hall.

The fanciful and convenient window-shades, or canopies, occasionally employed in this style, may be made of canvas, supported by a light iron frame, or of light wood, painted to resemble an awning. Handsome striped Italian canvas for this purpose may now be had in New York.

A building in this style will be greatly heightened in effect by being well supported by trees, the irregular forms of which will harmonize with the character of the archi-tecture. A Lombardy poplar or two, judiciously intro-duced in the midst of groups of round-headed trees, will have a happy effect. The beautiful wooded situations on the banks of our fine rivers are, many of them, admirably suited for an Italian villa of this kind.

Construction.—We have sup-posed this villa to be built of wood, the bracketed construction giving it a character of light-ness; but the effect would be even better if built of more solid materials, and brick and stucco, well constructed, would be very durable under the shelter of the broadly projecting roof. The forms of brackets given in Fig.

FIG. 51.

44 of our last design are equally suitable here, D being the bracket for the eaves in front. A portion of the veranda is shown in Fig. 51. In this the upright columns enclosing the lattice are supposed to be octagonal, and four inches in diameter, the lattice itself being much heavier and more durable than it is usually made. Its ceiling is made of beaded and planed stuff, forming the sheathing for the roof, and the rafters are in like manner beaded and plainly shown. The chimney-tops of the main building should come out at the ridge of the roof, which will be effected by *drawing over* the stacks in the garret. The roof should project at least 3 feet on every side. The principal story should be 13 feet high in the clear, and the chamber story 10 feet.

Estimate.—The cost of this villa, handsomely finished, will be about $6,800. [For the height of principal story we would say not over 12 feet, and for the cost say $10,000. —ED.]

LAYING OUT THE GROUNDS.

The grounds attached to this villa are supposed to be about one hundred and fifty acres in extent, and we have

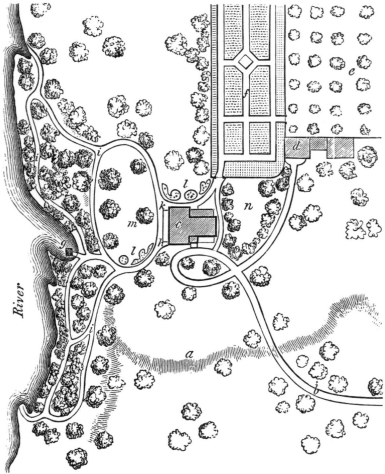

Fig. 52.

therefore been able to represent in the annexed engraving, Fig. 52, only a small part containing the house, and the more ornamental portion bordering the river. The house is situated on a plateau elevated about eighty feet above the river, and the ground falls off somewhat rapidly from this level along the river bank, and in the direction indicated by the waved lines, *a*.

The approach, *b*, leads to the house, *c*, in gently curved lines, and from thence to the stable and other out-buildings, *d*. There is a large orchard, a small part of which is seen at *e*, the kitchen garden is located at *f*, and at *g* is a bathing-house on the river bank.

This place, like a great many in this country of its character, we will suppose to possess a richly wooded hanging bank on its river side. This will afford us a fine opportunity to create a most agreeable series of walks, *i*. These walks may be conducted in easy directions, through the wood and along the bank, occasionally intersecting each other. They may often approach each other very near, without being visible one from the other, in consequence of the thickness of the foliage in some places, or the irregularity of the surface in others. They will be full of variety,—now leading to a point where a lovely view suddenly bursts upon us, and again plunging into a secluded portion, where the dense foliage of evergreens shuts out all other objects, and gives a quiet and secluded character to the scene. Rustic seats, Fig. 53, placed here and there in the most inviting spots, will both heighten the charm and enable us to enjoy at leisure the quiet beauty around. A very great advantage which

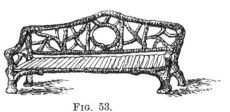

FIG. 53.

walks made in such a situation have, is the trifling care and expense necessary to preserve them in order. But few

weeds grow in the shade of large forest trees, and the character of the place renders it unnecessary that the walks
should have a very trim and neat appearance. The repose,
the variety, and the beauty of a series of walks of this
kind in several places that we could name, created with
very trifling trouble, render them, in our opinion, far more
delightful than twice the same distance of walks in a common level flower garden.

These walks commence at the veranda at h, and form a
connected promenade terminating at the other end of the
veranda at k. Near the house, in the space commanded
by the drawing-room and library windows, are some borders of handsome flowering plants at l. At least the oval
area of lawn, m, and the space between the porch and
where the ground descends at a, should be kept constantly
mown, and in the highest order, so as to heighten, and render more forcible by contrast, the wilder and more picturesque beauty of the sylvan walks i.

A turfed area for bleaching and drying clothes is set
apart and concealed by shrubbery at n.

When a situation like this is selected for a villa residence, with a bank richly clothed by a natural growth of
forest trees, and with, perhaps, scattered groups of large
trees here and there elsewhere, the art of the improver
should lie in harmonizing all his improvements with the
main features of the place already existing. Almost every
place of this kind has a natural character of dignity or
picturesqueness, derived from the rich banks of wood, the
noble river, and the finely undulating surface, which must
be kept in view in all embellishments. The trees which
are planted in the larger breadths of lawn should be elms,
oaks, horse-chestnuts, and maples, or other species of large
growth, so that they may correspond in expression, when

somewhat grown, with those already existing. No formal avenues or straight lines should be planted, to raise a discordant expression when viewed in the same *coup d'œil* with the existing groups and masses of foliage; and the larger breadths of lawn at a distance from the windows of the house should not be broken up by any frippery walks or parterres which might detract from the breadth and simplicity of the scene. In a place where there is a character of dignity and simplicity arising from extensive prospect, large and lofty trees, and considerable breadth of lawn, we should be extremely cautious about introducing too much of the little details of flower garden or shrubbery ornaments in the fore-ground, lest they should degrade or weaken the original and higher character of the scene. We should rather place the latter in a more secluded spot, where they will form objects of beauty to be considered entirely by themselves, and not in connection with other objects. For this reason it will be seen that we have in this plan, and a previous one, confined the flowering plants to three or four beds cut in the turf near the drawing-room windows of the house.

The orchard and fruit garden.—A small portion of the orchard, *e*, appears on the plan, but as we have supposed a place of this size to have a large and well-stocked orchard and fruit garden, we shall here give a list of superior fruits, which, having been tested, are known to be of first-rate excellence in the climate of the Middle States. A fine orchard and fruit garden, producing an abundant supply of fruit at all seasons, is one of the greatest sources of enjoyment in a country life; and when we consider how easily good fruit is generally obtained in this country, without the aid of walls or anything more than a moderate degree of attention, it would certainly appear a matter of just reproach, wherever there is sufficient room, not to have a first-rate collection of fruit.

Horticulture, but more especially pomology—that branch of it devoted to fruits—has received so much attention both in Europe and at home, that within the last twenty years the number of delicious fruits capable of being raised in the open air has been more than trebled. The Pear, especially, has been greatly improved and ameliorated, and has indeed taken the first rank among dessert fruits, in consideration of the variety in flavor, time of ripening, duration, and beauty of the numerous sorts. The late autumn and winter varieties are a very valuable acquisition to our dessert at these seasons. Added to this, many of the new sorts come into fruit at one-half or one-fourth the age necessary to the bearing of the older kinds.

Where a variety of *soils* occurs, as is frequently the case in a large orchard, it is well to know those peculiarly adapted to each fruit tree. Apples are found to thrive best in a strong deep loam—if stony it is preferable; pears and cherries in a mellow gravelly loam; plums in a strong clayey loam, and peaches in a light sandy loam. Apples may be planted in an orchard at from thirty to forty-five feet apart; cherries and pears, from twenty-five to thirty feet; peaches and plums, from twenty to twenty-five feet. In transplanting all fruit trees, be mindful not to commit the common error of setting them *too deep*.

LIST OF THE FINEST VARIETIES OF FRUIT

For the Orchard and Fruit Garden.

CHERRIES.

Knight's Early Black.

Mayduke, *fine for the table and for cooking.*

Black Tartarian, *large and of fine quality.*

Black Eagle.

Bigarreau, or Graffion, *large and delicious.*

Downton.

Downer's Red, *late and delicious.*

Carnation, *valuable for preserving.*

Belle de Choisey, *fine.*

Elton, *handsome and fine.*

Belle et Magnifique.

Belle d'Orleans.

Early Purple Guigne.

Coe's Transparent.

Early Richmond.

Rockport.

Napoleon Bigarreau.

Great Bigarreau.

Ohio Beauty.

Governor Wood.

Pontiac.

Empress Eugene.

Reine Hortense.

Donna Maria.

Imperial Ottoman, *best early.*

Green Gage.

Imperial, or Flushing Gage.

Coe's Golden Drop, *handsome, very late, and excellent.*

Coe's Late Red, *very late.*

Bleeker's Gage, *hardy and excellent.*

Jefferson, *yellow, large, and fine.*

La Royale.

Lawrence's Favorite.

Washington, *excellent.*

Magnum Bonum, or Egg Plum, *for preserving.*

Smith's Orleans, *productive.*

Violet Imperatrice.

German Prune.

Purple Gage.

Autumn Gage, *late and fine.*

Purple Favorite, *best purple.*

Dennison's Superb.

Prince's Yellow Gage.

McLaughlin.

Prince Englebert.

Prune d'Agen.

Transparent Gage.

Guthrie's Late Green.

Bavay's Green Gage.

Pond's Seedling.

Lombard.

PLUMS.

Early Scarlet, or Cherry Plum, *very early.*

PEACHES.

Early Royal George.

George IV., *very fine.*

Morris White Rareripe.
Red Rareripe.
Crawford's Late.
Snow Peach, *handsome.*
Red-cheek Melocaton.
Brevoort's Morris, *fine.*
Columbia.
Malta.
Large White Cling.
Early Newington.
Early York (serrate).
Heath Cling, *late and fine.*
Grosse Mignonne.
Old Mixon Free.
Troth's Early.
Large Early York.
Susquehanna.
Hale's Early.
Ward's Late Free.
Cooledge's Favorite.
Honey.

APRICOTS.

Moorpark, *one of the very best sorts.*
Large Early, *excellent.*
Breda, *sure bearer.*
Blenheim or Shirley.
Peach.

PEARS.

1. *Early Varieties.*

Madeleine, *early.*
Bloodgood's Early, *excellent.*
Dearborn's Seedling, *delicious.*
Doyenne d'été.
Beurré Giffart.
Rostiezer.
Tyson.

2. *Medium Period.*

Flemish Beauty.
Seckel, *first quality.*
*Doyenné, or Virgalieu.
Stevens's Genesee.
Golden Beurré of Bilboa.
Fondante d'Automne.
*Gansel's Bergamot.
Louise Bonne of Jersey.
Urbaniste, *excellent.*
Beurré Bosc.
Dix.
Beurré d'Anjou, *excellent.*
Thompson's.
Doyenné Boussock.
Beurré Diel, *large and good on Quince's stock.*
Duchesse d'Angoulême, *do.*
Bartlett, or Williams Bonchrétien.
Brandywine.
Clapp's Favorite.
Baronne de Mello.
Beurré de Waterloo.
Ananas, d'été.
Edmunds.
Maréchal de la Cour.
Do. du Cornice.
Howell.
Onondaga.
Souverain d'Esperen.
Sheldon.
Beurré Superfin.
Paradise d'Antonine.
Fulton.
Buffum.

3. *Late Varieties, from Nov. to May.*

Glout Morceaux.
Beurré d'Aremberg, *very fine.*
Columbian.

---

* These sorts only for favorable localities.

Winter Nelis.
Lawrence.
Emile d'Heyst.
Dana's Hovey.
Doyenne d'Alençon.
Josephine de Malines.
Beurré Gris d'Hiver Nouveau.

NECTARINES.

Early Violet, *good and productive.*
Downton.
Elruge.
New White.

APPLES.

Many of the best winter varieties are enumerated at pages 87, 88 ; the following are choice dessert fruits.
Red Astrachan, *a very beautiful and early sort.*
Yellow Harvest, *large and excellent.*
Strawberry Apple.
William's Favorite, *beautiful.*
Lady Apple, *beautiful dessert fruit.*
Northern Spy.
Ladies' Sweeting, *fine.*
Esopus Spitzenberg, *high flavor.*

Green Newtown Pippin.
Yellow Bellflower.
Baldwin, *very productive.*
Porter.
Fameuse.
Sops of Wine, *early and handsome.*
Rhode Island Greening, *excellent.*
Fall Pippin.
Hubbardston Nonsuch.
American Golden Russet.
Cogswell.
Evening Party.
Garden Royal.
Primate.
Mother.
McLellan.
Grimes' Golden.
Haskell Sweet.
King of Tompkins Co.
Klaproth.
McLellan.
Mother.
Melon.
Ohio Nonpareil.
Richard's Graft.
Summer Pippin.
Wagener.
Washington Strawberry.

In addition to these, we would recommend some of the smaller fruits of choice varieties. The Delaware, Allen's Hybrid, Adirondac, Concord, Iona, and Israella grapes, and some of the hardier foreign sorts, as the Golden Chasselas, Black Cluster, and White Muscadine; the large Red and the White Antwerp Raspberries; the Large Early Scarlet, Hovey's Seedling, and Burr's New Pine Strawberries; the frizzled and prolific English Filberts, and the Large White and Red Dutch Currants, may all be named as indispensable in every fruit garden. [In addition to the above the following fruits are to be recommended :— For *Raspberries*, the Orange, Franconia, Clark, and Kennett's Giant. For *Strawberries*, the Triomphe de Gand, Jucunda, Boston Pine, Crimson Cone, Agriculturist, and Charles Downing. For *Currants*, the White Grape, the Cherry, the Versaillaise, May's Victoria, and Black Naples.—c. d.]

In the cultivation of fruits but little difficulty will be experienced if a *keen watch* is kept *on insects*, destroying every appearance of a nest, brood, or swarm, as soon as it makes its appearance. One man may often do more to subdue and exterminate a troublesome insect in an hour or two, when it first appears, than a host of men would after it has had time to multiply, as it often will in a week, by thousands and tens of thousands.

In the case of the peach tree, examine the trees at the root every spring and autumn, and take out the peach worm, before it girdles the tree, with your knife; and destroy every sickly-looking tree, especially every old one, on your premises the moment it becomes fairly diseased— the *Yellows*, to which this fruit tree is liable, being a contagious disease, spreading from tree to tree, so that it is quite needless to plant healthy young trees where old ones are suffered to stand in their neighborhood. This fact alone, when understood, is sufficient to solve all the apparent difficulties in cultivating this fruit of late years. The *knots*, to which the plum is liable in some districts, are caused by an insect, and the limbs infected with them should be cut off and burned early in the spring. If the fruit fall from the tree prematurely, it is probably caused by the sting of the curculio, and the remedy lies in destroying all the curculio for the next season by gathering the fruit as soon as it falls (which contains the larvæ), and throwing it into the hog-pen; or in planting your stone fruits in an enclosure by themselves, and letting the swine run in it during the season when the green fruit is falling.

DESIGN VII.

An Irregular Cottage in the Old English Style.

THE situation for this cottage may be in a richly wooded plain, or a sequestered valley. It belongs to that class of richly decorated rural Gothic edifices, abounding in carved verge-boards and pendants, clustered chimney tops, and irregular outlines. There is something of freedom, or at least quaint richness in its details—something indicating a certain license of architectural imagination, not to be precisely measured by the standard of the rule and square, or the strictly utilitarian view. Now a cottage of this class must not, in any case, be erected on a bare plain, or even one comparatively so, as in such a place all its picturesqueness would seem out of keeping—unmeaning— and absurd. But let it be partially hidden, or half concealed by clustering foliage, and assimilated, as it were, with nature, by the interlacing and entwining branches and bowers around it, and of which its ornaments are in some degree a repetition, and we shall feel it to be in perfect unison with its situation. Whoever has seen one of these cottages, with its rich gables breaking out from among the intricacy of tall stems and shadowy foliage, will readily confess that he has rarely beheld anything more harmonious and delightful than the charming effect thereby produced.

Some one has truly remarked that the architecture of our dwellings is most appropriate when it embodies and breathes forth a *home expression;* a character to which we think the rural Gothic, with its quaint, independent, comfortable and extended air, seems fully to lay claim.

DESIGN VII.

AN IRREGULAR COTTAGE IN THE OLD ENGLISH STYLE.

Fig. 54.

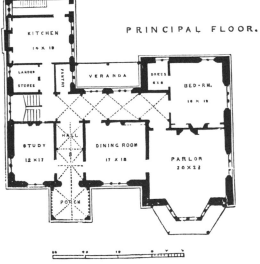

Fig. 56.

In arranging the plan of the interior of this cottage, Fig. 56, we have had convenience, as well as elegance, in our mind. The neat porch which shelters the front door is provided with suitable seats on either side, which should be made to correspond with the architecture. On opening this door we find ourselves in the vestibule, or entrance hall. This we shall suppose fitted up with a dado or base, three and a half feet high, of wood grained in imitation of oak or black walnut, and the walls painted of some grave color, to give greater effect to the rooms. The vestibule opens on the left into a pleasant little room, twelve by eighteen feet, which may be devoted to a study or library, and neatly fitted up with book-cases. In building, it will be found that recesses may be left in the walls for these book-cases, so that they will occupy but little space in the apartment. On the opposite side of the hall is the living or dining room, seventeen by eighteen feet. This room is lighted by one of the large, square mullioned windows, so common in the old English houses, which should be finished on the inside with a window-seat. A china closet is made on the right of the chimney-breast in this room, and on the other side of the hall are a pantry and a store-room, of good size, very conveniently disposed.

The dining-room communicates with the parlor or drawing-room on its right. The drawing-room is, of course, the finest room in size, aspect, and proportion in the house, being twenty-two by nineteen feet, with a fine semi-hexagon bay, which, projecting boldly, will give three distinct views to a person standing within it. We would have the ceiling of this and the dining-room ribbed, and perhaps slightly arched, in the form of two inclined planes, rising eight or ten inches from the side walls to the highest part of the ceiling. The wood-work of the whole of this story should be finished simply and consistently, that is, with suitable Gothic mouldings, and the whole should be painted and grained in imitation of oak, or of black walnut. The effect of the rooms will be still more pleasing if the walls are colored some harmonious neutral tint. The furniture should be in strict character with the style of the house, which may be easily obtained, without any additional expense, by choosing simple and suitable forms.

At the end of the hall leading to the drawing-room is a bed-room, 19 by 13 feet, with a closet. This would make a convenient bed-room for the master and mistress of the house. Adjoining it is a dressing-room, which, if neatly and tastefully fitted up with everything appertaining to a lady's toilet, will give this bed-room a highly comfortable and refined air.

The staircase is placed at the other extremity of this hall, and it may be made more private or secluded, if it is thought desirable, by an oaken screen of open woodwork. Under this staircase is constructed a descending flight leading to the cellar.

On the sides of the passage leading from the hall to the kitchen are the pantry, the larder, and the store-room. By placing these most useful and convenient appendages in this position, we not only make them at once easily accessible from the kitchen or the dining-room, but we also remove the kitchen, with its concomitant noises and odors, to some distance from the main hall, and these may be still further lessened in effect by having a door at both ends of this passage, to be shut when required.

The kitchen itself is sixteen feet square; it is amply lighted and ventilated, and communicates directly with the open air by the passage at the farther side. In this

passage is a servants' staircase, communicating with the
apartments in the chamber story.

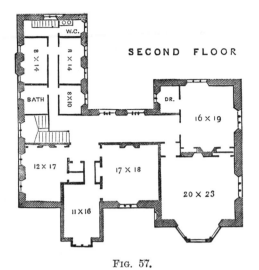

FIG. 57.

The chamber story contains abundant accommodation
for a cottage. There are three handsome bed-rooms, and
two of a smaller size. That over the drawing-room being
the largest, and the most beautiful in form, may be kept
as the "state bed-room," being fitted up with all the appli-
ances of comfort in its furniture and fixtures. The little
room over the porch will make a delightful room for a
bachelor; or if one of the young ladies takes a fancy to it,
it will make a little *bijou* of a boudoir, the oriel window
giving a character of novelty and beauty to the whole
apartment. On the second floor of the kitchen wing are a
bath-room, near the main hall (which may be supplied
with hot water by pipes leading to a boiler in the kitchen
below), and three servants' bed-rooms. There is also a
water-closet at the end of the passage in this wing, the
discharge-pipe from which is concealed in the partition, in
a closed trunk or chamber.

This class of dwellings abroad is frequently covered with thatch, which has a pleasing rustic effect. But our snowy and changeable climate will soon destroy so frail a material, and it is therefore unfit for covering the roofs of buildings for habitation. Our best shingles, however, afford an excellent material for covering roofs, and if those of good size and thickness are chosen, and shaped as we have directed in a former page, they will have a pictu-resque and agreeable effect, and make a very durable roof when painted with the cheap, coarse paint now so gene-rally used for this purpose. The roof of this cottage should

FIG. 58.

be extended boldly, say two to three feet, to give force and expression to the exterior, and to protect the walls fully. The ends of the rafters are projected, so as to ap-pear as visible supports at the eaves. A verge-board is shown on a larger scale in Fig. 58. This would be suitable for the porch gable, and the others may be made simpler and still bolder with good effect. The chimney-tops should be characteristically made of ornamental moulded bricks, or shafts may be selected of pretty patterns in cut stone. Although the partitions in which the dining-room and study flues are carried up are not in the centre, it will be easy to draw over these stacks in the garret, so as to bring them out at the ridge or apex of the roof, which will have the best effect. A plan of the bay window is shown in Fig. 59, in which the inside shutters fold into boxes on each side.

COTTAGE BAY WINDOW.

FIG. 59.

In a country where good bricks are abundant and easily obtained, we should prefer to build this cottage of good smooth brick. The raw and disagreeable color of new brick we would destroy by painting it three good coats in oil, of some one of the neutral shades given in a previous illustration, perhaps that one designated by F. By building it of brick, in the best manner, we should not only have solid enduring walls, but, to those familiar with English cottage architecture, it would have an agreeable effect by creating an allusion to the same material chiefly employed in that country.

All the exterior wood-work in this cottage (except the roof) we would either make of real oak, and oil it, when it would assume a warm rich tone of color by the effects of time, or we would paint and grain it in imitation of oak. If either of these modes should be considered too expensive, it may be plainly painted the same color as the house, or a few shades darker.

Should the execution of such a design as this fall into the hands of an ordinary country carpenter, without suitable working drawings from an architect, the probability is that he would destroy its beauty and character by reducing all its characteristic features to the most meagre level, until all the boldness and spirit of the style would be lost. He will cut the gable ornaments out of thin boards, make the mullions of the windows of slender timber, reduce the projection of the roof and the irregularity of the ground plan. If the amateur builder is so unfortunate as to fall into the hands of such a person, he will be very likely to get the *emaciated shadow* of the rural Gothic cottage, not its bold, picturesque, and striking reality. We mention this to put our reader, whose taste may lead him to build a cottage in this style, on his guard ; and we advise him, as in the end the most economical and most satisfactory mode, to employ a competent builder, and to procure accurate working drawings from an architect of ability before he commences.

Estimate.—The cost of this cottage, built in the manner we have here suggested, would be about $7,600. [The cost now would be from $17,000 to $20,000.—ED.]

THE GROUNDS OF THIS RESIDENCE.

In designing this cottage, we have had in view a quiet, sequestered situation in a long valley, or rather dale, in which there are ten or twelve acres of nearly level land, pretty well clothed with a natural growth of forest trees, and backed on either side by wooded hills fifty or eighty feet above the level of the dale.

There is an entrance lodge at the point where the approach diverges from the main road *b*, Fig. 60, which is to be built in the same style as the cottage, but in a more simple and rustic manner. From this point the approach

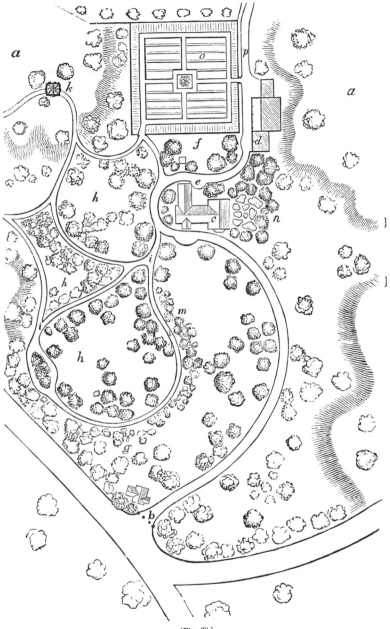

[Fig. 60.]

leads by a graceful curve to the house *c*, and from thence to the stable and other farm buildings *d*, having a gravel sweep for turning carriages in front of the porch, and another for discharging articles from a cart at the kitchen door *e*.

In its original state, the whole of the surface of this dale from *f* to *g*, is thickly covered with wood. This we propose to thin out and render an ornamental and interesting part of the place, by leading through it the series of plants marked *i* in the plan. These walks would be cool and shady in summer, and would have a delightful sylvan character at all seasons. In thinning out a natural wood on a place like this, a good deal of care and judgment is necessary to obtain a pleasing effect and preserve the best trees in good condition.* Were we to go into the wood and thin out the trees here and there, so as to leave the finest specimens standing singly, the probability is that these trees, thus suddenly losing the support of their fellows that had grown up in close contact with them on every side, would be blown down and destroyed by the first severe autumnal gale accompanied with rain. Good judgment, as well as good taste, will rather dictate that we should thin them out in masses here and there, leaving pretty open glades *h*, at intervals, which being soon covered with a fine green turf, and catching the gleams of sunlight, will be a charming contrast to the groups and thickets around. The trees thus left in groups and masses will afford each other protection and support against the wind, and will gradually strengthen and expand in their roots and heads, until they become luxuriant and spreading. We should

---

* Always lay bare the roots, and dig or cut out the tree below the surface of the soil. This will leave the ground clear, and not covered by straggling stumps which it is afterwards more difficult to extricate than to cut the whole tree out properly.

bear in mind, also, not to trim off the lower branches of such trees, unless they are dead or unsightly; as they will probably never be replaced, and the highest beauty of a tree as an ornamental object consists in its being *park-like*, that is, luxuriantly feathered with foliage quite down to the ground.

These walks, after traversing the little wood, lead to the summit of the hill, where a rustic arbor, *k*, serves as a resting-place, and affords a pleasant view. On the supposition that the surface on the right of the walk, *i* (where it first leaves the house), is open, or clothed with a few scattered trees, we will introduce a rich belt, *m*, of flowering shrubs on the side of this walk. This belt will be a pleasant contrast, in its lively show of blossoms, to the graver character of the forest trees, and it will serve the important purpose of concealing this walk from a person coming up the approach, and *vice versâ;* a circumstance which should never be lost sight of in places of moderate size, where it is always desirable to increase their apparent dimensions.

On the line of this approach, as there were not trees in sufficient abundance to give it a wooded appearance, we should plant some fine maples, elms, and sycamores, and near the house some European larches, Scotch elms, and other exotic trees. As the trees already clothing the place are large, and as all newly planted trees will therefore be likely to look somewhat insignificant for a few years, we should be careful to *prepare the soil thoroughly*, as previously described, before planting them. This will not only cause them to grow much more vigorously, but it will give them almost at once a luxuriant appearance, which goes very far to lessen the apparent disparity between a large tree and a small one; as we never despair of that which we see making rapid advances.

A regular, symmetrical flower garden is only in good keeping with a Grecian, Italian, or other highly architectural building. For a cottage of a highly rural air, like the present, something is required of a less formal character, and which shall leave a little more room for the exercise of the fancy. Such an irregular flower garden, *n*, we have designated (on a very small scale) on the right of the house, which is looked into from the drawing-room windows. It will be seen that the beds are irregular, and that the whole garden is surrounded by an irregular plantation of small ornamental trees and flowering shrubs.* The beds may be surrounded by turf kept neatly mown, or by gravel. [A very excellent and speedy way of mowing a small lawn is by the Excelsior Improved Lawn-cutter—cutting fourteen inches wide, and so light a lady can use it. It may be procured of C. Lawson, successor to L. M. Smith & Co., Newburgh.—H. W. S.] Or a gravel walk may be led through the centre of the space between the beds, and a border of turf left on either side wide enough for walking upon. The latter will perhaps be the preferable mode, as in damp weather the hard, firm gravel will be preferred, and in warm sunny days the soft turf will be more agreeable to the tread.

The kitchen garden *o*, is placed in the rear of the house, in a sheltered position between the rising ground on either side. From the barn and stables a lane *p*, leads to the farm land in grass and tillage beyond, which has a separate back entrance leading into the public road.

When a place like this occurs, as it occasionally does, in the midst of a more cultivated and less wooded neighborhood, it will be a delightful surprise, with its highly

* A larger plan of a flower garden of this description may be found in our " Treatise on Landscape Gardening."

picturesque air, to a stranger entering it for the first time. It will be a much easier place to render effective than a level plain with few trees, if we carefully study the natural expression of the scene, and only attempt to heighten, not to alter it by our improvements. In the wooded walk, which is the principal feature of interest in this place, there will doubtless be many beautiful wild plants growing naturally. These we should by all means foster, and we may increase their charm by collecting from other and richer localities all the ornamental indigenous plants which may be made to thrive in such a situation.

A Cottage in the same Style, suitable for a Gate Lodge for this Residence, or for a small Family.

In the opposite illustration, Fig. 61, we have indicated a very simple cottage in the same style as Design VII., which would be well adapted for a lodge at the entrance gate *b*. In this situation it would probably be occupied by the gardener, the farmer, or some family in the employment of the proprietor of this residence. When a stranger entered the place, this cottage would of course first arrest his attention, and, with its old English and pretty rural expression, would serve as a prelude or agreeable preparation for the more varied and extensive cottage of the owner of the demesne.

It would otherwise make a neat and picturesque dwelling, if properly located, for a small, respectable family, who wish to lead a quiet and simple life. Although its accommodation is limited, yet it may be made to assume an air of taste and neatness, always agreeable to the mind, and often more striking in its effect, when met with in

DESIGN VII.*
A SMALL COTTAGE, OR GATE LODGE.

Fig. 61.

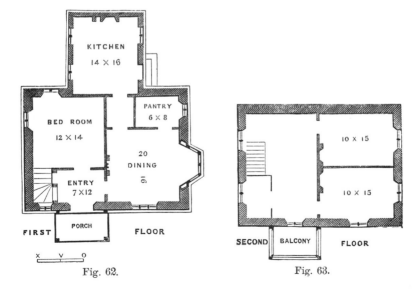

Fig. 62.

Fig. 63.

perfection in a charming little cottage, than in a stately mansion.

An examination of the plans of the interior, Figs. 62 and 63, will show the arrangement of the rooms. There is a parlor or living-room, lighted by two windows, one of them a bay-window, and adjoining it a pantry, a bed-room, and kitchen on the first floor. On the second floor are two bed-rooms, a large closet or wardrobe, and a smaller closet for linen. The kitchen is a wing added in the rear, with a gable and roof joining the main roof in a similar manner to that over the porch in the view of the front. The construction of this cottage is so similar to that of Design VII., just described, that we need not repeat the details.

Much of the pleasing effect of the most ornamental English cottages of this kind arises from the employment of vines and other climbing plants of different sorts, which, growing over and partly concealing portions of the exterior, render them, rich with blossoms, verdure and fragrance, perfect wonders of rural beauty. For this purpose our Virginia Creeper, the Trumpet monthly Honeysuckles, the Boursault, the Double Prairie, and the English White Climbing Roses, are most suitable in this climate.

Estimate.—This cottage may be built of wood for $830. [The cost now would be $1,600.—Ed.]

DESIGN VIII.

A Villa in the Italian Style.

This is a design in the modern Italian style, some of the merits of which we have previously pointed out. It will be at once perceived that, while this mode retains much of the expression of the Grecian style, it has far more variety, and a much more domestic character than the latter. The characteristic quality of the purest specimens of Grecian architecture is *elegant simplicity*, and it is a quality which is most appropriately displayed in a temple. On the other hand, we should say that the characteristic quality of the modern Italian buildings is *elegant variety*, which is most fitly exhibited in a tasteful villa. The great simplicity of form of the first is highly suited to a temple, where the singleness of purpose to which it is devoted appears symbolized in the simple Oneness of the whole edifice ; the irregularity of the second is equally in unison with the variety of wants, occupations, and pleasures which compose the routine of domestic life.

In our last design we have shown a cottage highly suited to a romantic vale, or sylvan nook, by the rustic picturesqueness of its *ensemble ;* the present one is equally appropriate for an open smiling plain, diversified by hill and dale, and sprinkled with groups and masses of trees. The more finished and architectural character of the building requires less the support of thickets of trees and intricacy of scenery to produce a harmonious union. The elegance of an Italian villa is produced mainly by the assem-

DESIGN VIII.

A Villa in the Italian Style.

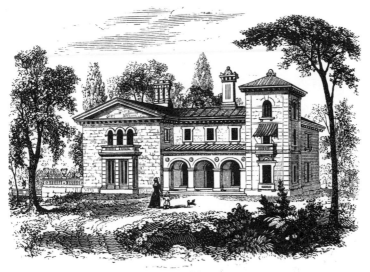

Fig. 64

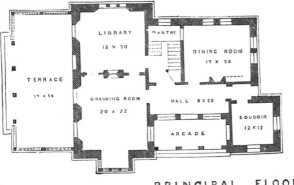

PRINCIPAL FLOOR

Fig. 65.

blage of simple and effective lines in its exterior, but it is also greatly enhanced by the introduction of such beautiful and refined features as the terrace with its ornamental balustrade and vases, and the balcony with its shade or canopy.

The terrace is a paved walk or smooth area, higher than the adjoining grounds, and twenty or more feet in width, surrounded by a handsome balustrade of stone, or of wood formed to imitate heavy Italian balusters. At suitable distances along the top of this balustrade may be placed vases of terra cotta, artificial stone, or more costly materials, and of classic forms, in proper keeping with the style of the building. As an object of taste the terrace is universally admired, because it serves to connect, by a gradual transition, so highly artificial an object as an architectural dwelling with the more simple forms of natural objects around. There is felt to be something incongruous in a highly finished house set down, as we sometimes see it, without the least reason or preparation, in the middle of a green lawn; but let the base of the house extend itself by a handsome terrace, and let the characteristic forms of the building be occasionally repeated near by, in the shape of a few pedestals with vases or other sculptured objects, and there is at once produced a harmonious union between the architecture and the landscape, or, in other words, between the house and the grounds.

As an object of utility, the terrace is a most comfortable and agreeable feature, affording a firm, dry, and secure walk, sunny and warm in the mid-day of winter, and cool and airy in the mornings and evenings of summer. From it, in many situations, access is had to the flower garden, the luxuriant creeping and climbing plants of which, enwreathing gracefully here and there the balustrade, or hanging in clusters of rich blossoms about the sculptured vase, increase the harmony growing out of this artistically contrived union of nature and art. [See page 235.]

In this cottage villa of very moderate size, we have endeavored to combine several of the peculiar beauties of the Italian style. Its façade, see Fig. 64, comprises a square tower or campanile, an arcade or Italian veranda, the triple round-arched windows, and the ridged or furrowed roof; and on the left is seen a portion of the terrace, which extends along the whole south side of the building. In the stack of chimneys to the left is shown the usual Italian form; in the central one, of loftier dimensions (which we have there introduced to improve the composition by giving it a more pyramidal outline), we have copied one not uncommon in Florence.

In its accommodation this house is moderate, and yet we trust it will be found convenient and agreeable. The front door is approached from the arcade, or veranda of the entrance front, Fig. 65. Opening this we arrive in the entrance-hall, which may be very completely connected with the veranda when the door and window are open in summer. The stair-case is conveniently and yet privately situated, as it is placed in a separate division of the hall, which may be excluded any time by a door between them. At the side of the hall opposite the front door is the dining-room, 17 by 20 feet, with a pantry opening into it on the left. Proceeding to the door at the left end of the hall, we enter the drawing-room, 20 by 22 feet, opening by its two casement windows to the terrace, and enjoying a fine view of the lawn through the large projecting window on the front. Directly in the rear of this room is the library, more quiet and secluded in its position, and of less size, but therefore more in character with the purposes for which it is destined.

We must not forget the *boudoir*, situated at the other extremity of the hall, which occupies the lower part of the tower. This may be very tastefully and prettily fitted up, and used by the lady of the house as a morning room for receiving social calls; or, if preferred, it would serve admirably as a dressing-room, and with a cabinet bedstead, as a bed-room at night when necessary. There is a private or back door to the hall, at the end of the passage leading into this *boudoir*.

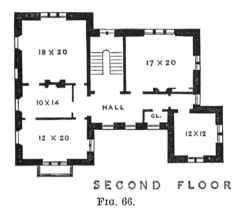

SECOND FLOOR

FIG. 66.

By a glance at the plan of the second floor, Fig. 66, the number and sizes of the sleeping apartments will be readily understood. There are five bed-rooms of different dimensions, including that in the tower, from which a light and fanciful open stairs may lead to the apartment in the campanile, serving as a belvidere or observatory. There is a large linen-closet in the front hall, and wardrobe-closets may be made in each of the bed-rooms.

The basement of this house may contain a kitchen directly beneath the dining-room, a cellar under the drawing-room, a store-room and laundry under the library, and a man-servant's bed-room in the basement of the tower.

Although from the strong contrasts of light and shade
in an Italian elevation like this, there is much boldness and
painter-like effect, yet, as these arise chiefly from the employment of a few strong lines and well-marked features,
the Italian, it will be perceived, is a comparatively easy
and an economical style. In this country, especially, it
will for some time be found that a building in this style
may be erected with less trouble than one like the preced-
ing design, because the ordinary mechanics are all familiar
with the details of Grecian architecture, which are chiefly
employed, with slight variations, in its execution.

An important advantage which the Italian architecture
possesses over the Greek, is the very great capacity which
its irregular form offers for additions that may be wanted
at any future period. One of our Greek-temple dwelling-
houses, on the other hand, is originally so complete in its
form that its fair proportions would be greatly marred by
adding any apartments that the comfort or convenience of
the family might suggest, when increased in wealth or
number. In carrying the present design into practice,
should it be preferred to enlarge or extend it by adding a
kitchen and offices on the first floor, a wing for this purpose might be extended to the right of the dining-room, a
little in the rear of the tower, which, if judiciously composed, would heighten the effect of the whole pile of
building, by giving it greater extent and irregularity,
two important elements of beauty in Italian villa architecture.

Construction.—We would either build this house of the
smoothest and best brick, and paint it in some soft, pleasing shade, or of the roughest brick, and coat it with the
best cement, colored to resemble a light mellow stone. The
solidity of the architecture would scarcely permit the em

ployment of *wood* as a material for the whole of this edifice, although the lighter character of
the bracketed Italian (Design V.) is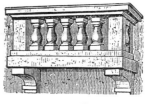
well suited to wood. Should econ-
omy oblige us to construct the balcony and terrace balustrades of wood,
they should be made in a bold manner, and thoroughly painted and sand-

FIG. 67.

ed, to imitate the material of the house. In Fig. 67 is
shown the Italian balcony; in Fig. 68, the arcade on the

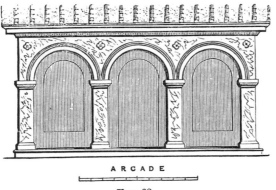

ARCADE

FIG. 68.

entrance front, both to a larger scale. The central Florentine chimney, which is of a very handsome description, is
 shown in Fig. 69. The body of this chimney-
top may be built of common bricks, and the or-
namental apex or summit of cut stone.

The roof is one of the most striking features
in this style, which arises (on the continent)
from its being made ornamental by employing
large furrowed tiles. When these are not at
hand, the effect may be easily imitated by a
covering of tin or zinc put on in the *ridge* man-

FIG. 69..

ner, the ribs being made bold and heavy. This is not only

a handsome, but an equally economical and a much more secure mode than the common one of *soldering* the whole surface, generally practised. The roof of a house in this style is made sufficiently steep to render the latter unnecessary. In painting it, either a dark brown or slate color should be chosen.

Estimate.—This design would cost $8,800 if the balustrades, etc., were cut of freestone. If made of wood, $7,600. [Would cost in brick $18,000, and in wood, $15,000.—ED.]

ARRANGEMENT OF THE GROUNDS.

A house like this would naturally demand a situation where some considerable extent of ground could be obtained. It would be highly suitable for a handsome villa residence in the country, of a moderate size, comprising from eighty to one hundred and fifty acres of land. A large portion of this would be kept under culture, and would serve to give employment to the proprietor in his character of an amateur farmer. Near the house ten or twenty acres may be devoted to lawn, all of which may be kept mown; that nearest the house being of course more neatly and more frequently clipped by the scythe, to accord with the air of elegance and polish always to be observed in the precincts of a handsome dwelling.

In the plan here given, Fig. 70, we have attempted to convey an idea of the arrangement of that portion of the grounds directly about the house, as our previous examples have probably given sufficient hints to the management of the more distant and extended portions, including the approach. The trees introduced in this design should be chiefly those of large, finely rounded heads, and graceful

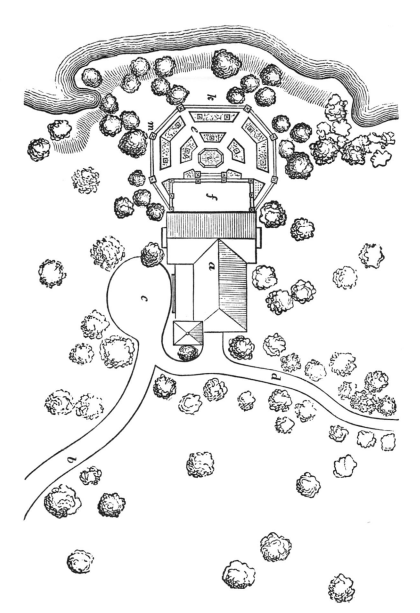

[Fig. 70]

sweeping branches, and they should be grouped in such a manner as to allow them to develop themselves in their utmost beauty of form on every side.

The dwelling *a*, we have placed on a little table of land descending gently on every side, and about one hundred and twenty feet distant from the shore of a pretty little natural lake on the left. The approach leading from the public road through the demesne to the house is shown, in part, at *b;* a gravelled sweep for carriages, *c*, is formed in front of the arcade, and the road *d*, leading to the stable and farm buildings, branches off at the right of the house.

The most important feature in this plan which we shall endeavor to describe here, is the architectural flower-garden *e*, which will be seen occupying a considerable space on the left of the house. The terrace *f*, the beauty and utility of which we have already insisted upon, lies in this direction, serving as a kind of beautiful extended base to the house. We shall suppose this idea still further carried out in the architectural flower-garden which surrounds this terrace, and which, lying directly below it, affords a fine display from the windows of the drawing-room and library.

We are not admirers of geometric or formal flower-gardens like this, considered by themselves, and merely as flower-gardens, because we think a natural arrangement is more replete with beauty and grace, and is capable of affording a much higher kind of pleasure. But this kind of architectural flower-garden, so common in Italy, and so appropriate an accompaniment to residences of this kind, requires to be regarded in another light. It is not only a garden for the display of plants, but it is a garden of architectural and floral beauty combined; it is as much an accessory of the building as a portion of the grounds, and therefore it very properly exhibits much of the regularity and symmetry of architectural forms and compositions. It contains plants, trees, and shrubs, it is true, in great profusion, but the beauty of these is heightened, and rendered more brilliant, by the introduction of elegant vases, sculptured urns, or perhaps a few statues of floral deities, or busts of distinguished persons. Those who have never seen the lively effect that may be produced by a garden of this kind, joined to an elegant villa, the architectural forms of which seem repeated in the garden and thus beautifully harmonized with nature, can scarcely conceive how charming it appears. A summer moonlight walk on this terrace, while we hear the silence broken only by the gentle murmur of the fountain at *e*, and see, softly gleaming in the silvery beams, the sculptured vases, clustered over partially by luxuriant climbers, and backed by dark masses of rich waving shrubs and flowers, would be sufficient to remind one, of even the most indifferent poetical temperament, of the garden of Boccaccio,

> Where, half concealed, the eye of fancy views
> Fauns, nymphs, and winged saints, all gracious to his muse.
> Still in the garden let me watch their pranks,
> And see in Dian's vest between the ranks
> Of the trim vines, some maid that half believes
> The vestal fires, of which her lover grieves,
> With that sly satyr peeping through the leaves!
>
> COLERIDGE.

In the example of this kind of garden attached to this house we should not expect to find so costly a decoration as marble vases introduced, but all the beauty of form, and nearly all that of material, may be obtained at a very moderate cost, suited to our more economical habits in this

country, in vases and ornaments of terra cotta, or artificial
stone.* The exorbitant price paid for some single article
of fashionable furniture, such as we not unfrequently find
in our country houses of this class, would embellish a whole
architectural garden with vases.

It should always be remembered that all
vases, urns, or other sculptured ornaments
for gardens and grounds, should be placed
on proper *pedestals*, plinths, or bases, to serve
as a firm support. A pedestal not only se-
cures a firm and an upright position, but it
gives a dignity and importance to the vase
as a work of art, which it would not have if
it were loosely and carelessly placed upon
the ground, or the gravel walk. A simple
form for such a pedestal is shown in Fig.
71, *b*, but a great variety of a more ornamental description will be suggested by a study of classical antique
designs.

FIG. 71.

This garden, octagonal in its form, we would surround
by a light and low balustrade-like fence, *k*, to be partially
concealed by creepers. At the angles of this fence we
would place pedestals for supports, *m*, each to be crowned
by a vase of some simple form. These pedestals, and
those in the interior of the garden that we intend for vases,
are designed by the × mark on the plan.

The beds or parterres for flowers we would border with
box, that being a very regular, architectural looking plant,
and a very permanent one for this purpose. The walks
should be of gravel, made hard and firm by the use of the

---

* Some specimens of terra cotta vases may be found at the Salamander Works,
Cannon Street, New York. Those in artificial stone may be had at Gibson's or
Goodwin's warehouses.

roller. The collection of plants chosen for the garden may vary somewhat to suit the taste of the proprietor, but the most satisfactory result will be attained by choosing such shrubs and herbaceous plants as are distinguished for richness and depth of color in their foliage, and for a massy and luxuriant habit of growth, as well as for beauty or delicacy of blossom. All lean, starved, and meagre-looking plants, mere botanical rarities, or such as are pretty for a short time, and then only remain to offend the eye and destroy the general *ensemble* of luxuriant verdure and bloom, should be rejected from a garden of this kind.

It will be a fortunate circumstance should a spring exist somewhere on a neighboring height, whence it may be brought in concealed pipes to supply this fountain. When this is out of the question, a cistern constructed in the upper story of some outbuilding, at no great distance, may afford a sufficient supply for playing in the evening, or at certain times during the day.

The French have an ingenious method of raising water from a well for this purpose, which has been put in practice in some places in this country at little expense. A small wooden tower or square building is placed in a convenient position over a well, and where it is not too conspicuous an object, and furnished with sails like a windmill, and a simple shaft and apparatus for drawing water by means of a pump to a cistern of good capacity in the top of the tower. This will furnish a fountain, or *jet d'eau* of moderate size, with a sufficient supply of water during the whole summer at little trouble, and without intermission, if the cistern be made large enough to hold a small over-supply for an occasional calm day. A still simpler mode of raising water for such purposes is the *hydraulic ram*, lately brought into common use, and sold at all the agricultural warehouses. Where a spring or small brook can be commanded, that will fill constantly a leaden pipe of one and a quarter inch in bore, the hydraulic ram may be used to raise water to the tops of buildings or the highest parts of the grounds at very moderate expense.

DESIGN IX.

A Cottage in the Italian or Tuscan Style.

THE design for this cottage, Fig. 72, has been kindly sent us for this work by J. Notman, Esq., Architect, of Philadelphia.

In the plan of the principal story, Fig. 73, there is an entrance hall with a handsome staircase, and an apartment on either side; that on the right being a parlor, and that on the left a dining-room. In the piers on either side of the staircase are spaces which designate hot-air flues, which proceed from the furnace in the basement, and by means of registers, warm all the apartments in the house, although the four principal ones have fire-places besides, for occasional use if necessary.

The first flight of stairs ascends half the story, and on a level with the landing here is the broad and airy balcony in the rear, entered by a fair round-headed window, opening to the floor. Underneath, this balcony forms a kind of partly enclosed apartment, serving as a wash-room or outer-kitchen in summer.

There is also a balcony over the recessed porch in front, which is a pleasant appendage to the chamber floor. This floor, Fig. 74, affords three pleasant bed-rooms, and there is a fourth of more ample size in the third story of the central portion of the cottage, which is, both with regard to its proportions and the fine bird's-eye view it commands, a very pleasant apartment.

The plan of the basement, Fig. 75, sufficiently explains itself. In the middle of the hall below is the furnace for

DESIGN IX.

COTTAGE IN THE ITALIAN OR TUSCAN STYLE.

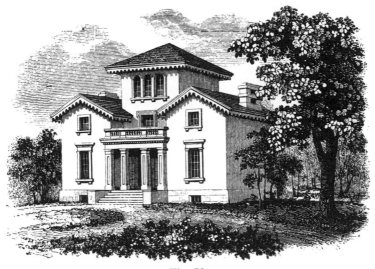

Fig. 72.

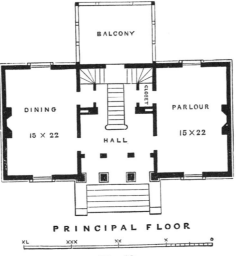

PRINCIPAL FLOOR

Fig. 73.

supplying heated air, and on either side are the kitchen, the store-room, and the fuel cellar.

This design, Mr. Notman remarks, might be altered and

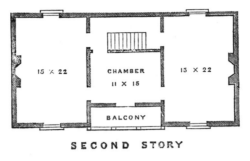

SECOND STORY

FIG. 74.

improved, without any variation of the present form, by elongating the flanks, and adding a suite of rooms in the rear. It may be built of brick and cement, or of wood; and a very simple kind of interior finish would be in the

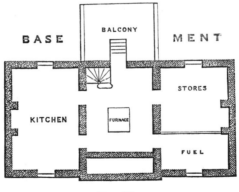

FIG. 75.

best taste for a cottage of this class. The roof may be covered with tin, zinc, or shingles, and the joints between the roof of the wings and the wall of the central portion should be well protected by broad lead or copper flashings or strips, running up a foot or more on the roof and wall, and being built in the latter in the usual manner.

Estimate.—This cottage, well constructed of solid materials, and neatly finished, would cost $3,000. If built of wood, filled in with brick, the expense might be slightly reduced. The design has been executed in a more elegant and costly manner near Philadelphia. [Would cost $5,000 to $6,000.—Ed.]

ARRANGEMENT OF THE GROUND.

For the sake of illustration, we shall suppose this to be a suburban dwelling, placed upon a long and narrow lot of ground, that being the most common form near towns, and the most difficult one to render agreeable or interesting. Its dimensions may be 120 feet broad by 375 feet deep, and it may extend from the street in front to another in the rear.

The first object of the proprietor of this cottage we shall suppose to be the production of a large crop of fruit and vegetables of every description, and the second, to render the whole garden rather tasteful and agreeable, by a skilful distribution of his materials and arrangement of walks. We shall suppose no trees introduced solely for ornament, except on the small lawn or area of grass in the front of the dwelling, and those bordering the irregular walk on the left; and even in these situations a preference will be given to ornamental *fruit-bearing trees*, as the Black Mulberry, the English Walnut, the Spanish Chestnut, and the thin-shelled Almond among trees, and the productive varieties of filberts, etc., among shrubs.

In the plan, Fig. 76, the entrance gates are placed at *a*, the house at *b*, the stable and yard at *c*. On either side

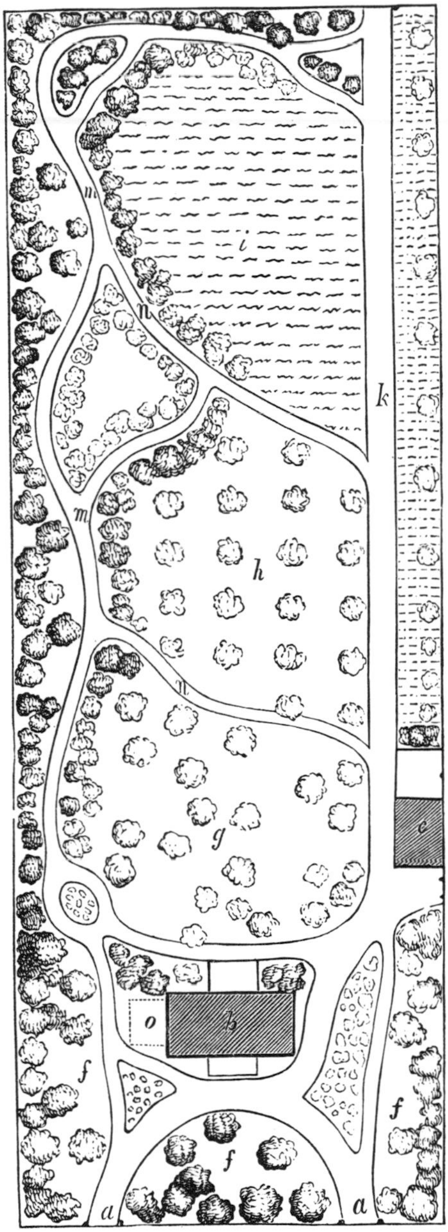

[Fig. 76.]

of the house is an area of turf, studded with a few ornamental trees of such species as are thought desirable. The
plot, g, in the rear of the house, is also devoted to grass,
but it is planted with a small orchard of fruits of the
hardier and more rapid growing kinds, cherries, pears, or
such other trees as will succeed tolerably well in a surface
kept in grass. This orchard is planted in the picturesque
manner, that is, in irregular groups, as it is seen directly
from the house, and therefore would be most agreeable in
this form. The second compartment, h, is another orchard
of such choice fruit trees as require more care, and the
ground around which is to be kept open by culture, and
may be planted annually with various crops of vegetables
with advantage to the trees and economy of space.

The third compartment, i, is the kitchen garden, the
area of which is to be kept free from trees and devoted
entirely to vegetables. There is a walk, k, sufficiently
wide for a cart or wagon, leading from the stable, c, to the
street in the rear, which gives access to the stable, and
affords an opportunity of supplying the garden with compost, or carrying away litter, or garden products, without
passing by the house, or having recourse to the front entrance. The long border, l, may be devoted, in different
parts, to grape-vines, strawberries, and other small fruits,
or to rhubarb, and other esculent plants.

As a counterpart to this long walk, which is strictly
useful in its character, we have another, m, on the opposite
side, winding and graceful in its direction, and bordered
by a miscellaneous collection of small flowering trees and
shrubs. These shrubs, as we have before suggested, may
be interspersed with the productive varieties of English
filberts, the Siberian crab, and other small fruits used for
preserves, and also with dwarf apples and pears, which.

growing only a few feet high, will, when in fine bearing, be very ornamental objects. The border or belt of shrubs, varying in width from three to fourteen or more feet, should be continued on both sides of this walk, as the object of it is, not only to render the walk interesting by the variety of shrubs, but also to render this portion of the garden complete in itself, by preventing, as much as possible, the eye from seeing the kitchen garden or other compartments on the right, at the same time with the scene formed by the walk and its boundary or fringe of shrubs. A person, after having walked along the whole course of the irregular walk, *m*, may vary the impression received, either by returning through the straight walk, *k*, of the kitchen garden, or, if it is preferred, he may return partly in a new course of curved walks, by taking the cross-walks, *n*, in his way.

We have indicated by the dotted outline at *o*, how a conservatory might be added on the left wing of this house, which might be warmed either by a flue, or by warm-water pipes connected with the fire-place of the dining-room, or the kitchen below. This should be on a level with the principal floor, and should of course be entered by a glazed door from the dining-room. As the wall of the house would form one side, or rather the back of the conservatory, it could be more economically constructed, and kept warm at less expense, than a detached green-house.

The grass on the areas *f* and *g* should be mown at least once a fortnight during summer. This, if it is successfully performed on the different portions, will go far towards supplying a horse or cow with green fodder during the growing season, and, by the frequent cutting, the beauty and verdure of the lawn will be greatly improved.

The grounds of a cottage orné, like this, while they

would afford a considerable quantity and variety of valuable products, would, we think all will admit, be far more agreeable and interesting than the common rectangular lots so general in the suburbs of our towns, and which are so entirely destitute of beauty of design.

DESIGN X.

A Villa of the First Class, in the Pointed Style.

THIS design of a Pointed Villa, by A. J. Davis, Esq., Architect, although a much larger and more elaborate composition than fairly comes within the scope of this work, we have introduced as a concluding example, both for the purpose of showing a more complete and extensive villa than we have hitherto presented, and as a specimen of the progress which architectural taste is making in this country; it having been recently designed by Mr. Davis for the country residence of J. Rathbone, Esq., of Albany.*

In the annexed view, Fig. 77, the artist has chosen a position showing the north and east fronts of the building, which are to be seen from the river, the entrance front being on the west side, a small portion of the open porch or *porte-cochère* being visible on the right of the house.

This villa, now completed, is undoubtedly one of the finest specimens of the Gothic or Pointed style of architecture in this country. Although the whole composition evinces unity of feeling, there is as much variety of feature as we ever remember to have seen introduced successfully in a villa; indeed, perhaps a greater variety of windows, gables, and buttresses than could be introduced in a building of that size with good effect, were it not supported by

---

* It is proper to add, that this design has not only been executed, but large additions have been made since its erection—which render it a much more spacious and complete residence than appears by our plan.

the corresponding intricacy and variety of the trees and foliage around it, which are here in admirable keeping with the picturesque outlines of the edifice.

Fig. 78 is a plan of the principal floor. A good deal of character is conferred on the west or entrance front by the projecting porch, which, extending entirely across the approach road fifteen feet, forms a dry, sheltered *carriage porch*, under which a carriage may draw up and the occupants alight dry and sheltered in all weathers.

If we now enter and pass through the vestibule, we shall soon find ourselves in a circular hall, sixteen feet in diameter, that forms a nucleus or radiating point from which all the principal apartments diverge. This (and through it the whole house) is heated by a furnace in the basement. Directly beyond the hall is the library, a sexangular apartment of much beauty of proportion, which will command a very striking view of the Hudson from the bay window at the eastern extremity. This bay window should be filled with rich stained glass, which would produce a mellow tone of light in this apartment, in admirable keeping with its character. On the right side of the library is another window, opening to the veranda or "umbrage," affording a delightful walk, with a noble view of the river in its southern course.

The dining-room is entered by another door on the right of this hall. It is sixteen by twenty-four feet in its dimensions, and the bay at the south opens into a conservatory for plants, which will give this apartment an air of summer even in the depths of a northern winter. This conservatory, forming as it does a portion of the veranda, may be entirely removed in summer if it should be preferred to have the whole veranda open, by having movable sashes, constructed so as to be easily taken out in the spring and replaced in autumn. The dining-room has a china closet on the right of the chimney breast; a dumb waiter on the left; across the staircase hall is the pantry, and the *stairs* descending to the kitchen and its offices is placed in most convenient proximity to the door leading to this passage.

The drawing-room opens on the left of the hall, and forms a *suite* with the library and dining-room. Its bay has a charming sylvan view to the north, and the two windows on the river front another looking east.

The two remaining doors of the hall lead, on one side to the staircase hall, and on the other into the family bed-room. The latter has three closets, a space for a wardrobe, and an alcove which may be used as a dressing-room, or a recess for placing a bed. On the south side of the vesti-bule is the office, or gentleman's own room, to be neatly and appropriately fitted up as a business room, or study, for the master of the house. The dotted triangular space at the corner of this office, indicates a place for an iron safe built in the wall. On the north side of the vestibule is a large closet for cloaks, umbrellas, etc. This story is thirteen feet in the clear, and the dotted lines in the hall and principal rooms show the form of the ribbed ceilings.

The second floor contains six sleeping apartments of various sizes, a bath-room, and a water-closet; and the attic furnishes sleeping accommodations for the servants. We regret that we are not able to show, by engraved plans, the ample and convenient arrangements of this and the base-ment story.

The whole internal arrangement of this villa by Mr. Davis is, we think, highly remarkable for its elegance, its compactness and the abundance and convenience of its accommodations. While any portion of the house may by itself be used by the family at any time, the effect of

DESIGN X.
A Villa in the Pointed Style.

Fig. 77.

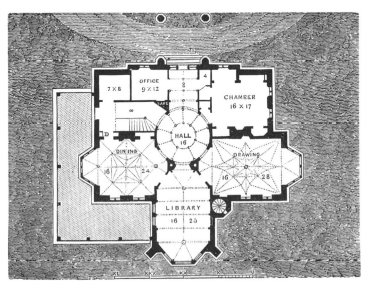

Fig. 78.

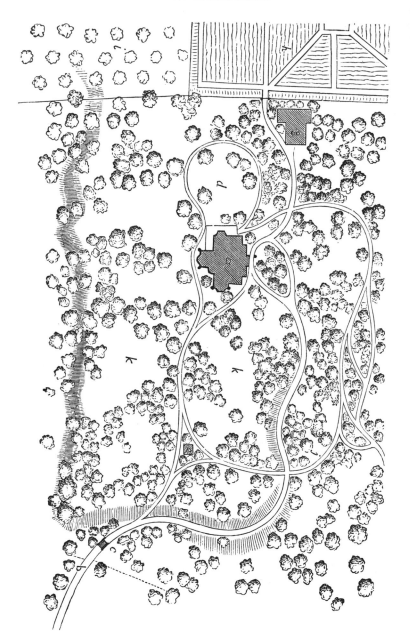

[Fig. 79.]

the entire first floor, when thrown open at once, would be more striking than that of many mansions we have seen of four times the size, where the rooms, having no connection and being badly arranged, produced little effect as a whole.

Estimate.—The estimated cost of this villa varies from $12,000 to $15,000, according to the material adopted, stone or bricks (either), and the degree of finish employed in the interior.   [This house would cost now from $25,000 to $30,000.—Ed.]

ARRANGEMENT OF THE GROUNDS.

The situation selected for this residence is a hill of considerable extent, commanding an extensive view of the Hudson, which is densely wooded with a natural growth of forest trees.   The preference was given to this site, as its natural picturesqueness and intricacy seemed to be admirably in keeping with the style of building in view; and also as it is found much easier to produce, in a short time, a satisfactory effect by thinning out and improving a suitable natural wood, than by planting and raising up new growths of sylvan accessories where none are already existing.

The grounds are about one hundred and twenty acres in extent.   In the accompanying plan, Fig. 79, a considerable portion in the neighborhood of the site for the house is shown.   There is a great variety of surface, caused by the undulations of the ground, upon this area, which will eventually, if proper advantage is taken of this circumstance, cause the demesne to appear of large extent.   In laying out the grounds, the course of the entrance road, *b*, was determined by a natural depression, which afforded a much more easy and suitable approach than could be found in any other direction. The road itself is not made in the *bottom* of the little dell, as this would render it wet, and even liable to be washed away at certain seasons of the year, but upon one side of the sloping bank, at a sufficient height above to insure the dryness and firmness of the road at all seasons. At *c*, the road is carried across a small stream, which affords an opportunity of introducing a pretty rustic bridge, constructed of the roots and stems of the trees felled in opening the road. An object of this kind, strictly useful in its character, when, as in this case, it can be legitimately introduced, always gives interest to a walk or road through the grounds, although it should never be made when there is not some obvious purpose beyond that of mere ornament.

There will be, eventually, an opportunity for creating a great variety in these grounds, but as an idea of this kind of situation can scarcely, like a flat surface, be conveyed by a mere plan, we shall only designate a few of the leading points of interest. There is an open lawn, *d*, at the south side of the house, to be enlivened by groups of flowering shrubs and plants, that will contrast agreeably with the dark verdure of the thicker groups of foliage on the other sides. At *e* is a rustic pavilion or summer-house, Fig. 80, on a knoll slightly elevated above the surrounding surface. The stable and other out-buildings are located at *g*, the kitchen garden at *h*, and the orchard at *i*.

The long and intricate walk, *j*, which may be led at pleasure a long distance beneath the shady, embowering branches of tall beeches, stately maples, and "melancholy pines," now threading little dells filled with mosses and ferns, and dark with forest verdure, and again emerging into sunny glades, opened among the forest trees here and

there, will be one of the most agreeable features of the place.
The greatest charm of this residence,
when it is completed, will be the
novelty and contrast experienced
in coming directly from the highly
artificial and populous city, only a
couple of miles distant, to its quiet,
secluded shades, full of wildness,
only sufficiently subdued by art to
heighten its natural beauty.

FIG. 80.

The principal difficulty in skil-
fully treating a residence like this, to be formed on an
entirely new surface, covered with wood, lies in thinning
out and opening the wood judiciously—in seizing on
the finer portions to be left, and selecting such as may,
with greatest advantage, be cleared away.   It must be
borne in mind, as we have previously urged, that few
single trees can be left, but that the thinning must be
done by opening glades boldly, *k*, and leaving the
trees in groups, masses, thickets, and groves.   Trimming
up the trees, beyond what is absolutely necessary in
removing dead branches, should never be attempted, but
unsightly underwood should be removed except in distant
parts, where it is desired to retain the wild and picturesque
character of the place for the sake of contrasting with the
more dressed air immediately around the house.   In short,
the *natural expression* of a place like this must be thoroughly studied before making any improvements; as otherwise the latter will, instead of heightening and developing
its original charm, only weaken and render it incongruous
and unsatisfactory.

DESIGN XI.

A Cottage for a Country Clergyman.

This little design has had its origin in some correspondence between a country clergyman in Massachusetts, a reader of the first edition of this work, and the author. His first letter was accompanied by a sketch of what he deemed the real wants of a family in his position; and the following extract from it may serve to place the subject more fairly before our readers.

"I recently purchased, and have read with much interest, your volume upon Cottage Residences. I have been wishing to procure a *home*—one, however plain and simple in its character, that might yet have something attractive about it, above the appearance of the unsightly fabrics that are too often classed under the head of dwelling-houses. And I turned over the pages of your volume in eager hope of finding something that would be adapted to my wants, and that would be so economical in construction that it might be made available for the comfort and convenience of a *poor country clergyman*, in the condition of him who addresses you. There were many of these snug cottages that charmed me, but I could not find in them what I cannot do without—*a study*. It was only in the more expensive structures, the cost of which places them wholly beyond my hope of possession, that the *library* found a place. With the expectation that others will aid me in the erection of a house, from absolute necessity I

A COTTAGE FOR A COUNTRY CLERGYMAN.

Fig. 81.

Principal Floor.—Fig. 82.

wish to restrict myself to the smallest possible outlay. Yet I have felt that the most modest residence might have something of true beauty in its character, and that there was no need, in any structure, of sinning against architectural propriety and law. I dare not think of having a house that shall cost much above $1,000 or $1,200, for I can ill afford to pay the rent of one that will much exceed that cost. [This design would cost now $2,800 to $3,000.—ED.] But is it impossible, that for about that sum we may be furnished with the conveniences we need? We have in prospect of possession a little bit of land, but half an acre, fronting south upon the road, which runs east and west. To the west and southwest we shall have a fine prospect, which we wish to enjoy by bringing the rooms mostly occupied upon that side of the house. The rooms we desire upon the first floor are a kitchen, sitting-room, bed-room, study, parlor, and pantries. We wish to place the house upon the east side of the lot, or very near the east side, that the garden may occupy the other portion. From your work, with my own cogitations, I have endeavored to approximate such a plan as we need, yet find it still defective; and I much desire to know whether it meets your approval, or if you can aid me in regard to its defective points. * * * My difficulties are to bring the kitchen nearer the sitting-room without giving up the bed-room; to get a back stairway underneath, which may be a way to the cellar; to obtain a room over the kitchen; and, finally, to know what should be the external appearance of such a house, that it may be neat and proper, yet without showing *pretension*—or how most economically it may be made acceptable to correct taste in its outward appearance. Which of the styles would afford a proper and economical finish? Poor as I am, for I possess not a

farthing aside from my salary of $700 per annum, I dislike
to be accessory to the erection of a house that shall be an
eye-sore to those who may rightly judge it.   We have few
houses here built with regard to good taste.   I appreciate
most fully all that you say about the proper construction
of houses; and now, when I am struggling to obtain one
for my own home, I desire that it may be, however humble, an approach to what a neat little 'parsonage' should
be—and that it may be a standing lesson to those who
belong to my parish, of the manner in which a pleasant,
unpretending home may be constructed—with the hope
that it may not be without a certain tendency, in its influence upon their minds, to an increased refinement and
moral elevation."

Entering into the views of our friend the country clergyman, we have retained all the principal features of his
ground plan, only modifying them so as to bring the whole
into a more constructive form and a more agreeable
arrangement.   Not being able to afford a back stair, we
have given something of the utility of one, so far as the
cellar-way is concerned, by shutting off the back entrance
from the front hall by a door at C, Fig. 82.   A door at D
opens on the veranda.   In the study there are book-cases,
with closets for papers, B, B.   There is a nice parlor, 13
by 16 feet, on one side of the hall, and a corresponding
dining-room on the other side—the latter having two convenient closets, so placed at the end of the room as to form
a kind of bay-window effect, that would be pleasing and
convenient.   There are also a kitchen, a bed-room for the
clergyman and wife, and a child's bed-room, all in connection.   The door at A should be glazed, in order to light
the back entry more completely.   If a communication
between the bed-room and the entry is thought more desir-

able than the closets, a door placed there instead of the closets would answer that purpose.

The second floor plan, Fig. 83, shows five good bed-rooms, with a closet to each. (This plan is drawn to a smaller scale.) Closets are shown at *a, a.* The dotted lines show the roof of the veranda. Fig. 84 is a small sketch of the rear.

FIG. 83.

The first story being 11 feet in the clear, the posts for the frame of this cottage would be 17 feet long. The outside would be covered with vertical boarding.

For the exterior of this cottage we have chosen a simple

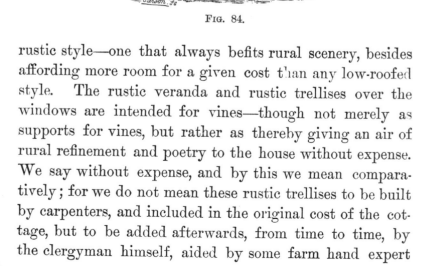

FIG. 84.

rustic style—one that always befits rural scenery, besides affording more room for a given cost than any low-roofed style. The rustic veranda and rustic trellises over the windows are intended for vines—though not merely as supports for vines, but rather as thereby giving an air of rural refinement and poetry to the house without expense. We say without expense, and by this we mean comparatively; for we do not mean these rustic trellises to be built by carpenters, and included in the original cost of the cottage, but to be added afterwards, from time to time, by the clergyman himself, aided by some farm hand expert

with the saw and hammer. They should be constructed
of *cedar* poles, with the bark on, which may be had almost
anywhere in Massachusetts for a trifle, and which, if neatly
put together, will be more becoming to such a cottage as
this than elaborate carpentry-work. By the addition of
such trellis-work and a few vines, a simple rustic cottage like this may be made a most attractive object in a
rural landscape.

DESIGN XII.

A Villa in the Elizabethan Style.

WE take this design from Brown's Domestic Architecture, and place it before our readers, partly as offering some good suggestions, and partly to enable us to point out some of its most glaring defects. As much benefit may be derived sometimes from the critical examination of designs which are defective, as from those which are nearly perfect.

The plan of this house, Fig. 85, is in many features a

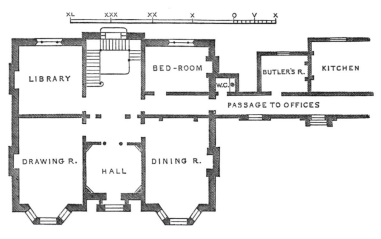

FIG. 86.

good one. The large space devoted to the staircase and hall gives the house a dignified appearance, while the rooms are of good proportion, and are conveniently arranged for privacy and home comfort, with studious avoidance of all effect produced by the connection of one apartment with another, etc.

A great blunder is however committed in the position of the fire-places and chimneys, by placing them on the *outer* instead of the inner walls. Change the chimneys to the side of the room directly opposite where they now stand, and you have them in a better position for draught, and for accumulating warmth in the house, while you have a space left to place a couple of windows in the drawing-room, and a broad window in the library, so as to command the light and circulation of air on the longest side of these rooms. The same remark applies to the dining-room. The exterior effect would be even more improved by this change of position in the chimneys than the interior—since nothing can be more ugly than a chimney springing from the lower edge of a steep roof instead of the higher part of the ridge, where it naturally belongs.

To this left-hand side of the house we would add a veranda, shading the windows we have just suggested in the drawing-room and library.

The exterior of this villa is pleasing in general character, though faulty in its details. Knock off the bedpost-like ornaments at the angles of the gables, adopt the finish shown in the gables of Design III., move the chimney-tops to the middle portion of the roof, as we have already suggested, put a correct and solid-looking oriel window in the place of the flimsy one over the front porch, break up the left or south roof-line by dormer-windows in suitable style, and omit the grotesque and absurd effigies of dogs on the springing stones of the porch, and this villa will have a dignified and agreeable air as the home of a country gentleman. It should be built either of stone or brick—and supposing the kitchen wing to be of moderate size, the whole would cost from $7,000 to $9,000.

DESIGN XII.

A Villa in the Elizabethan Style.

Fig 85.

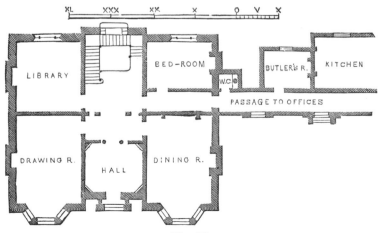

Fig. 86.

A Small Cottage for a Toll-Gate House.

Fig. 87.

Fig. 88.

DESIGN XIII.

A small Cottage for a Toll-gate House.

THIS picturesque little villa was designed by Mr. Wild, and originally published in Loudon's Supplement as a village inn. But it would be much better adapted here for a toll-gate house upon one of our turnpikes or plank roads. The gate itself should be directly connected with the tower, and might easily be arranged so as to be opened by

FIG. 89.

the inmates from the inside of the building. Devoting it to this purpose, *a* (Fig. 88) would be the porch, *b*, the entry, *c*, the living-room, *d*, bed-room or parlor, *e*, veranda, *g*, back-entry, *m*, wood-house, *l*, back porch, *h*, pantry, *i*, store-room, *k*, milk-room.   There is a bay window at *o*, with a seat outside, *n*.   The upper floor would be divided into two good-sized bed-rooms or three smaller ones.

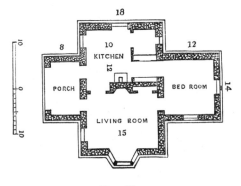

FIG. 90.

This building would look well of wood, put on in vertical boarding, and painted a warm drab color; or it would be more picturesque if covered on the outside with shingles—in the manner of many of the Dutch farm-houses in the State of New York—which make a more durable covering than inch-boards.   If the shingles were rounded on the lower edge, or cut into diamonds or hexagons, it would add still more to their good effect at but a trifling increase of expense.   The estimated cost of this building, of wood, is $930.   [Present cost, $2,000.—ED.]

Figs. 89 and 90 show a sketch and ground plan of a small toll-gate house or lodge, in a massive, simple archi-tectural style, quite opposite in character to the foregoing.

The whole is supposed to be built of rubble-stone, and the cost, when this kind of stone is abundant upon the ground, would be about $500. [Present cost, $1,600.—E<small>D</small>.]

DESIGN XIV.

A Cottage in the Rhine Style.

THIS residence was designed by us for our neighbor, J. T. Headley, Esq., and has been built in a picturesque and highly appropriate position, where its steep roof-lines harmonize admirably with the bold hills of the Hudson Highlands. Though spirited and irregular in composition, it is simple in details, Mr. Headley's object being to erect a picturesque rural home in keeping with the scenery, but without the least unnecessary outlay for decoration.

The plan of the principal floor, Fig. 91, shows an entrance hall, eight feet by thirty-six feet. Out of this open the three best apartments—viz., the library and dining-room, each sixteen by twenty feet, and the drawing-room, seventeen by twenty-two feet. The library has a ceiling prettily ribbed, and the book-cases are in recesses formed in the walls. On this floor are a kitchen, pantry, closets, etc., with spacious verandas on two sides of the house.

The plan of the chamber floor, Fig. 92, shows four bed-rooms of good size, and one smaller one in the tower, which may be either used as a dressing-room or a child's bedroom. From the north bed-room there is a private passage to the bath-room and water-closet, by descending a few steps. (The closets taken out of the spaces each side of the chimney have been omitted in the drawing.)

The high roof of this style of building affords considerable space in the attic, which is finished in three good bedrooms for servants, or other uses.

RESIDENCE OF MR. HEADLEY, NEAR NEWBURGH.

Fig. 90.

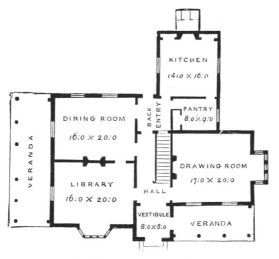

Principal Floor.—Fig. .91

Fig. 98.

The first story is twelve feet in height; the chamber floor nine and a half feet. The kitchen is nine and three-fourths feet in height.

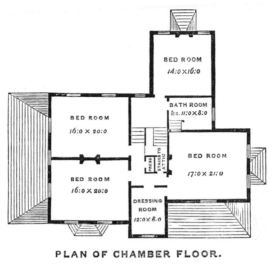

PLAN OF CHAMBER FLOOR.

FIG. 92.

This house is built of brick—the first story walls one foot thick, the second story eight inches; the foundations are heavy blue-stone. Water is forced to a cistern in the garret (and thence is led over the house) from a spring about 150 feet distant—the elevation being overcome by a hydraulic ram, worked by the overflow of the spring through a pipe of one and a quarter inch bore.

This very picturesque dwelling was erected at a cost of $4,800, exclusive of the water-pipes.

[In 1871 this place was purchased of Mr. Headley by R. H. Pardee, Esq., of New York, who directed us to make certain additions and alterations, which are shown in the additional engravings introduced below. At the front entrance a carriage porch was placed, stretching over the drive-way, and forming a sheltered approach to the front door. (See Fig. 98.) The window over this, in the second story, was cut down to the floor, in order to reach the balcony over this porch, from which a rather better river view may be obtained than from below. The dressing-room shown on the second story plan (Fig. 92) was taken away, and the attic stairs—before enclosed by a partition—were taken down, and a new broad open flight to the attic put up in their place. By these alterations the second story hall was made to occupy the whole extent of space from the front to the rear of the house.

The small one-story kitchen-wing was taken down, and a new wing erected in its place, as shown on the plan (Fig. 93), two full stories and an attic in height, and containing a kitchen and laundry in the first story, and two quite pleasant chambers in the second story. The butler's pantry was completely remodelled, and new cupboards and shelves put up, besides a butler's pantry-sink for washing dishes, etc. The laundry was fitted up with large closets and three laundry wash-trays, and the kitchen was supplied with range, boiler, cast-iron sink, and a large dresser in the corner at the side of the range.

In the second story the old chambers were provided with closets (Fig. 94), and with permanent wash-bowls supplied with hot and cold water, and the bath-room was refitted with bath-tub, wash-bowl, and water-closet.

The wood-work was remodelled to some extent throughout the house, and the whole exterior repainted a cool gray color, and all was done at an expense of about $4,000. Such a house as this is now could be built at the present time for about $15,000.

Figures 95, 96, and 97 represent a small stable that was put up at the same time by Mr. Pardee. It is of brick, built on a side-hill, sloping towards the east, so that the

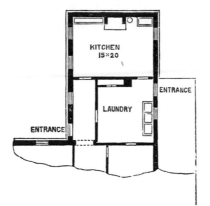

Fig. 93.

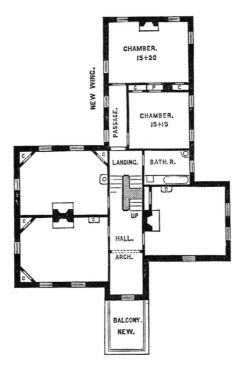

Fig. 94.

basement is entirely out of ground on that side. In this basement are cow-stalls, a manure-pit, and storing places for farm-wagons, etc.

The principal story has a carriage-room twenty by twenty-two feet; stalls for four horses, each five feet six inches by nine feet; a harness-room and a feed-closet, and a stairway to the second story.

In the second story is a sleeping-room for a man, besides ample storage for hay. [This stable cost about $2,700. G. E. H.]

Fig. 95.

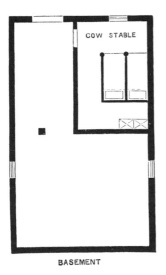

BASEMENT

Fig. 96.

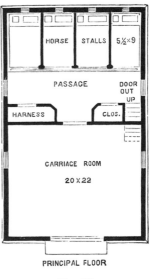

PRINCIPAL FLOOR

Fig. 97.

Fig. 99.

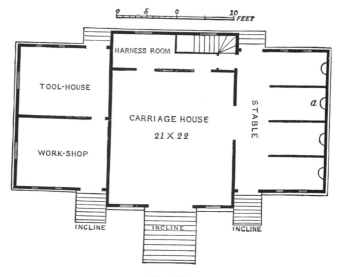

Fig. 100.

DESIGN XV.

A Carriage-House and Stable in the Rustic Pointed Style.

As this stable, which has been erected from sketches furnished by us, upon the estate of M. Vassar, Esq., near Poughkeepsie, is both convenient and ornamental, we present a perspective view and ground plan for the benefit of our readers. The composition is, we think, pleasing—the ventilator upon the top being as valuable in adding to the picturesqueness of the building as to its comfort.

The plan shows a carriage-room, twenty-one by twenty-two feet, double-floored and ceiled all round, with a harness-room and separately enclosed stairway in the rear. On the left is a tool-room, work-shop, etc.; on the right a stable, with stalls for four horses. Over the whole is a large loft for hay, with mouths in the floor to feed the racks, *a*, in the stable below, without the necessity of carrying or throwing it down.

As this stable is built upon sloping ground, it has beneath it another story—a basement stable—for farm horses, cows, cellar for roots, etc., not shown in this elevation, making altogether a very complete building. It is constructed of sound timber, sheathed with matched pine plank, battened, and the whole filled in with brick. The walls of the cellar story are blue-stone, laid in mortar, and the whole is finished in a very substantial and excellent manner. The cost was about $1,900—but in many parts of the country, where lumber is cheap, the whole may be built for about $1,000. [Present cost $2,500 to $2,800.]

NEW DESIGNS

FOR

COTTAGES

AND

COTTAGE VILLAS.

Fig. 101.

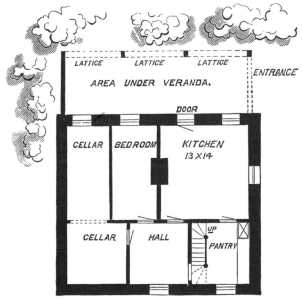

Fig. 102.

DESIGN XVI.

A small Side-Hill Cottage.

THIS cottage was designed for a situation where the ground descends very rapidly away from the line of the front, and this peculiarity was taken advantage of to get a kitchen and servants' room below the main story—though entirely out of ground on one side and the greater part of another side, making them quite as dry and pleasant as the upper story.

Fig. 102 shows the plan of the basement. Under the veranda is an area, the floor of which is two feet above the ground, and paved with bricks. This area is neatly latticed up, so that the whole space is quite private, and forms a pleasant working place in the summer-time. The kitchen opening from it is thirteen by fourteen feet, and adjoining it is a large pantry containing a dumb-waiter rising to another pantry in the floor above, besides a stairway up, and sundry shelves and cupboards. There is a hall opening into a servants' room, eight by fourteen, and into two good cellars, both of which have floors laid on chestnut beams bedded in grout, as in fact have all the other basement rooms.

The cellar is eight and a half feet high in the clear, and the walls are of stone with the exception of those fronts which are exposed—they being of brick and painted.

The principal story (Fig. 103) has an entrance hall ten feet square, and a staircase hall of the same dimensions, separated from each other by a screen made of chestnut. The stairs are three and a half feet wide, and under them is a closet for coats. The pantry is ten feet square also, and is fitted up with cupboards, and has a butler's pantry sink for washing dishes in, supplied with hot and cold water from the range.

The parlor and dining-room are both of the same size, fifteen by sixteen feet. The first has a large French window, through which one can pass to the yard (see Plate, Fig. 101), and the dining-room has a similar window opening out upon a large balcony. Both rooms connect with a veranda nine feet wide. This story is ten and a half feet high.

In the second story (Fig. 104), a small hall-way or passage at the head of the stairs opens into three chambers, two of which are thirteen feet square and the third about six and a half feet square. This story is ten feet high in the middle of the rooms, falling away to three feet at the extreme eaves, where they are furred out to make the finished height six feet in the lowest part. The spaces furred off may serve as closets.

This cottage was designed to be a frame cottage boarded and clapboarded, and also filled in with bricks for greater protection against cold. The interior finish of pine stained, or of chestnut simply oiled, and the floors of all of the first story of Southern pine laid with a border of black walnut all around twelve inches wide. The floors of the second story of narrow pine plank. The estimated cost is $3,200.

This design, with perhaps some slight alteration in the plan, would make a very suitable parsonage for the small church illustrated in the frontispiece.

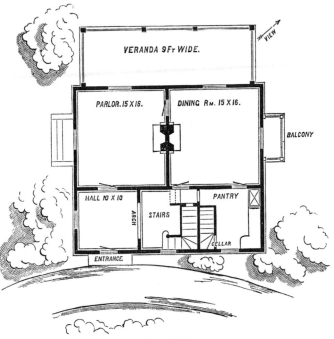

Fig. 103.

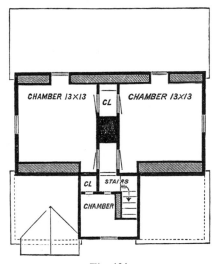

Fig. 104.

DESIGN XVII.

A Plain House.

THIS is a very plain and inexpensive but roomy house, suitable for a village lot.

The veranda at the entrance is nine and a half feet in width, and is approached by a broad flight of six steps from the path.

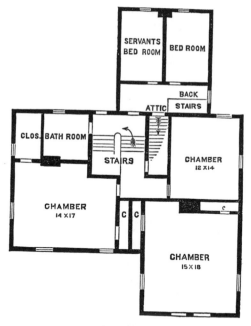

Fig. 107.

The hall is eight by eighteen. The library is thirteen by fourteen, and back of it is a bed-room eight by fourteen. The parlor is on the rear of the hall, and back of it is

DESIGN XVII.
A Plain House.

Fig. 105.

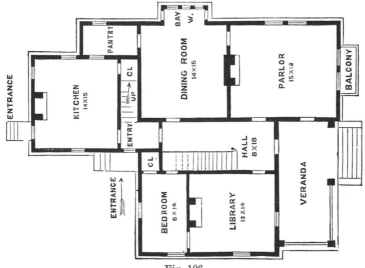

Fig. 106.

the dining-room, with a bay window projecting from it. There is a back entry with a private staircase in it, and opening from it is the kitchen, which is separated from the dining-room by a large pantry. (Fig. 106.)

The second story (Fig. 107) contains five chambers in all, and a bath-room and five closets.

The attic story is unfinished, but may be divided off into three large rooms, with several closets. The attic stairs rise from the back hall, the floor of which is somewhat lower than the second story hall of the main house.

The cellar is unfinished, and extends under the whole house.

The first story is ten feet high, the second is nine feet, and the cellar seven feet. The rooms in the attic may finish eight feet high.

This house may be built for $4,000.

DESIGN XVIII.

A Gate House.

Tʜɪs design partakes somewhat of the Swiss style, and would make a very good gate house or gardener's house on a large country place. The outline is simple, but the details are rather bold, giving deep and heavy shadows, which make up much of the picturesqueness of its appearance.

The veranda at the entrance (marked A) is eight feet in width, and the front of it is enclosed by a lattice-work, with oval openings in each bay between the posts for light. The hall, B, is seven and a half feet wide, and in it is the stairway to the second story. C is the parlor, fifteen feet square, having a square bay window projecting from the front, and communicating with the room D, which may be used as a bed-room. This room is fifteen feet square. E is the living-room, fifteen feet square also, and G is a large store-room or pantry, through which we pass to the passage, K, and the kitchen, F. M is a closet, and L is the back stoop leading to the grounds. The kitchen is thirteen by fifteen feet, and is in a one-story wing attached to the rear of the house. In the second story (Fig. 110) are three good-sized bed-rooms and five closets.

The principal story (Fig. 109) is nine and a half feet high, and the second story nine feet in the clear.

The cellar is unfinished, extends under the whole house, and is seven and a half feet high in the clear. It stands about two-thirds out of ground—the top of it, or the level

Fig. 108.

Fig. 109.

of the main floor of the house, being about five feet above the natural grade of the ground. An artificial terrace or banking occupies three and a half feet of this height, and the rest is made up by the underpinning, which may be of granite, or brick painted. The banking—which is an almost universal feature in some parts of New England, though seldom to be met with in this neighborhood—is designed to be neatly graded with loam and then carefully covered all over with sods, so that it may have a strong, healthy coat of grass over it.

This is a frame house, with vertical boarded and battened sides and a slate roof. The cost would be about $2,800.

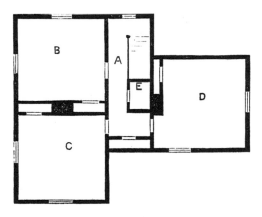

Fig. 110.

DESIGN XIX.

A Rambling Cottage with Low Walls.

THIS house would cost about $6,000, and we think com-
bines convenience with a rather comfortable appearance
of exterior, which appearance is due mainly to the low
walls, steep roof, and ample piazzas with which it is provided, offering a pleasant retiring-place on every side of
the house, and for every hour of the day.

The veranda nearest in the picture is the one by which
we approach the house, and projects considerably beyond
the front of the gable in order to give it a width of ten
feet, which for a cottage of this size is an unusual width.
Such a lounging-place cannot fail to be attractive.

The hall is seven and a half feet wide, and on the left
is the parlor, fifteen by twenty, the width of which is
increased some four feet by the bay window projecting
from the side opposite the fireplace.   (Fig. 112.)

At the rear of the parlor is a veranda seven feet wide,
and both the windows of this room extend down to the
floor and have casement sashes.   These windows, too, are
about four and a half feet wide, which is a foot and a half
wider than they are ordinarily made, so that in the summer, when both are open, the verandas really become
portions of the room; in fact, in case of an entertainment
at any time, when extra space is needed, the two verandas
may be very easily enclosed by boarding, and the available
space increased very considerably; the room would really
be fifteen feet wide and thirty-seven feet long.

DESIGN XIX.

A Rambling Cottage with Low Walls.

Fig. 111.

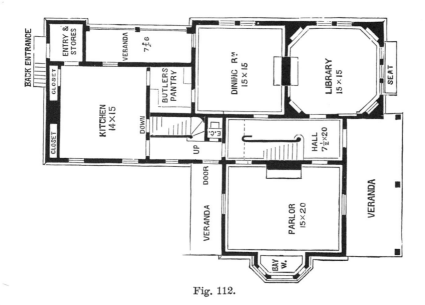

Fig. 112.

In the winter-time it would probably be necessary to cover these windows with an extra sash screwed on the outside, otherwise, by reason of their size, there might be too great an escape of heat through them.

The library is a very pleasant room, octagonal in shape, with two large windows on the outsides and bookcases let into the walls in the corners, and having on another side a broad old-fashioned fireplace, made expressly to burn big logs of wood in, being provided, of course, with bright brass andirons and a wire fender; the fireplace opening should be at least three feet broad and about two feet four inches high, and the mantel-piece should be broad and high, built of wood, carved here and there, or faced with tiles of some of the pretty patterns which may be found in abundance now-a-days. The ceiling might be panelled in wood, oiled or shellacked, so as to show its genuine color; or painted in parti-colors, say a rich blue for the panels, relieved by lines of light, and a chocolate for the ribs, picked out with some bright contrasting color. Whatever the decoration may be, however, care should be taken not to overdo it, as the room is small and may be easily overloaded.

The dining-room is fifteen feet square, and from it a casement window opens out upon the side veranda, which, being a considerable height above the ground, by reason of the falling off of the grade towards the rear, is protected by a strong railing. This veranda may be the *smoking-room*, if perchance the "actual" head of the house should object to the indulgence of the "horrid" habit inside the walls. Or, if it should happen to face the south, it might be enclosed in winter and turned into a very convenient conservatory, getting the required heat from the kitchen or from the room below by means of a drum.

The butler's pantry connects the kitchen with the dining-room, and has all the usual fittings. In the back entry there is a private staircase to the second story, under which is another to the basement. There is also an earth-closet placed here in a convenient yet retired position. The kitchen is 14 by 15 feet—has two closets, besides a large store-room, and a door with a stoop leading to the grounds at the rear.

The rear of this house is entirely out of the ground, and the laundry, which is under the kitchen, is entered by a door under the last-named door and stoop. The rest of the cellar is occupied by a milk-room, furnace-room, coal-cellar, vegetable-cellar, and a large store-room.

In the second story (Fig. 113) are three large chambers

Fig. 113.

and two small ones; there are eight closets in all, and a bathing-room and two stairways.

The principal story of this house is 11½ feet high, and the second story 10 feet—unusual heights for a small house, but desirable in this particular case.

The material is wood, with a slated roof, and the basement is brick where showing above the ground, and stone elsewhere.

DESIGN XX.

A French Roof House.

THIS design represents a style of house very commonly found in Eastern New England, and is a fair example of a plain, economical house containing a considerable accommodation.   It measures 32 by 40, with the addition of a two-story projection at the rear, as shown on the plans.   The roof of this projection is flat, and comes just under the cornice of the main house, but does not interfere with it at all, the curved roof covering the square 32 by 40 only.

The plan (Fig. 115) shows a portico about eight feet square, opening into a hall eight by nineteen, in which are the main stairs to the second story.   On the left is the library, occupying the front of the house, and behind it, connected by folding doors, is the parlor.   These rooms are on the south side, and opening from them by long windows is a veranda nine feet in width, extending along the whole of the south side.   There is another narrower veranda at the rear, sheltering the back entrance to the house.

On the right of the front hall is the dining-room, and back of it, separated by a narrow passage in which is a stationary wash-bowl, is the kitchen, measuring 12 by 16 feet.   The back entry and private stairs are close by, and also a store-room and three large closets.

The second story (Fig. 116) contains four pleasant chambers of good size, each one of which has a closet attached. In the passages connecting each pair of chambers are permanent wash-bowls, supplied with hot and cold water.

DESIGN XX.

FRENCH ROOF HOUSE.

Fig. 114.

Fig. 115.

The bath-room is of good size, and there are two large closets besides those attached to the chambers. The attic or roof story is finished off, and in it are four chambers over those in the second story, and of the same dimensions, with the exception of a space against the outside wall, furred out one foot, to give better height in the rooms, and to support the framework of the roof. Above the

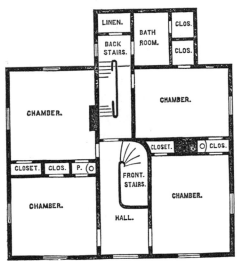

Fig. 116.

rooms in this attic story is a space of about six feet in height in the centre, running down to about three at the sides, which serves both as a trunk-room and as a ventilating chamber for the whole house.

The cellar is of stone, with a split and dressed granite underpinning 18 inches high. The laundry is under the kitchen, the coal-cellar under the dining-room, the furnace under the hall, and the balance of the space is used as an open cellar for fruits, vegetables, etc.

There is an outside cellar-door under the end of the back entry.

The cellar is eight feet high; the principal story ten and a half feet; the second story nine and a half feet, and the attic story nine feet.

It is a frame house, boarded and clapboarded, and having a slated roof. The frame is made of spruce timber, and the following are the suitable dimensions for the several parts: Posts, plates and girths, four by eight, except the third story girths, which are one and a quarter by six, notched into the studs and nailed fast to every one.

Sills, eight by eight; floor-beams, two by ten and two by nine, and placed sixteen inches from the centre, and crossbridged between the points of support; trimmers and headers, four by ten and four by nine, and kept two inches clear of the chimneys; rafters of lower pitch, three by five, and twenty inches from their centres; rafters of the upper pitch, two by nine, and the same distance apart, all placed double at the openings; studs, two by four, and sixteen inches from centres and double at all the openings; partition heads, four by four; braces, three by five; posts in attic to support the roof, four by eight and four by six.

These dimensions may be varied a trifle to suit different localities, but nothing smaller should be used unless the frame is to be built in the balloon manner—without mortises—in which case they may be considerably lighter.

This house was built near Boston some years ago at a cost of about $7,000.

DESIGN XXI.

A Cottage for a Village Lot.

THIS design represents an inexpensive cottage suitable for a village lot of about one hundred feet in width.

The material is wood, the frame being covered with tongued and grooved boarding and rosin-sized paper and then clapboarded with narrow pine clapboards. The roofs are also boarded and papered and then slated with small-sized slates of one or two colors.

The cellar wall is of stone, with an underpinning of brick or of split granite in long sections, laid on top of the stone wall so as to show about eighteen inches in height below the wood-work or sill of the house.

There are some ornamental features upon the exterior, but nothing of an elaborate or expensive kind, the most noticeable being a cresting on the ridge of the roof, which can be put on complete for about $100.

The plan (Fig. 118) affords the following accommodation: A veranda, eight feet wide, at the entrance, opens into the vestibule, six by eight, which connects with the hall containing the principal staircase. This hall is seven feet wide and the staircase is three and a half feet wide, and under it is a closet for coats and hats, etc. The parlor is sixteen by nineteen feet, and the dining-room adjoining it is sixteen by seventeen feet. Both of these rooms open out by casement windows upon a pleasant balcony. The dining-room has a bay window and a large china closet. The butler's pantry separates it from the kitchen, and is filled up with shelves and cupboards for china, etc. Conveniently placed to the kitchen is a private staircase for access to the upper stories, and a large store closet. The back entry opens into the main hall, the kitchen, and out upon the back stoop, and also connects with the cellar by a stairway under the back stairs. The kitchen is fifteen by sixteen feet. The study opens from the main hall and is fifteen feet square.

In the second story (Fig. 119) are three good sized

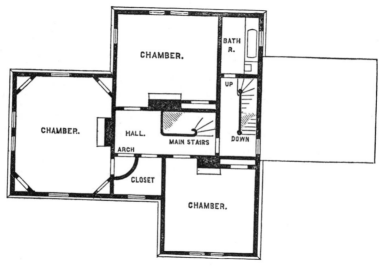

Fig. 119.

chambers, being in fact the same dimensions as the lower rooms. There are seven closets in all, one of which, over the vestibule, may be used as a linen-closet. The bath-room is over the butler's pantry, and is supplied with a bath-tub and a water-closet. The attic stairs are over the private stair-case, and in the attic are two good rooms for servants' use.

Fig. 117.

Fig. 118.

The cellar contains a coal-cellar, a furnace-room, a vegetable-cellar, and a large lock-up store-closet. The floor of this cellar is grouted and the ceiling lathed and plastered.

The principal story is ten feet high in the clear, and the second story nine feet.

The cost would be $4,200.

DESIGN XXII.

A Stone Cottage.

A COTTAGE of similar exterior to this design, but differing somewhat in plan, has just been erected under our direction near Newburgh.

The material is stone taken from the immediate neighborhood, of a dark-blue color, and the trimmings are of blue-stone from the Kingston quarries.

The walls are laid double, the outside stone wall being twenty inches thick, with a space of three inches between it and a lining or inner wall of brick, four inches thick, which wall is joined to the outer by iron ties every fifth course, and two feet apart. This method of building makes a very substantial and dry wall, though somewhat more expensive than the ordinary method of building. The plastering is laid immediately upon the brick wall, and, as the partitions are all of brick, the house is almost fire-proof as well as rat-proof.

The front porch is of stone, and has a floor of encaustic tiles of various colors. The main hall is nine feet wide and extends through the house, with doors at the rear similar to those in front (Fig. 121). The floor of the hall is also paved with tiles.

On the left is the parlor, measuring fifteen by twenty feet, and beyond it is an old-fashioned square landing staircase, near to which are a water-closet and a cloak-closet.

Fig. 120.

Fig. 121.

On the right of the hall the front room is the library, fifteen feet square, and behind it a dining-room, fifteen by twenty feet. This room is octagonal in shape, two of the corners being occupied by closets—one by a niche in the hall for a piece of statuary, and the other by a passage leading to the kitchen. There is a butler's pantry connecting the dining-room with the kitchen, and a store-room near it.

The back entry is marked E, and from it rise the private stairs to the second story of the wing, the cellar stairs being under these.

The principal story is eleven feet high. The second story has four chambers in the main house and five closets, one of which is a linen-closet (Fig. 122). In the wing are two

Fig. 122.

rooms for servants, a bath-room, and a stairway leading to the attic. This second story, though the external appearance of the house is that of a cottage, has full square rooms nine and a half feet high, except in the kitchen wing, where the rooms are five feet high at the sides, and nine in the centre. There is a fine open attic, capable of being divided into four good sized rooms.

All the rooms have open fire-places, and in addition there is a large furnace in the cellar, with hot-air pipes to the several rooms. There is a large cistern to supply a tank in the attic with rain-water by means of a force-pump, and from the tank the water is carried over the house to the water-closet, bath-room, butler's pantry, kitchen, and furnace.

The whole interior finish is of ash, oiled and rubbed down, and the window and door furniture is of bronze.

The walls are finished with a rough sand finish preparatory to receiving polychrome decoration.

The roofs are all slated with Peach Bottom slates (which are the best quality, costing some $18 per square of ten feet, while the ordinary qualities are worth about $14), and are surmounted with an ornamental cast-iron cresting, made purposely for them.

The whole of the work is of the very best quality throughout.

Such a design as this, built upon the plan here offered, would cost $18,000 to $20,000; but one of similar design and plan, but with simpler and plainer finish, and ordinary fittings, may be erected for about $15,000.

DESIGN XXIII.
An Architect's Residence.

Fig. 123.

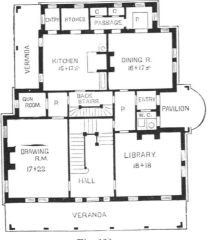

Fig. 124.

DESIGN XXIII.

An Architect's Residence.

THIS is a comfortable villa of moderate size, erected during the past year for his own residence by Mr. Gilman, architect, of New York. Fronting the south, and the side towards the road being on the east, the principal rooms are so disposed as not only to take advantage of the view, but also to receive the sun in its best and most desirable aspects during the year. Although a frame house, the construction has been done with great care and thoroughness, so as to render it warm and dry at all seasons. The framing is first covered with a fair quality of one-inch spruce boards, tongued and grooved, and well nailed to every post, stud, and rafter. A covering of thick heavy tarred felting is next placed over this boarding, the joints being everywhere lapped and double-nailed with care. Over this again is placed the exterior sheathing, furred out five-eighths of an inch, of extra clear one-inch white pine stock, in regular widths of eight inches, also tongued and grooved—the groove in each case marked with a bevelled rebate, which gives a sharp line of shadow to all the joinings of the exterior finish. Inside, the walls are first lathed directly on the studs, and plastered with one thick coat of hair mortar for "back plastering," then furred out over this first coat one inch more, and again lathed and plastered with two coats of lime and sand mortar, making a most hard and durable finish to receive either paint or paper, as may be desired. It is believed that no style of material and no mode of building are better adapted to all the exigencies of the American climate than these, a triple air-chamber being secured throughout; and that in comfort and (if kept well painted) durability a house of this kind will compare most favorably with those of much higher cost and pretensions.

The style of design is in that simple form of *Renaissance*, with Mansard roof, so common in the country houses in the vicinity of Boston. On the north-east angle the walls are continued up square in a somewhat higher story, so as to form the low tower seen on the extreme right in the view. There are in this house seven chambers of good size, with two dressing-rooms (one with bath) and two servants' chambers, besides a trunk or lumber room over the hall in the third story. The cost, complete, has been about $15,000.

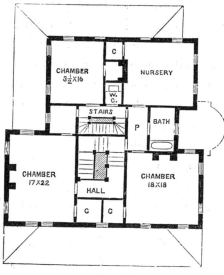

Fig. 125.

But this house, although a very comfortable dwelling, of moderate accommodations, is chiefly remarkable for the extreme beauty of its situation. Placed on the easterly slope of the highest ridge of land on Staten Island, and backed on the north and west by rich woods, the view from the two principal fronts is one of unsurpassed variety and beauty. The elevation of the site is computed to be about 400 feet above the level of tide-water; but as the approach is gradual for a mile and a quarter from the landing, the ascent is nowhere so steep as to become inconvenient, and the road is so laid out that no glimpses of the view are seen or suspected until the visitor, turning a sharp angle in the highway, comes out suddenly on the terrace in front of the eastern side. The panorama of land and water which then breaks upon the eye is so striking and varied in its attractions as rarely to fail in calling forth expressions of surprise and delight from the visitor who sees it for the first time. Immediately in the foreground a sharp open declivity falls away, for about a third of a mile in extent, to the village at the foot—the ground covered with a crisp turf, strewn here and there with moss-covered bowlders of the blue granite peculiar to the Island. In the middle distance lie the villages of Stapleton and Clifton, and the green slopes of the embankments of Fort Wadsworth, fringed by thick clumps of trees, from the midst of which rises the gray spire of St. John's Church, a thoroughly English model of quiet and picturesque beauty. The Hudson River, here forming in its lower portion the magnificent harbor of New York, finds its junction with the sea at the "Narrows," just beyond the ramparts of the fort—the white sand-hills of Coney Island stretching out into a point across the picture, as if to emphasize the deep blue of the open ocean beyond. The view in this quarter terminates only with the skyline of the broad Atlantic, in a fair day perhaps twenty miles away, and dotted in every direction with the white sails of the commerce of the great metropolis. Southward lies the long, low, wavy range of hills which terminate in the renowned Sandy Hook, the calmer waters of Raritan Bay interposed like a mirror between. To the east, the opposite shore of Long Island, covered with rich woods and sprinkled here and there with villas of neat and tasteful character, stretches away in the distance; the eye distinctly catching the white lines of the surf on the beach at Rockaway, while beyond the landscape fades away in blue and purple tints among the farming lands of Kings and Queens Counties, the historical battle-grounds of so many skirmishes of Revolutionary memory. Northwardly lie the dense thickets of Greenwood, and the mass of roofs and spires that mark the cities of Brooklyn and New York; while the eye, ranging along the heights of Weehawken and the receding line of the Palisades, and resting for miles on the broad bosom of the Hudson, finds its limit only in the high lands of Yonkers, some six-and-twenty miles away. When it is considered that a spot so charm ing is reached by clean and admirably appointed ferry-boats in a sail of twenty-five minutes and a short drive beyond—forty-five minutes in all—from the heart of Wall Street, it appears singular that every available spot in the vicinity of this hill has not long since been occupied by residences of the highest character. Let those New Yorkers who deem it necessary to travel in search of the picturesque, but take the opportunity to bestow a couple of hours upon a trip to Castleton Heights, and they will be repaid with a view for which, in its every aspect of loveliness, they may search over many a weary mile of distance to find a parallel.

This view has been engraved in Bartlett's "American Scenery," with descriptions by N. P. Willis (published in London some twenty years ago), Vol. I., p. 35.

DESIGN XXIV.

A Picturesque Brick Cottage.

This design was made for a gentleman in Newburgh last year, but was not carried into execution, the owner preferring to build of wood instead of brick, and upon a plan differing in many points from this.

The house was to have been placed between the public road and the river, with the entrance front—that shown in the picture—facing the west, while the living-rooms and the veranda are on the opposite side, towards the water.

The front porch is large, and is raised but one step above the ground, and from it we enter the vestibule. This is separated from the hall by an ornamental screen of chestnut, having carved tracery between the posts, and the floor is paved with encaustic tiles of ornamental patterns, costing about $1.50 per square foot. The main hall measures twelve feet by twenty, and in it are the stairs to the second story, which are three and a half feet wide and of easy ascent. The library is on the right of the hall, and measures fifteen feet square, and opening out of it by wide sliding doors on the south side is a place marked " Flower Alcove," which is in fact a small conservatory, having large windows occupying nearly the whole of the sunny side. This alcove is fitted up neatly with flower-stands, and the doors connecting it with the library are entirely of glass set in a light frame like French casement windows, and are made to slide on brass ways into the partition on either side.

Next to the library, occupying the south-east corner of

the house, is the parlor, a pleasant room sixteen feet by twenty, opening upon the veranda on the east by French casement windows, and having a bay window projecting from its south side. This room connects with the library by folding doors, and with the hall by a short passage, as shown on the plan,—in which is a niche for a piece of statuary. The dining-room is on the north-east corner, and measures fifteen by nineteen feet. This room is octagonal in shape, and in the corners are small china-closets. There are two French casement windows leading to the eastern veranda. The butler's pantry, adjoining, has a dumb-waiter rising from a corresponding pantry below, and is fitted up with cupboards and a butler's pantry sink supplied with hot and cold water. The stairs leading down to the kitchen are under the principal flight. This story is ten feet high, and all the rooms have neat cornices. The finish is entirely of chestnut.

The basement is divided in the same manner as the principal story, the partitions being all of brick, to afford a strong support for those above. The kitchen is under the dining-room, and, as the ground slopes away on that corner, it is almost entirely out of the ground, having three large twelve-light windows on the north and east sides. Under the parlor and library are open cellars, unfinished, but with cemented floors, white-washed walls, and plastered ceilings. The kitchen, pantry, and basement hall are all finished rooms.

In the second story (Fig. 128) are three pleasant chambers measuring respectively fifteen by seventeen, fifteen by twenty, and fifteen by fifteen. They are well lighted and have ample closet room. There is a servants' room over the vestibule, and a place for the storage of trunks, etc., above it, in the upper part of the tower.

DESIGN XXIV.

A Picturesque Brick Cottage.

Fig. 126.

Fig. 127.

The finish of the interior is of the simplest character, slightly stained and shellacked—chestnut in the principal story and clear white pine elsewhere. The hall floors are of southern pine in narrow strips, with a black-walnut

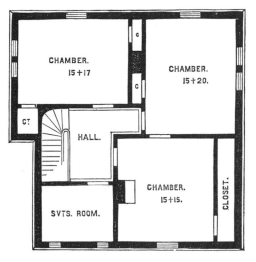

Fig. 128.

border twelve inches wide all around. In the rooms the floors are of narrow white-pine floor-plank. The second story is ten feet high, and the basement eight feet eight inches in the clear.

There are open fireplaces in all the rooms, adapted for burning coal in grates or wood on the hearths, and provision is made for a portable furnace in the cellar, to take the chill off from the halls and certain of the rooms.

The material of the house is brick trimmed with blue-stone neatly dressed, the bricks for the outside facings being selected for uniformity of tint and sharpness of outline, and laid in dark-colored mortar. The roofs are slated and surmounted by ornamental cresting of cast iron.

The estimated cost is $8,000.

DESIGN XXV.
The Brick Cottage of Judge Monell.

THE house is built of selected North River brick, well laid with white sand, relieved with Milwaukie brick, of a soft buff color, placed over the arch of the porch door, over the windows of the lower story, and as a moulding around the summit of the ample clustered chimneys.

It stands in the centre of a field, facing the south, and commanding a wide view of mountain, plain, forest, and river for many miles. Yet, owing to its broad, expanding proportions, its deep sheltering roof, with overhanging hooded windows, it has not the bare, exposed appearance that dwellings so prominently situated often have.

Its pretty terrace-garden on the river-side, entered from the broad piazza, thirteen feet wide, and connected by that with the parlor and library of the house, gives an air of cheerfulness and brilliancy in summer, with its flower-beds, balustrade, and vases glittering with blossoms and gay-colored leaves.

On the east side this is balanced by a bay-window in the dining-room, overlooking a shrubbery, and also by a small terrace piazza with a balustrade, but without a roof, on the south-east, in front of the dining-room windows, affording a pleasant shaded seat before the sun is low enough in the west to allow the large veranda to be occupied.

After entering the porch, which projects some ten feet from the house, we come upon a broad tiled hall, running from south to north, from which open the doors of the parlor and library on the west and the dining-room on the east. Beyond the entrance of the latter rises the ample staircase, with a landing from which there is a door open-

DESIGN XXV.

The Brick Cottage of Judge Monel.

Fig. 129.

ing upon a passage to the bath-room, linen-closet, and servants' bed-rooms, and from which a private staircase leads to the kitchen, and another to the garret.

From the above landing there is a window controlling an extensive northern view. And opposite to it you rise by a few steps to a square hall, from which open the five bed-rooms. From the lower hall and from under the staircase is a door leading to a passage which connects on the right with the butler's pantry and dining-room, and on the left with the kitchen, between which and the pantry is a small convenient room for any domestic use.

The woodwork of the principal floor, and the mantels throughout the house, are of black walnut and chestnut.

The chimneys are in the centre of the house, so that no part of the heat may be lost by outside exposure; while the central position of the furnace under the main hall enables you to carry the warm air easily into the several rooms of the house.

The bath-room is heated by a hot-air chamber attached to the kitchen range.

The ceilings of the first floor are ten and a half feet high, those of the second story nine feet.

There are open fireplaces throughout the house, and while the furnace gives heat enough for ordinary purposes, the wood fire is used for extra warmth and ventilation, added to its great comfort and beauty, as well as the atmosphere of health and well-being it always promotes.

The expression of the house is that of domestic comfort. It is easy of access, has a sheltering porch, and is invitingly connected with the terrace garden and piazzas, besides enjoying the luxury of a southern and eastern exposure. The roof and chimneys are boldly treated, so as to indicate the purposes for which they are adapted.

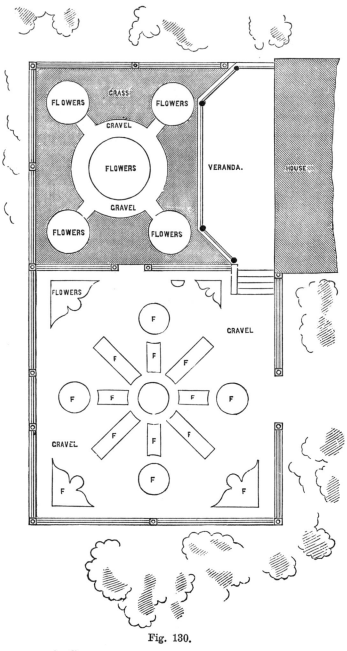

Fig. 130.

A GARDEN BELONGING TO DESIGN XXV.

DESIGN XXVI.
A River Cottage.

Fig. 132.

DESIGN XXVI.

A River Cottage.

THIS cottage, Fig. 132, designed by Mr. R. G. Hatfield, Architect, of New York, is intended to be located upon a sharp declivity, where a fine view, either upon a river or extended valley, is to be had from the lower side.

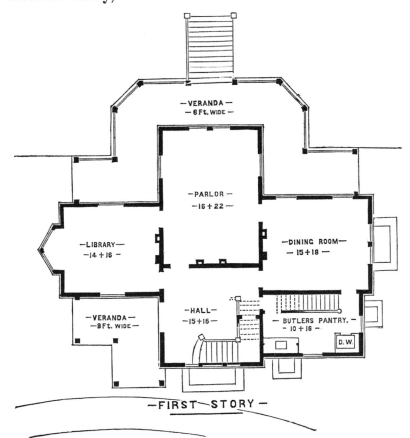

Fig. 133.

It has, therefore, a road front and a river front,—the former having the entrance porch extended out beyond the line of the house, to answer the purpose of a porte-cochère, and the latter provided with an ample veranda, connected with the lower lawn by a flight of steps.

On the principal story floor, Fig. 133, the entrance is on the south side of the central gable into a large stairway hall, 15 × 16 feet, from which doors open into all the rooms. At the centre is the parlor, which extends out on the river front, and by its end and side windows affords a view either up, down, or across the water; the size of this room is 16 × 22 feet.

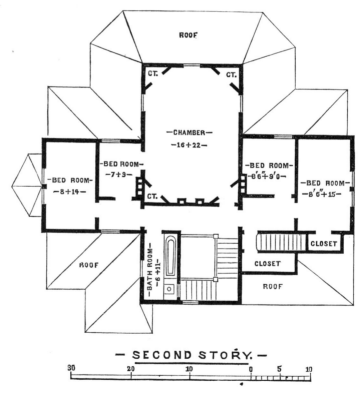

Fig. 134.

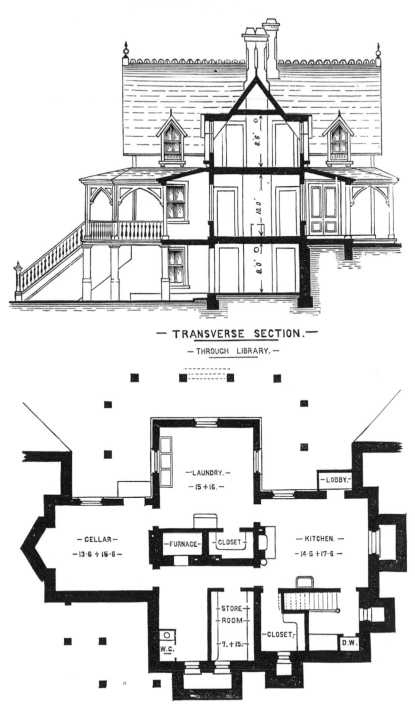

Figs. 135 and 136.

The parlor opens at the left into the library,—which is 14 × 16 feet, and has a bay window at the south end,—and at the right into the dining-room.

This room is 15 × 18 feet, and opens in front into a pantry, 10 × 16 feet, containing a dumb-waiter descending into the basement, a private stairs leading down to basement and up to second story, cupboards, shelves, etc.

All the windows opening on the rear veranda should descend to the floor.

The second story or attic floor, Fig. 134, contains six rooms. Over the parlor is the principal chamber, which is 16 × 22 feet, and has three corner closets.

This opens into a small child's room on the left, which is 7 × 9 feet. The three other small bedrooms are 8 × 14, 8′ 6″×15, and 8′ 6″× 9 feet, respectively. The bath-room is in the stairway-hall, and is 6 × 11 feet; it contains the bath and water-closet.

The basement, Fig. 136, contains, on the right, the kitchen, 14′ 6″× 17′ 6″, provided with pantry, closet, and store-room in front; at the centre the laundry, with wash-trays, closet, stove, etc.; on the left the cellar for fuel, etc.; and in front a passage containing a water-closet, the furnace, etc. There are two exterior doors, one opening from the cellar and one from the kitchen, the latter enclosed in a lobby.

The side of the basement towards the river is entirely above ground, as shown by the section, Fig. 135. The height of basement is 8 feet, of first story 10 feet, and of attic 8½ feet in the clear when finished.

The walls of the basement, where against the ground, should be built of stone, and the side where above ground, towards the river, may be of brick. Above the basement the building is of wood, but should be filled in with brick to the roof, as its position is evidently one of great exposure in winter, and it could scarcely be made comfortable without.

The detail of the finish, both on the exterior and interior, is intended to be plain, leaving the good effect to depend rather upon good proportion than embellishment.

The cost would depend upon local advantages, and would average $5,000.

DESIGN XXVII.

A Rural Church.

(See Frontispiece.)

WE introduce here a design for a small and inexpensive country church. The plans were made for a town in the West, and the estimate upon them was $3,200, last year. In this locality, the cost at the present time would be about $3,500.

The main building measures 25 feet by 48, and has a small recess at the eastern end for a sanctuary.

There is a tower at the south-west corner with a covered porch at the front doors. The entry in this tower is 8 feet square, and over it is a ringing-room, with the bell-deck just above it. The entire height of the tower is 48 feet, and on the peak is an ornamental finial of cast iron. The height of the ridge-pole of the main building is 30 feet. The building is of frame, filled in with bricks, and boarded and clapboarded on the outside, except in the upper parts of the gable ends, which are boarded up vertically and battened with 3-inch battens.

The projections of the gable are finished with a simple verge-board or false rafter 4 inches high. The roofs are boarded and shingled with pine shingles, a part of which are cut on the lower edges.

Fig. 139 is a sectional drawing, showing the general appearance of the chancel end, together with the finish of the roof and the framework which supports it. This framework is all of pine, finished carefully, and left exposed to view, the ceiling itself being of narrow pine or chestnut stuff nailed to the under sides of the common rafters, following the slant of the roof—so that the church inside is about 28 feet high in the centre.   There are eight ventilators on the roof, which can be opened or shut at will by means of ropes from below.   The windows are all stained glass—a plain enamelled with a colored border, set in lead quarries—and each one has a ventilator in the lower section.

There is one aisle or passage down the middle, with a row of seats each side (Fig. 139).   The seats are designed

Fig. 139.

to hold 6 persons each, and there are 27 in all, making the capacity of the church about 162 people.   The sides of the church are ceiled up to the line of the window-sills with narrow ceiling, and the space above that, to the spring of the roof, is lathed and plastered, and finished with a rough sand finish (this rough surface being better for tinting than the plain hard-finished wall).

The chancel is at the east end, raised three steps (or twenty inches) above the floor of the nave, and it measures about 14 feet square. A space is partitioned off by a carved chestnut screen on the north for a robing-room, and on the south for a small book-room. The robing-room has a separate entrance from the grounds. The altar is in the eastern recess, the floor of which is 5 inches above the chancel floor, and over it is a triple-light chancel window. The sedilia and the bishop's chair are at the sides, and the altar-rail directly in front.

The lectern and pulpit (marked L and P) are at the sides of the chancel steps.

At the western end near the entrance is the font. The interior woodwork, including all the furniture, may be of chestnut, simply oiled three or four times and well rubbed —the expense of it being not much greater than that of pine of a suitable quality for the purpose. The exterior should be painted in two tints of a quiet gray color, the trimmings being a trifle (and only a trifle) darker than the main body of the building.

FURTHER HINTS

GARDENS AND GROUNDS

OF

COTTAGE RESIDENCES.

In many small cottage residences there is not room to attempt much arrangement of grounds of any kind; but there may still be a strong taste for flowers and plants. A little flower garden, or, at least, a *parterre* of flower beds, may be laid out and managed by the mistress of the cottage.

There are two very distinct ways of laying out even the smallest flower garden. One is to make it consist solely of flower beds and borders, with alleys or walks of gravel between. The other is to have for the ground-work or general surface of the flower garden, a smooth piece of turf or lawn, and in this lawn to cut out such forms of flower beds as may be adopted.

Each mode has some advantages. Almost any common laborer can hoe, dig, and dress the first kind of flower garden, — at least with some occasional superintendence and assistance from the owner. The flower garden on turf requires a neat and practised *mower* to keep it short, by cutting it at least once a fortnight; for upon the shortness and closeness of the lawn the good effect of the flower garden largely depends.

But as regards the relative beauty, there is, to our taste, no comparison to be made between the two modes, especially in this climate. A flower garden composed only of flower beds and walks, looks pretty well in the moist and growing weather of the early season. But as soon as the hot weather of the American summer commences it presents quite another appearance. Instead of rich foliage and gay flowers, the eye reposes on beds of earth, perhaps only half covered with vegetation, and walks of gravel that only reflect the glare and dryness of the parched soil.

If we contrast such a flower garden with one in which the beds are cut in the turf, how much will not the latter gain by the comparison. The green, close turf is always such a pleasant setting, because its color is so refreshing to the eye, and because it shows off the colors of the flowers in the beds by contrast to so much more advantage than bare walks.

In modern flower gardens, especially those made upon turf, it is the practice to choose, for the most part, low-growing flowers—say not exceeding six inches or a foot in height—and to plant these in *masses*, sometimes filling a whole bed, or at others only part of a bed, with the same flower. This produces a brilliancy of effect quite impossible in any other way; and as the object in a flower garden is gayety, this *bedding* or *massing* of flowers is certainly the most complete and beautiful mode of attaining it.

In order to add still more to the perfection of the modern flower garden, it is also the custom to reject all plants that bloom but a short time, and then leave a blank space in the garden; and to choose those plants that bloom the greater part, or a large portion, of the summer and autumn. Certain annuals, like the Petunias, Portulacas, etc., come under this head, and by employing these, in conjunction with certain dwarf and showy herbaceous plants, like the Double White Campanula (*C. persicifolia, pl.*), a constant succession of bloom may be kept up in the masses all the summer season.

In all gardens where a gardener is employed the year round, or where a pit or green-house is at command, another class of plants has of late years become very popular for flower gardens. We mean exotics, that require to be kept from frost in winter, but which grow and bloom from May to November in the open flower garden. As examples of these, we need only mention the Verbenas and the Scarlet Geraniums, plants which, in their many varieties, their brilliant colors, and their power of withstanding heat and dry weather, have done more to give an air of perpetual beauty to our flower gardens than all other plants together. [We would add the many beautiful varieties of tricolors.—H. W. S.] As a few pots of cuttings of these, planted in August, and kept through the winter in a frame, a green-house, or even a warm room. will furnish a whole garden with beauty, hardly any one but those who have the humblest gardens need be without them.

Next to these, the greatest ornaments to the flower gardens are the ever-blooming roses. We mean by this (when we speak for the Northern States) those China roses known under the name of Bourbon, Bengal, and Noisette roses—since they will all thrive well in open beds, if very slightly covered with straw or branches of evergreens in winter. Among those, the *Bourbons* are the hardiest and the most beautiful.

For all the country south of the Potomac, in addition to the foregoing ever-blooming roses, the *Tea* roses may be added. As these are, in our estimation, the most lovely and delicious flowers in the world, and as they bloom, in

beds of light rich loam, all the season, they afford, in their
many shades and colors, the most admirable materials for
enriching the flower garden. To produce the finest effect
with them, small round beds—say three or four feet in diameter, surrounded by turf—should be planted with roses
of a single color, such as one bed of white, another of red,
a third of rose-color, etc. The branches should be pruned
and pegged down (*i. e.* fastened along the surface of the
ground by small forked pegs), so that the entire surface
of the soil in the bed shall be covered with foliage and
bloom. In this way they will produce a far richer effect
than if left to grow in an upright and loose manner.

It is not necessary that the soil for flower gardens should
be very rich—though a moderate annual dressing of well-
decomposed manure or poudrette is indispensable ; but it
is very important that the soil in the beds should be *deep*,
in order that the plants in them may send their roots
downwards, out of the reach of the heat and droughts of
August. A rich soil may induce a rapid and luxuriant
growth early in the season, but a soil two to three feet
deep in all parts will continue that growth and maintain a
fine verdure through the whole of the summer and autumn.

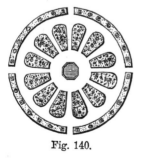

Fig. 140.

The smallest flower gardens are
called *parterres*, and Fig. 140 may be
taken as an example of the simplest
symmetrical arrangement in this way.
When a parterre is small, like this,
and depends for its good effect very
much on the arrangement of the beds,
care should be taken not to destroy
this effect by planting in the beds any flowers whose tall
growth might partially or wholly hide it. On the contrary, such a little parterre should, if possible, be planted

with the dwarfest flowers. We would therefore put into the four outer beds forming the margin, verbenas—say white verbenas in the first bed; pink verbenas in the second; purple verbenas in the third; and scarlet in the fourth. In the centre of this parterre we would place a sun-dial, or a vase upon a pedestal. The twelve beds that surround this we would plant as follows:—Every alternate bed we would devote to bulbs and annuals; that is to say, crocuses and hyacinths should be planted in them at pretty good distances apart, and the spaces between these should be filled every year with showy dwarf annuals, such as Gillia tricolor, Portulacas, Sweet Alyssum, Collinsia bi-color, Eschscholtzia, etc. The bulbs would bloom and give beauty to the parterre early in the spring; after they had passed, the annuals would supply their place. The remaining six beds we would devote to that fine dwarf scarlet geranium, the Tom Thumb, and the varie-gated-leaved scarlet geranium, etc. The latter is not only pretty in its bloom, but a bed composed of its parti-colored leaves is almost as handsome as one of flowers. Two beds of the scarlet geranium, two of the variegated, and two of the finest purple petunia, would, with the border of verbenas, make the parterre gay and bright the whole summer through.

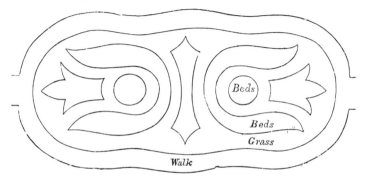

Fig. 141.

Fig. 141 is a pretty arabesque design for a parterre on a lawn, by the late Mr. Loudon. The beds are grouped in the turf so as to produce a pleasing pattern, and there is a walk running around the whole, so that the spectator may see the parterre, when the grass is wet with dew, without being obliged to walk upon the damp lawn. Of course, each bed here should be planted with a single kind of flower, or, what is still better, with one kind of flower for the bed, but a border or margin of another kind—when the bed is wide enough to permit it. [A charming garden is composed entirely of the new variegated leaf geraniums in stripes or ribbons.—H. W. S.] When the beds on opposite sides of the figure correspond in shape, they also produce a better effect when the same colors are introduced into such opposite beds—and even the same plants.

Fig. 142.

[Fig. 143.]

Another very tasteful design for a small flower garden is shown at Fig. 142. This consists of 8 arabesque beds, B, cut in the turf, A, and surrounding a ninth circular bed, C, in the midst of which is a vase or a fountain.

This garden would have a very satisfactory appearance if it were planted as follows :—The four larger beds at the corners to be filled with ever-blooming roses—one bed entirely with pure white roses, such as the White Daily, White Madame Desprez, Aimée Vibert, etc. ; another with deep crimson roses, such as Cramoisie Supérieure, Comice de Seine et Marne, Paul Joseph, Queen of Lombardy, etc. ; a third with rose-colored varieties, such as Hermosa, Pink Madame Desprez, Bouquet de Flore, etc.; and the fourth with creamy, fawn, and shaded roses, such as Madame Bosanquet, Saffrano, Jaune Desprez, Queen, and Souvenir de Malmaison. By keeping each color distinct, we get a marked and striking effect, entirely unattainable by mixing all colors together; and by using only ever-blooming roses, the beds are always in an ornamental condition. The four smaller intermediate beds may very properly be filled with verbenas, or scarlet geraniums, or any other dwarf and showy flowers.

A flower garden which has been much admired is one near Vienna, in the grounds of Baron Hügel, a distinguished amateur. The plan is shown in Fig. 143. In this flower garden the beds are in turf—and the general style is mixed —partly arabesque and partly geometric. The central beds, *l*, *m*, *n*, *o*, *p*, are, perhaps, faulty in taste, on account of their unmeaningly jagged outlines, out of keeping with the rest of the design, and inelegant in themselves. Filled with masses of gay flowers, well contrasted, no doubt the effect is better in reality than upon paper. The prettiest and most novel feature in the plan is the running *guilloche* pattern of the beds which form the boundary. These beds are very carefully planted with low-growing flowers, of such sorts as bloom very freely and constantly, and do not grow high enough to obscure the pattern, for everything depends upon this. In order to make this guilloche bed as brilliant as possible, the centre circle, *c*, of each bed is planted with some brilliant color, alternating with white: —for example, supposing the centre, *c*, to be white, then the next centre would be dark red, the next white, the next blue, the next white, the next yellow, the next white, scarlet, white, purple, white, and so on, repeating the primary colors all round the figure. The interlacing beds, *d*, may be planted upon the same principle, but omitting white, and the effect will be best if the contrasting or complementary colors, such as yellow and purple, blue and white, etc., are placed near each other.

The two centres, *i, i*, are occupied by handsome vases. Such a garden as this ought always, as in the case of Baron Hügel's, to form a scene by itself, by being shut out from all other objects by a belt of shrubbery or trees, at least on three sides.

Fig. 144 is a plan for a geometrical flower garden with curved lines, which would answer remarkably well for a situation near a fine villa, when it is desirable to give the flower garden something of an architectural character. If we suppose A to be the terrace directly around the house, from which a flight of steps descend to the level of the flower garden, then the walks of the flower garden commence at B. In a situation where water is abundant, the dark figure in the centre and the four dark squares marked E might be handsome fountains; the four smaller squares, marked F, might be vases or pedestals; or, if water is not at command, then the larger spaces might be occupied by

statues and the smaller ones by vases, or even large orange
trees in tubs.   The whole surface of the beds, D, might be
filled with low flowers in masses—or the garden might be
a mixed flower garden, so arranged that the taller plants,

Fig. 144.

like dahlias, fill the centre of the beds, and so gradually
lessening in size, till verbenas, and other plants only two
or three inches high, occupy the space next the walk.

It is sometimes desirable, in a residence of a particular
character, that the style of art adopted should be carried

out very minutely in the surroundings. The flower garden, especially, may partake of this character in some
cases, and particularly in the Italian and the Elizabethan
or Renaissance style. In this latter style the garden was
always formal and geometric, and was generally placed
close to one side of the house, usually under the drawing-
room windows. Fig. 145 is an example of an Elizabethan

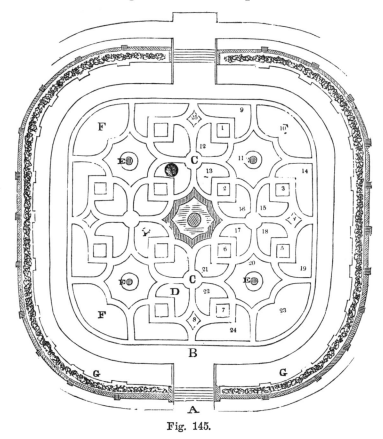

Fig. 145.

flower garden, which we give for the sake of variety. This
garden is supposed to be surrounded by a parapet walk, G,
"which has piers at regular distances, surmounted by
vases; at each of the flights of steps there are two statues,

one on each side of the entrance at the upper steps, and a vase at each of the lower steps."* A clipped hedge of yew, or holly, or hemlock, would be equally characteristic and less expensive. The centre is intended to be occupied by a fountain and a basin of water, and the four circles, E, by vases or statues. This garden would undoubtedly have the best effect if treated as a parterre, and wholly planted with masses of low-growing flowers—a single sort and color in each bed. In this way it would, if well grown, have the same pretty effect as a handsome and gay carpet. In order to give the richest effect, however, the colors ought to be harmonized and balanced : they may be harmonized by placing the beds of those colors next each other which agree, and balanced by making the corresponding figure or bed of the pattern on one side balance the same figure or bed on the other. To assist the novice, we give the following list for the beds on one side, premising that the other side should be exactly the same :—

1. *Blue.* Salvia patens.	13. *Orange.* Eschscholtzia crocea.
2. *Yellow.* Eschscholtzia californica.	14. *Lilac.* Hebe petunia.
3. *Blue.* Campanula carpatica.	15. *White.* White verbena.
4. *White.* Alyssum maritimum.	16. *White.* White petunia.
5. *Blue.* Lobelia gracilis.	17. *White.* White petunia.
6. *Yellow.* Calceolaria rugosa.	18. *Lilac.* Eclipse petunia.
7. *Blue.* Gillia bicolor.	20. *Scarlet.* Tom Thumb geranium.
8. *White.* White verbena.	21. *Orange.* Tropeolum minus fl. pleno.
9. *Purple.* Purple verbena.	22. *Orange.* Eschscholtzia crocca.
10. *Yellow.* Portulaca thorburnii.	23. *Yellow.* Œnothera macrocarpa.
11. *Scarlet.* Defiance verbena.	24. *Purple.* Prince of Wales petunia.
12. *Orange.* Eschscholtzia crocea.	25. *White.* Achillea ptarmica, pl.

Another accompaniment to the antique style of residence is the *labyrinth*, of which Fig. 146 may serve as an example. The amusement and interest in a labyrinth

---

* Loudon's Gardener's Magazine.

grows out of its being planted densely with shrubs and evergreens, so as to shut out one walk entirely from another. The visitor enters at A, pursues his way onward,

Fig. 146.

is stopped by the sudden termination of the walk, starts again with little better success, or, perhaps, only to reach the centre, B, where a large aloe or a rustic covered seat meets his eye; here he may rest awhile, or continue his walk, as much at a loss to find his way out as before; and a stranger may spend an hour or more in this way, in a state of "pleasant vexation." A labyrinth is, however, it must be confessed, the most interesting to the children of the family, who are never weary of this part of the grounds, preferring it to all the rest for daily amusement. The Arbor Vitæ, Privet, Buckthorn, and Tartarian Bush Honeysuckles, are the best shrubs for the thickets of a labyrinth. They should be *cut-back* at first, so as to render them thick and bushy at the bottom, like a hedge, and also sufficiently topped now and then to make them preserve this habit.

A plan like Fig. 140, planted thickly with shrubs, so arranged as to form masses of verdure, highest in the middle of the bed, and gradually lessening to the front, would make a very interesting *shrubbery* for a special scene in a country place. Or it might be planted wholly with evergreens of moderate size, and thus make a pleasant winter garden on a small scale.

In presenting all these various modes of arranging flower gardens, we must be allowed to say that the modern taste of discarding any set flower garden, and, instead of it, arranging the beds of choice perpetual blooming plants in and around a small lawn, in graceful and harmonious forms, is by far the most satisfactory in the majority of cases. It is especially so in all small places, where the ornamental grounds are too limited to allow of separate scenes. In such cases, the grouping of beds of flowers round a lawn, having only one or two colors in a bed, heightens the beauty of the lawn itself, while the flowers are enjoyed, perhaps, more than in any other way. Fig. 147 is a design of our own of this kind, which has been carried out and found extremely pretty and satisfactory. In this, A is the dwelling-house; B, the conservatory (a detached building on one side of the lawn); C, the lawn; D, flower beds; E, vase, fountain, sun-dial, or rustic basket filled with flowers. Round the whole runs a boundary belt, F, of trees and shrubs—shutting out all that portion of the grounds not strictly ornamental. In practice, it is found that small circular beds, about 3 feet in diameter, grouped in twos and threes (like those on the left of D), are more convenient and effective than the irregular beds; partly because a three-feet circle is large enough for a mass of a single color in a small garden, and partly because a circular bed, like a tree, always looks well either

alone, or grouped with other circles. It is also adapted to
any position, which an irregular bed is not.

In order to give the lawn, c, a more picturesque character, we have introduced a few single specimens of trees,
such as grow into beautiful forms when standing alone.

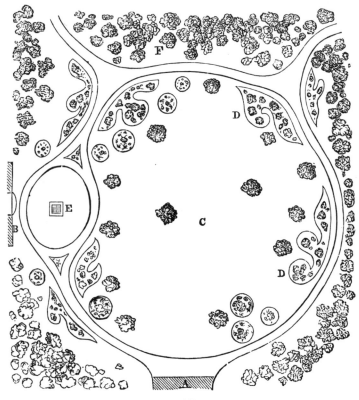

Fig. 147.

We may mention, as peculiarly adapted to such sites, the
Chinese Magnolias (*M. conspicua* and *M. soulangiana*),
very hardy and beautiful; the Weeping Ash, Weeping
Beech, Purple Beech, and Weeping Silver Lime, all striking in habit and foliage; the Ash-leaved Maple or Negundo, for its lively green foliage; the Virgilia, of Kentucky,

with snowy white blossoms; the Virginia Fringe tree, etc. As evergreens, to plant there singly, we may enumerate the Deodar Cedar, the Norway Spruce, the Himmalaya Spruce, the Irish Yew and the Silver Fir. A lawn and flower gar-

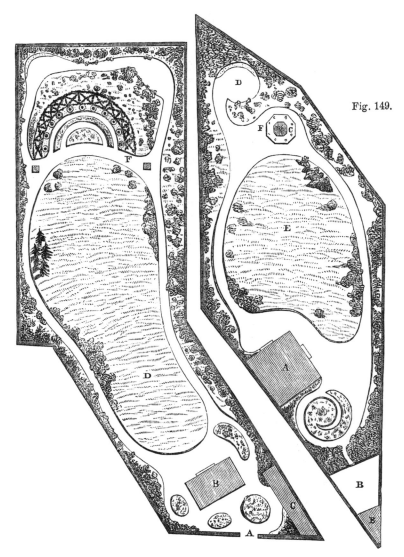

Fig. 149.

Fig. 148.

den combined and planted in this way, would have a tasteful and beautiful effect in any situation, or in connection
with a residence in any style.

To waive the subject of flower gardens, and consider
again the whole grounds of the residence, let us examine
for a moment some clever plans for cottage and suburban
residences by French landscape gardeners.

Figs. 148 and 149 are examples of the mode of laying
out two small places, where the boundaries are very irregular. In Fig. 148, A is the entrance gate; B, the house; C,
the stable; * D, the lawn. At the further end of the lawn is
a semicircular parterre, backed by vases of terra-cotta, filled
with scarlet geraniums, *lobelia gracilis* and other delicate
climbers Behind this is a semicircular arbor, F, covered
with vines, and affording a shady walk.

In Fig. 149, which contains half an acre, A is the dwelling, directly on the right of which is a fanciful flower bed
or parterre. This is backed by a thicket of shrubbery,
through which a walk leads to the tool-house or shed in
the corner, B, with ground for compost, etc. The lawn, E,
extends upon the other side of the house. At its further
extremity is a pigeon-house or aviary (or, still better, a
summer-house), C, surrounded by vases of flowers, F. At
D is an alcove for seats, surrounded by thick shrubbery.

In placing two suburban cottages near each other, the
lots of ground upon which they stand may sometimes,
when the houses belong to intimate friends, be thrown into
one, and laid out so as to add to the general effect, and
give more space for air and exercise. Fig. 150 is an example of this mode of arrangement, in which A and B are the
two houses, behind which are the two lawns, C and D, each

---

* Quite too near the house.

bordered with shrubbery, prettily grouped. A light iron fence, of trellis pattern, might be run through the middle bed of shrubbery, on the division line between the two lots, with light iron gates, where the two walks cross it. This would be so inconspicuous, if painted dark green, as not to look like a barrier; and as the gates could be locked when occasion required, the two places might be used either separately or singly, as might be most agreeable to the proprietors.

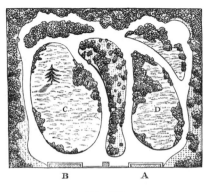

Fig. 150.

A tasteful *jardin paysager*, of an acre, which may be taken as one of the best examples of the modern style of laying out grounds in Germany, is shown in Fig. 151. In this, A is the dwelling-house; B, the main walk or promenade; G, the lawn, bordered with groups and masses of shrubs and trees, planted in turf. At the further extremity of the grounds is an elegant circular temple or summerhouse, D, in the classical style, surrounded by a series of vases or pedestals, C, and backed by a thick plantation of evergreens and deciduous trees. A handsome statue is placed in the open space at E, and at F is a rustic open summer-house, built of branches, with the bark on, in which, and upon the grass around it, the family take tea out of doors in summer afternoons, in that agreeable, easy, social manner so common in Germany.

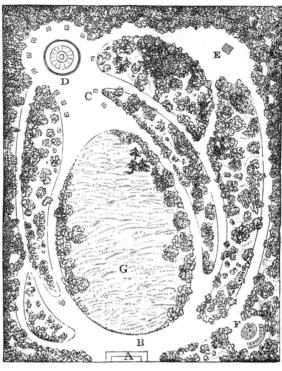

Fig 151.

A common fault in all the continental grounds, which may be noticed in the foregoing examples, is the unartistic manner in which the walks are arranged, by which they are not kept of any uniform width, but run into great open spaces of gravel round the house and in various other parts, where several walks meet, as in Fig. 149. This has a bad effect in itself, and is a waste of valuable space, that would appear far better if covered with green turf. There is, too, in most of the French plans, a lack of necessary attention to utility and convenience, especially as regards the kitchen offices, etc. In these respects, as in many others, the English plans for smaller places are models—showing how the most may be made of the least piece of ground.

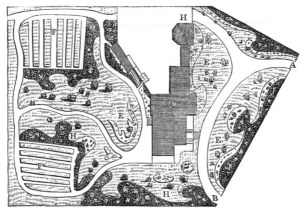

Fig. 152.

Fig. 152 is an example of this kind. In this, c is the house, placed back far enough from the public road to give it some privacy, and having a double entrance, A, B. Behind the house is a spacious kitchen yard, H, where all the outbuildings are entirely shut out from view, while they are placed in the most convenient position—being entirely masked from the front by a conservatory and summer-house, which forms the right wing of the house— while on the rear of the outbuildings a thick belt of trees and shrubbery effects the same object. The ground-work of the whole is a lawn, E, nicely kept, of which the back-ground is an irregular belt of trees and shrubs, nicely grouped, and the fore-ground beds of flowers, in arabesque patterns, cut in the turf. Neat kitchen and fruit gardens, F, F, are laid out in the rear, which are so arranged as to give all the convenience without marring the beauty of the scene; and a back entrance allows access to the kitchen yard, outbuildings, kitchen garden, etc., without being seen from the more elegant parts of the grounds. There is a great deal more merit in such a plan as this than in Fig. 148, although the latter may appear more prettily on paper,—because the former combines beauty with the greater utility,—so that the possessor of such a place gets his every day satisfaction from each separate source without feeling it to be at the expense of the other

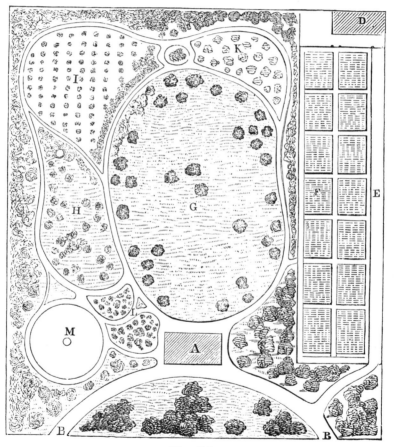

Fig. 153.

A plan of our own for a pleasant suburban residence, which is thought to have a good effect, is shown in Fig.

153. In this, A is the dwelling, B the carriage entrance, D the stable. The lawn, surrounded with beds or masses of flowers, is designated at C, and around it is grouped a choice collection of the most ornamental trees and shrubs, forming shady walks in some portions, and sunny, open ones in others. A circular parterre of showy summer flowers may be laid out at M. The kitchen garden, F, is arranged so as to be conveniently cultivated, and is placed near the stable, for the convenience of getting manure for hot-beds, etc., while it is shut out from the ornamental grounds by a belt of trees and shrubs. A fruit garden of dwarf trees, I, is shown beyond, and something of an ornamental character is given to an orchard at K, by grouping the trees picturesquely, instead of planting them in straight lines.

By studying carefully such plans as the foregoing, almost any person who has a little talent in drawing may be able to compose a design for a small place, that will exhibit more or less taste, and combine with it the advantages of entire convenience and usefulness. The first point, in the smallest place as well as the largest, is to get as much expanse of green lawn as possible. After this, to conceal the boundaries with trees and shrubs, so grouped and arranged as not to form a stiff hedge or verdant wall, but a picturesque, irregular, natural-looking boundary. Care should be taken in planting, not to intercept any fine views or vistas, but in such points (if any boundary plantation must be made) to compose it of shrubs or low-growing trees. Shrubs, trees, and grass, with a few walks, gracefully and naturally curved, are the materials with which a pleasing little landscape may be created in any site, when the soil is such as to favor the growth of vegetation; and it will generally be found that the more simple and natural the arrangement, the more lasting will be the pleasure derived from it. There is no error so frequently committed as to suppose that *beauty*, whether in houses or grounds, depends on *variety* and *expense*. Chasteness, good proportions, agreeable and expressive arrangement of simple forms,—these are the elements of the beautiful, which are always captivating to persons of pure and correct taste, whether that taste be natural and intuitive, or whether it has been refined by the long familiarity with all that is most satisfactory in nature or art.

SUGGESTIONS CONCERNING ITALIAN GARDENS.

BY HENRY WINTHROP SARGENT, ESQ.

THERE is hardly any improvement in the adornment of country places, within the last few years, more effective than what are called in England "Italian gardens." So universally popular is this new accession to a house of any pretension, that there are more Italian gardens in England than in Italy itself.

There is seldom a place, large or small, but what has this new and very charming feature attached to one side of it. And, in fact, the present fashion of ribbon gardens seems peculiarly adapted to the long, stately terraces and formal figures—parterres of embroidery set in stone or box and surmounted by balustrades and vases, somewhat in the style of the annexed view of a small garden of this description at Wodenethe, on the Hudson, as also at Judge Monell's, in the same neigborhood.

An English place, as a general rule, consists, first, of its park, the outer portion of which is often a rough forest or chase, abounding in cover of furze thorn, ferns, laurel, and the common sort of rhododendron, and filled with game. One passes from this to the Home or Deer parks, where the picturesque beauty and wildness of the chase gives place to stately groups and masses of trees, grand vistas, and glades of soft verdant turf, kept short and fresh by horses and cattle, and deer and flocks of sheep, feeding up to the very entrance-gate. Of course there are not on this side of the house any flowers or shrubs or ornamental plants; everything is quiet and simple, and, in places of any size, grand and stately. Should the house face the east, there is usually on the north side a dense mass of ever-green plantation, concealing the offices, stables, and stable-yard (this last an important feature in England), and separated from the park, which surrounds it, by a ha-ha, a brick wall, or a wire fence.

On the south and west sides extend the Italian gardens, if possible in terraces, the west garden being two or three feet lower or higher than the south, the whole surrounded by a low brick or stone wall, surmounted by a heavy stone balustrade, with vases on the pilasters every fifteen or twenty feet, filled with splendid specimens of Geraniums or Luccas, and other formal plants. Around the outer por-tion of the gardens runs a walk ten to twenty feet wide; and adjoining the balustrade, and immediately bordering it, are long formal beds densely planted in ribbons, Centaurea Candidissima, Mrs. Pollock Geranium, Silver Queen and Tom Thumb Geranium, and Lobelia Paxtonii. The Lobe-lia and Centaurea coming together form a beautiful con-trast, the edging of these beds being white marble or stone six inches high, and as wide.

From this outer grade or platform you descend perhaps three or four stone steps to the centre garden, which is sunken to this extent, and this is entirely filled with charm-ingly arranged patterns or figures of architectural designs, sometimes in scrolls or arabesque forms, in stone or marble edgings,—precisely as we employ box in this country,—the beds themselves forming a species of embroidery each representing one color.

The broad straight walks are likewise bordered at inter-vals by tubs or square boxes, containing Irish Yews or Junipers and Portugal Laurels, cut into round-headed balls.

DESIGN XXVIII.

Italian Gardens.

Figs. 154 and 155.

The whole of these gardens abound in fountains, statues, vases, and China seats; and being all in immediate connection with the house, from being on the same level as the floor of the living-rooms, with which they communicate by French windows opening to the ground, the effect is most captivating.

In fact, the Italian garden is an outside drawing-room, thoroughly isolated from the park, and generally four or five feet above it, accessible only from the different rooms of the house except through a gate from the park, which is always kept locked. It is reserved entirely for the family and their friends, and being always in evidence, is kept in scrupulously nice order.

While there is something dreary and unsafe in windows opening to a lawn exposed to cattle or intrusive strangers, as we have them in the country, you entirely lose this feeling in England, from, as I have said, the gardens being raised several feet above the rest of the place, and, in addition, having a wall and balustrade, with perhaps a haha beyond, so as to render the garden inaccessible to outsiders.

From the Italian garden you descend by a flight of steps, through a locked gate, to the pleasure grounds, Arboretum, Pinetum, Rosarium, kitchen garden, etc., all separated from the park by the brick wall or ha-ha.

HERBACEOUS GARDENS.

We have gone through several gradations of gardening, from the stately Italian school—with formal and architectural beds and borders—to the highly ornate and elaborate designs and patterns of the "bedding-out system," as it is so called—parterres of embroidery, each bed representing a color and a series of beds of different colors, forming designs, scrolls and embroideries of the most complex, dazzling and intricate styles, and certainly, when well done and artistically arranged, quite captivating from its very perfection, with the single drawback of monotony having no variation during the summer months, and inevitably destroyed with the first frost, requiring the same work in striking and storing the plants, and in forming and arranging the designs, year after year.

Though this style has still many advocates, yet the tide has commenced to turn and is slowly rolling back to the good old herbaceous borders of the past. Mr. Disraeli, in his charming description of Corisande's garden, in *Lothair*, has perhaps contributed to this change. I cannot illustrate this garden better than by using the words of a late article in Mr. Robinson's Magazine describing this style of mixed planting.

"Let us recall," he says, "the charming diversity of color and of form which they, the annuals, perennials and bulbous plants of spring, present to our admiration. Of form, from the tall Imperial Fritellaria, having the resemblance of crown and sceptre, also the prostrate Stone-crop carpeting the ground beneath. Of color, what a range! what a variety!—all colors, primary and intermediate, brilliant and soft, positive and neutral. Colors to harmonize, colors to contrast, colors which I like, colors which you like—all of them are here. Does your eye delight in the glow and brightness of the more vivid tints? Look at that Anemone—well named Fulgens—all afire in crimson glory. Regard these Tulips! General Garibaldi in his scarlet uniform—or royally named and royally apparelled 'Rex Rubrorum,' King of the Reds. Gaze upon that Gentian (vernal), luminous, gleaming like the breast of a humming-bird, with an intense and dazzling blue. Watch that clump of yellow Crocus as they ope to receive the kisses of the sun, and what is there in the stone or summer garden, in Orchid, Allemanda or Calceolaria, which can vie with it in its velvet sheen?

" Or have you what is called a more quiet taste? Bend over this bed of Myosotis Dissetifolia, bluer than the Turquois—blue as the heavens; or turn to that patch of exquisite, dainty little Scilla, or to that sheet of roseate Silene, blue Mountain Anemone, purple Pansy, pale yellow Primrose, bright yellow Cheiranthus, lilac Aubretia, or to those snow-white masses of Candy Tuft (Iberis Corrœfolia, the fairest of the fair), of Alyssum, Arabis Saxifrage, Daisy, and Snowdrop.

" Now glance at that combination—at that bed of golden Feverfew, dotted here and there with purple Crocus; of white Candy Tuft, from which, at intervals, the bright red Hyacinths arise; or of Cerastium, with small circular patches of scarlet Anemone, or Clieneden Pansy, or Erica Carnea, with the golden Arabis intermixed; or of Sedum Acre Aureum, with white and red Tulips, inserted à la pincushion.

" What foliage so attractive in the summer garden as that of the gold-tipped Stone-crop (Sedum Acre Aureum); of the Daisy, which has leaflets of green and gold ; or of the exquisite variegated Thyme? Is not the golden Feverfew brightest in the spring ? Are not the variegated Arabis, Euonymous and Periwinkle, and the silvery Cerastium, Centaurea, Graphalium, and Santolina most beautiful in their early growth? And then, what fragrance from the Violet and Primrose, Hyacinth and Wall Flower! All herbaceous plants can be multiplied quickly and will soon cover the ground, having the additional advantage of becoming stronger and more beautiful every year, and do not require annual renewing, like ribbon gardening."

With a view of assisting beginners, we add the following names :—

FOR SPRING.

Alyssum saxitale. Adonis vernalis. Anemone apennina. Coronaria and Sylvestris. Arabis albida. Asperula odorata. Aubretias bulbocodium vernum. Wall-flowers, including cheiranthus. Marshallii. Various kinds of crocus. Lily of the valley. Decentra eximia and spectabilis. Erica carnea. Erysimum ochroleucum. Ficaria grandiflora. Hepaticas. Different kinds of Iberis. Iris nudicaulis. Premila and reticulata. Snowdrops. Lithospernum prostratum. Myosatis dissitiflora and sylvatica. Orobus vernus. Daffodils. Phlox reptans and lubulata. Ranunculus monspeliacus. Montanus and the double-blossomed Aconitifolius. Sweat rocket. Scilla siberica and bifolia. Triteleda uniflora. Tulips and Violets.

FOR SUMMER.

Acanthus latifolius. Achillæa upatorum. Ptarmica pleno. Millefolium roseum. Aconitum japanicum and variegatum. Alstrosmeria aurea. Anchusa italica. Auterrhinums. Aquilegia glandulosa, cærulea and truncate. Aster Pyrenæus. Baptesia Australis. Betonica grandiflora. Double-blossomed Calystegia putrescens. Campanulas of various kinds. Catananche cærulea. Centranthus ruber. Coreopsis lanceolata and tenuifolia. Corydalis lutea. Different kinds of Larkspurs. Dracocephalum ruyschianum. Dictamnus fraxinella and albus. Erigeron peiboldie. Gallega officinalis. Gentiana asclepiadea. Geranium ibericum and sanguineum. Helianthus rigidus. Numerous species and varieties of the Flag (Iris). Everlasting Peas. Lilies of various kinds. Linaria dalmatica. Lychnis chalcedonica (vars.) and vicaria plena. Lythum. Salicaria roseum. Lavatera ungueculata and thuringiaca. Lupins malva, alcea, and moschata. Monarda didyma. Œnothera fruticosa. Mæro-carpa riparia. Margineta speciosa. Platycodon grandiflorum. Phlomis russelliana. Herba vente. Herbaceous and other Phloxes. Pyrethnm carneum. Rudbeckia speciosa. Salvia argenta spiræa. Aruncus palmata and venusta. Statice latifolia and tartarica. Symphyandra pendula. Symphytem bohemicum. Tradescantea Virginica and varieties. Trollius. Tropeolum polyphyllum. Veronicas and Verbascum chaixii.

FOR AUTUMN BLOOMING.

Acio autumnalis; Hollyhocks; Aconitum autumnale; Anemone japonica and varieties; Arundo conspicua; Asters; Astilbe rivularis; Chrysanthemums; Eupatorium purpureum; Gaura lindheimeri; Merendera bulbœodium; Platycodon autumnale; Pyrethum serotinum; Polygonum cuspidatum and vaccinifolium; Sparaxis pulcherrima; Sternbergia lutea; Stevia purpurea; Tritoma uvaria, and others.

The following perennial plants have fragrant flowers:

Adenophora litiafolia; Allium fragrans and odorum; Asclepias cornuti; Speciosa Douglasi; Calamintha glabella; Clematis flammula; Crambe cordifolia; Crinum capense; Daphne cneorum; Puicks; Dictamnus fraxinella; Funkia Iliboldii; several species of Iris Lavender; Leucojum vernum; different sorts of Lilies; Lupinus polyphyllus; Malva moschata; Mirabilis jalapa; Muscari moschatum; Narcissus major and jonquilla; Pancratium maritum; Tussilago fragrans; Viola odorata; Wall-flowers and mignonnette.

In the narrowest borders such things as House-leeks, Stone-crops and Saxifrages would do well; and among them might be planted bulbous plants, such as Crocus and Squills.

ADDENDA.

Building Contracts. The great disproportion frequently occurring between the estimate or contract and the final cost of a house, is a very constant source of disappointment and vexation to persons who engage for the first time in building. The cottage or villa is contracted to be built by the mechanics at a fair, or even a low price, quite satisfactory to the proprietor; but when the building is complete, the bills are often found to exceed the contracting price by one-third or one-half the original sum.

This result will always, on experience, be found to arise from two causes. The first of these is the want of a well-digested and thoroughly satisfactory plan before the contracts are made. A general idea of the arrangement, or a mutual understanding to copy pretty nearly the house of Mr. A. or B., in the neighborhood, is very often as definite a shape as the matter assumes before the house is commenced. While it is in progress, the subject opening on the mind of the owner, new arrangements or alterations in the plan are suggested: an additional room here, a closet or staircase there, would, it is discovered, add so greatly to the elegance or convenience of the house, that they are of course at once introduced. There are not wanting mechanics, who, finding perhaps that they shall obtain but a moderate profit on their original contracts, and being secure of the whole work, charge at a greatly increased price for these additional items, knowing that no other builder can now be brought into competition with them, to reduce the rate by a lower estimate.

The second source of multiplied expense is the want of

proper *specifications*, when the building is proposed to be estimated upon. The specifications of a building to be contracted for at a certain price are supposed to embrace every portion of it, and every item of the expense. Now, to draw up a full and complete list of specifications for a house of considerable size, requires a very accurate knowledge of everything relating to building—a knowledge that neither the generality of proprietors nor many artisans among us will generally be found to possess thoroughly. Usually, these specifications for a country house are drawn up, at the suggestion of the proprietor, by one of the master workmen, and include all the particulars that occur to him or his employer. But in carrying them out, it is found that so large a number of items have been overlooked, that the *bill of extras*, at the close of the work, amounts to 20 or 30 per cent. on the whole estimate.

To obviate these evils it is evident that it is highly necessary to have perfectly satisfactory drawings, showing every portion of the house necessary to a perfect understanding of all its parts before it is commenced or contracted for, *in order that no material alteration need be made while it is in progress;* and also to procure from some experienced and competent architect, or master-builder, very complete and full specifications for the whole work.

We have in these remarks supposed the contract mode of building, because experience has led us to believe that in most parts of the country the work may be done in this way in an equally excellent manner, and at a much lower cost, than by the day's-work system. This is owing partly to the fact that a great deal more judgment and proper economy will always be exercised in the purchase of materials, etc., by a master-builder for himself than for the proprietor; and partly, also, that in all buildings there is a great deal of labor of secondary importance, which may be performed at a cheap rate to the master-builder by his apprentices, and which would otherwise be paid for at the journeyman's rate in the day's-work system. At the same time the architect, owner, or superintendent of the work retain the power to inspect and reject all workmanship of materials not of a proper and specified quality.

The most economical mode of building in the United States will therefore be found to be that of employing only the best master workman, building by contract, and undertaking the work only when provided with complete plans and specifications.

Employment of architects or professional men.—The most mortifying feature, to a person of cultivated taste, in the architecture of our country houses built within the last ten years, is the frequent violation of correct proportions, of unity of decorations, and of appropriateness of style, so frequently seen, even in our finest residences. This arises sometimes from the indulgence of the fancy or caprice of the proprietor, and sometimes from the bad advice or worse plans of the country carpenter or mason in his employ. Although such buildings please their owners at first, yet with the dawnings of a more extensive knowledge, obtained either by the examination of really admirable edifices, or by a greater familiarity with the subject, they almost certainly regret, when it is too late, the errors they have so hastily committed.

To those who are not thoroughly informed and competent themselves (a class yet very small in all countries), we would strongly recommend the employment, in any building of importance, of the best professional talent. They may then feel assured not only of having a satisfactory production, but one which, being correctly designed, will rather grow than lessen in their admiration, as their knowledge or taste for architectural beauty increases.

When we have really decided to build, the difference between a common form and an excellent one may at once be secured in favor of the latter, by applying to an architect of talent and experience. The small addition (say two and a half per cent.) which this will make to the whole cost of the building is certainly a consideration of trifling consequence, when we reflect that in the *design* lies the whole *individuality* of the building, whether it shall be full of beauty, grace, or picturesqueness, or abound in uncouthness, incongruity, and foolish conceits—a matter of the more importance as it is to continue before our eyes and become identified with ourselves, perhaps, for a lifetime! Many persons within our knowledge have been deterred from applying to a professional man for advice in building a house, or laying out their grounds, from a mistaken idea of the enormous charges to which they would be subjected.

But this is a matter that is in reality greatly misunderstood. The established rate among architects of reputation on both sides of the Atlantic, for furnishing a complete design, is $2\frac{1}{2}$ per cent. on the estimated cost (that is, $125 for a house to cost $5,000, and in the same proportion for buildings of greater or less cost). Now, when a proprietor of moderate means is about to spend $5,000, he says to himself:—"I shall save $125 at least by planning for myself." This he accordingly does—but unless his house is a fac-simile of his neighbor's, so that the builder has only to copy what he has already done, the alterations and additions the owner is obliged to make before he gets the edifice completed cost him double the architect's charge for the design; so that he is absolutely the loser, even in money, putting out of the question the superiority of that plan which has been carefully studied and composed by a man of talent, taste, and experience, in a particular and difficult branch of knowledge.

The same thing is true, in a larger sense, in the case of buildings of greater extent, with regard to the *superintendence* of a building while in progress. The usual charge for superintendence made by architects, in addition to the charge for the design, is also $2\frac{1}{2}$ per cent., making 5 per cent. on the whole cost. This includes working drawings for every part of the interior and exterior, and a constant supervision of the work in progress. Not only does this insure a thorough and satisfactory execution of the plans adopted, without any personal annoyance to the proprietor, but, in the case of all architects of standing, experience proves that a building of any considerable cost can be far more economically and substantially erected by an architect than by any proprietor not familiar by long practice with building.

It is proper to state, that all architects make sketches and studies for particular purposes at lower prices than the rates we have stated. Every man *may* be his own lawyer or his own architect, but he usually has to pay much more dearly for the privilege, when he has any business of importance in hand, than he supposes; and we cannot counsel him to undertake the perplexity and vexation that generally result from it, if he can find a professional man of integrity and ability to perform the task so much more satisfactorily for him.

REMARKS CONCERNING THE PROFESSIONAL SERVICES OF ARCHITECTS.

BY THE EDITOR.

In order to more clearly make known to persons interested in the subject the customary charges for the services of Architects at the present time, we give below the substance of the schedule of charges adopted by the American Institute of Architects in 1866, which schedule is followed by all Architects of reputation in this country and in Europe, having been modelled upon that of the Royal Institute of British Architects.

For full Professional Services, including a General Superintendence of the work, the charge is five per cent. upon the *actual cost* of the work, payable in instalments as may be agreeable to both parties. We have usually followed the custom of calling for a payment of one-half the commission calculated upon the contract price at the time of signing the contract, and sundry other payments on account while the work is in progress; and then, when the work is completed, the balance remaining due of five per cent. upon the *actual cost* of the work including that of the extras: for instance, if an architect superintends the erection of a house, the contract price for which is $10,000, then, at the time the contract is signed by the owner and builder, the architect receives a payment of $250.00, which is one-half of five per cent. on $10,000; then, when the house is finished, if there have been extras added, at the desire of the owner, so that the house has cost $12,000, the architect's commission is calculated upon

$12,000, and the balance due him (if no intermediate payments have been made) is $350.00.

In buildings of greater cost a more exact system of payment is adopted; namely—2½ per cent. on the contract price upon the signing of the contract by the builder and owner; 2½ per cent. upon the amount of each payment made to the builder; and then, in case of extra work, five per cent. upon the amount of all bills for extras as soon as audited.

The charges for *Partial Services* are as follows :—

FOR PRELIMINARY SKETCHES, ONE PER CENT.

FOR PRELIMINARY SKETCHES, GENERAL DRAWINGS AND SPECIFICATIONS, TWO AND A HALF PER CENT.

FOR PRELIMINARY SKETCHES, GENERAL DRAWINGS, SPECIFICATIONS AND DETAIL DRAWINGS, THREE AND A HALF PER CENT.

These charges (provided the further service of superintendence is not required) are based upon the estimated cost, and the payment thereof is due when the drawings are completed; as—for example—if an architect, after a due amount of consultation with a client, makes studies and sketches for a house, and gives an approximate estimate of the cost of it, which estimate we will say is $8,000, and the client concludes not to build immediately—then the architect's charge is $80.00, and is due him when the said sketches are finished. If, at the same time, the client orders plans and specifications based upon these sketches, then the charge is $200.00, due also when finished.

If the sketches are made and paid for, and the plans and specifications are not ordered immediately—but at a later period (within a reasonable limit of time)—then the sum paid for the sketches is considered a part of the whole sum to be charged, and the deduction is made accordingly—as it will be seen that the charge for each class of service includes the charges for all that precede it.

For designs for FURNITURE or for MONUMENTAL or DECORATIVE WORK, special charges, in excess of the above, are made for each particular case.

For buildings at a distance from the office of the architect, the actual travelling expenses are charged in addition to the percentage for superintendence.

With regard to *superintendence*, a word or two may not be amiss here, as it is a subject which seems not to be thoroughly understood by the public generally. After having made all the drawings and specifications necessary to properly construct the proposed building, the architect's further duty is to prepare the contract, setting forth the conditions upon which the work is undertaken, the cost, the time of completion, and the manner of making the payments; to witness the signatures of the parties to the contract; to locate the proposed buildings, and to give the necessary directions about preparing the site; to give advice to the owner upon all matters connected with the work, and proper verbal and written instructions to the builder about carrying out the design in difficult and obscure parts; to give the orders for the several payments to the contractor, as fast as they shall become due; to advise concerning, and to give the orders for, any alterations that the owner may desire to have made in the works; to act as sole and supreme umpire in case of any difference of opinion between the owner and contractor with regard to the meaning and intent of the plans and specifications; and, finally, to exercise a *general supervision*, by means of periodical visits to the works while they are in progress, the frequency of these visits depending upon the character of the building and the distance which it may be from the office of the architect. During these visits the architect examines the work already completed, to see if it has been done in a proper and satisfactory manner; and if, upon such examination, it should appear to him that there is any deficiency, by reason of imperfect materials or bad work, then he has the right to order such deficiency made good, even if it should involve the taking down of work already finished—and the loss occasioned thereby falls upon the contractor.

The architect's further duties consist in examining the bills of extras, and arranging the final settlements between the owner and the contractor.

In order more effectually to insure the faithful performance of contracts, they have a custom in England of employing, upon each work of any importance, a person in the employ of the owner, called the "*clerk of the works*," who gives his whole attention to the work upon which he is engaged, receiving instructions from the architect, and frequently reporting to him, and keeping a constant superintendence upon all the different branches of the work, to see that the requirements of the plans and specifications are being fully carried out.

It is desirable that this system should be adopted in this country; and indeed, to some extent, it has been done upon large works, though not so generally as we would like to see, and very seldom in the erection of private houses. We should consider it money well spent in any case, though not absolutely necessary in small cottages.

But there is one point which should never be forgotten: none but the most reliable and capable builders should be employed upon any work; for as it is not to be supposed that an architect can give his whole attention, or any considerable part of it, to any one work, as his visits must be periodical, it may occur that during the intervals between these visits a dishonest or a careless builder may put in both inferior work and inferior materials, which, being immediately covered up, it will be almost impossible to detect. An interval of a single day may enable a person so disposed to put up work much at variance with the "true meaning and intent" of the plans and specifications.

Competent and reliable builders there are in abundance, and they only should be intrusted with the carrying out of any work, whether large or small; they may possibly require higher prices, but it is only because they expect to be fairly paid, and expect to do what is right for their employer in return. The cheapest is very seldom the best, and it is far better to employ a first-rate man at a fair price, than to agree to pay a tricky man two-thirds the proper price, and then be obliged to watch him day after day for fear he will take advantage wherever he can to make himself whole in his short bargain; and this leads us to strongly deprecate the custom of submitting plans for indiscriminate public competition among builders—a custom which places the good man on the level with the bad, and allows every advantage to the latter; if this must be done, then the proper course for the owner is to have it understood beforehand that he does not bind himself to accept the lowest, or any proposal that may be offered— which leaves him free to exercise his own discretion in the matter, and to intrust the building of his house to whomever he pleases.

By far the best thing to do, if a person wishes to have a good house and the true value of his money, is something like the following:

After the plans and specifications have been completed, let them be given to, say, four builders, whose reputations are undoubted, and whose names are a guarantee that, with the proper co-operation of the architect, the work will be *good* in every respect. Give each of these parties a proper length of time to estimate in, and in this case let it be understood that the lowest bidder receives the contract. Appoint a time to receive the proposals; let them be taken, sealed, to the office of the architect, and there opened in the presence of the bidders, and the contract given at once to him who is the lowest. After this let the articles of agreement, already prepared by the architect, be signed, and the work commenced, and in due time we will guarantee that the owner will see the realization of his wishes, in the shape of a convenient, comfortable, and satisfactory home.